JL

Jl

"OVERPAID, OVERSEXED, AND OVER HERE"

The American GI
in World War II Britain

by Juliet Gardiner

"OVERPAID, OVERSEXED, AND OVER HERE"

The American GI in World War II Britain

by Juliet Gardiner

CANOPY BOOKS

A division of Abbeville Press, Inc.

NEW YORK

Frontispiece: Short back and sides Yankee style. The barber's shop of the 381st Bomb Group at Ridgewell.

First published in the United States of America in 1992 by Canopy Books, a division of Abbeville Press, Inc., 488 Madison Avenue, New York, NY 10022.

First published in Great Britain in 1992 by Collins & Brown Limited, Mercury House, 195 Knightsbridge, London.

ISBN 1-55859-408-6

Editorial Director: Gabrielle Townsend
Editor: Jennifer Chilvers
Designer: Ruth Hope

CONTENTS

PREFACE

I N JUNE 1940, WITH FRANCE DEFEATED and Dunkirk hastily evacuated, Britain feared a German invasion from across the Channel. Elaborate official plans and enthusiastic amateur ones were laid to defend the British Isles from Operation SEALION – which never came.

But eighteen months later, on 26 January 1942 – fifty years ago – the American invasion from across the Atlantic began to arrive in Britain little more than a month after the bombing of Pearl Harbor brought the US into the Second World War. At first it was a trickle but by May 1944 there were over a million and a half US troops, soldiers, sailors and airmen, stationed in the UK poised to launch an Allied attack on Hitler's 'Fortress Europe'.

In the resonant words of John of Gaunt, 'This land . . . this dear, dear land . . . is now leased out,' and the leaseholders were to have their wartime lives profoundly affected by this occupation – albeit a friendly one. The GIs who poured into a country smaller than the state of Iowa or North Carolina came from a land where, until very recently, the war in Europe had seemed a world away. They were better paid, better fed and better dressed, and they had an immediate impact on British life and resources, on the men, women and children, pubs, language, music and ways of having fun – and ultimately on post-war attitudes and expectations.

As it was war that had brought the GIs as far as 6,000 miles to Britain, so it was only victory that would take them home again. Their way home had to be fought across Europe by land, sea and air, and this would require considerable Anglo–American co-operation. The policy was hammered out by the political and military leaders: the reality had to be forged by the men.

This book aims to give a picture of those years of the American invasion. It could not have been written without the memories of the men and women who were part of the GI occupation – both those who came 'over here' and those whose lives they changed. I am most grateful to the large number of people who wrote or talked to me in response to my various requests for information and filled in the exhaustive questionnaire I sent them. Their vivid and varied stories are the substance of this book. I am also very grateful to the authors of the unpublished papers, letters and diaries that I have consulted and who have given me permission to quote from them. In this regard I am indebted to the Department of Documents at the Imperial War Museum, the Mass Observation archive at the University of Sussex, the Public Record Office, Iowa Historical Society, the National Archive in Washington; to Tony Davies for allowing me to quote from his unpublished work *Stars and Stripes in Salop, 1942–6*, to Robert Lafore for allowing me to quote from Laurence Lafore's unpublished memoirs, to John W. McClane and to William E. Ruck. I would also like to thank those correspondents who did not wish to be quoted but who nevertheless were prepared to help me with my enquiries.

PREFACE

The book could not have been written either without the existing literature on the subject from official histories to personal, privately printed memoirs and the wide range of literature on various aspects of the military, political, social and cultural history of this aspect of the history of the Second World War. The bibliography indicates my debt to those sources.

In gathering this information, there are many people to whom I owe thanks: the editors of the newspapers, magazines, journals and newsletters both in Britain and the US who published my requests for information; the staff in the departments of documents, printed books, photographs and film at the Imperial War Museum; the staff at the Mass Observation archive, in particular Dorothy Sheridan; the staff of the Public Record Office at Kew, in particular Nicholas Cox; the staff of the London Library, in particular Douglas Matthews; the 8th Air Force 2nd Division Memorial Library in Norwich, and in particular Tony North; the staff of Camden library service; Lea Bridge Road library, Cambridge public library; the various librarians and county record offices throughout Britain who answered queries and suggested local sources; the secretaries of local history societies who did the same; John Oxley of Central Television who brought *The Village Who Met Them Again* for me to see; and Lavinia Warner of Warner Sisters who let me see *GI Brides*; the Women's Voluntary Service in London, in particular Megan Keable; the British Red Cross; the National Archive and the National Air and Space Museum, Washington DC; the American Red Cross, and in particular Barbara Pathé; New York Public Library; University of Iowa Library; Chicago Historical Society; Madison Historical Society; Iowa State Historical Society; USAAF Museum at Dayton, Ohio, the Veterans of Foreign Wars Association and the numerous representatives of Bomb Group Associations both in Britain and the US who have publicised my search in their publications and answered my questions.

For hospitality, advice and information, I would like to thank Quentin Bland, Pat Everson, Anona Moser, John Oxley, Connie and Gordon Richards in Britain and Helen Angell, Bill and Kitch Aydelotte, Eileen and William Barry, Mary Clark, Robert Edberg and Averil Logan in the United States.

Quentin Bland, Terry Charman, Henry Horwitz, Jerome Kuehl, Tony North, Connie and Gordon Richards, Gillian Tindall and Gavin Weightman have read drafts in whole or in part and I am deeply appreciative of their suggestions and corrections while recognizing that any errors that remain are mine. I would like to thank my editor, Jeremy Lewis, for making it a better book, and Jennifer Chilvers and Gabrielle Townsend for precision and encouragement. For help with illustrations, I am indebted to Quentin Bland, Pat Everson, Jacqueline Guy, Philip Kaplan, Philippa Lewis, Harriet Orr, Connie and Gordon Richards, and all the GIs and friends of GIs who sent me photographs.

I am also indebted to various friends for suggestions, references and encouragement; to Sarah Guy for help with typing; to my children, Alexander, Sophie (who also typed) and Sebastian Gardiner for enthusiasm and critical insights. It is to my husband, Henry Horwitz, that I dedicate this book in thanks for his indefatigable securing of books, following up references, textual improvements, but above all for his sustained interest and his native ability to save me from the grossest of my misunderstandings about American life and habits.

CHAPTER ONE

WAR ON A FAR FRONT

I CAN REMEMBER ON THE DAY THAT GERMANY invaded Poland, September 1 1939, my father who owned the Willows Garage in Salem, Connecticut, drew a rough map of Europe in the dirt in front of the garage with a stick . . . He said to me, 'Before this is over, you'll be in it, Bob. Yes, and Duncan too.' How right he was!

The sun was breaking through a hazy sky over Dufferin Quay, Belfast, at 11 o'clock in the morning on 26 January 1942. The Union Jack and the Stars and Stripes fluttered together in the breeze from a flagpole as a band of the Royal Ulster Rifles struck up with 'The Star-Spangled Banner', the American national anthem:

> *O, say, does that star-spangled banner yet wave*
> *O'er the land of the free and the home of the brave?*

The bandsmen and some Irish dock workers watched as the gangplank was hauled into position against a tender and a line of US soldiers scrambled ashore, looking for all the world like veterans of the First World War trenches in their 'soup plate' tin helmets and gaiters – and on closer inspection it seemed as if the stripes on the sleeves of their uniforms had all been stitched on upside down.

Sir Archibald Sinclair, Secretary of State for Air, who had come to Northern Ireland on behalf of the British government, detached himself from the huddle of assembled dignitaries on the quayside and stepped forward to welcome the contingent of American soldiers. 'From the prairies and teeming cities of Iowa and the North-West,' he began, 'these American troops have come thousands of miles, not to sojourn amongst strangers, but among grateful friends and among comrades of the British fighting forces who would be proud to share with them the place of honour in the battle.' The doughboys would join in the defence of 'any assault upon this island fortress . . . and would sally forth with [Britain] to carry the war into the enemy's territory and free the oppressed people of Europe. Their safe arrival marks a new stage in the World War.' He saw it as 'a gloomy portent for Hitler' and predicted that its 'significance would not be lost on General Tojo'.

The correspondent from *The Times* who was covering the event noted that 'finer young troops in physique or bearing would be hard to find;' and indeed the GI who was welcomed ashore as the first United States soldier to set foot on British soil was a particularly fine specimen. Private First Class Milburn H. Henke of the 34th US Infantry

Division was a clear-faced, handsome young man from Hutchinson, Minnesota, with an engaging smile whose photograph in the British newspapers was to bring him sacks of fan mail – though *The Times* added a slightly sour note by pointing out that 'the first ordinary soldier to land on British soil was the son of a naturalized German'.

In fact, Private Henke was not the first Yank ashore – he was the 501st. A column of infantrymen was already marching smartly off to camp, for a whole contingent had come ashore in Belfast without anybody noticing. Nevertheless, the vanguard of some 4,000 US Army soldiers destined for the European Theater of Operations had finally arrived after an uncomfortable but uneventful journey during which their ships had zigzagged across the Atlantic to avoid the German U-boats.

But despite the gathering of military top brass on the quayside, *The Times* found the occasion 'curiously subdued' in contrast to its 'historic importance'. The writer and politician, Harold Nicolson, was also perplexed at the low-key British response to America's entry into the war, noting in his diary that 'We simply can't be beaten with America in. But how strange it is that this great event should be recorded and welcomed here without jubilation. We should have gone mad with joy if it had happened a year ago.' But a year ago the United States had still been determined to keep out of the conflict raging more than 3,000 miles away in Europe – when for the last time Americans could thank heavens for the Atlantic Ocean.

Their President, Franklin D. Roosevelt, was in the habit of having what he liked to call 'fireside chats' over the radio with the American nation. On the outbreak of war between Britain and Germany, on 3 September 1939, he made the position clear to the millions listening to him across the country. 'You must master at the outset a simple, but unalterable fact in modern foreign relations between nations. When peace has been broken anywhere, the peace of countries everywhere is in danger. But,' he stressed, 'let no man or woman thoughtlessly or falsely talk of sending its armies to European fields.' America was to remain neutral – and he concluded on a note which brought reassurance to the families clustered round their crackling radio sets: 'I have said not once, but many times, that I have seen war and I hate war . . . as long as it remains within my power to prevent it, there will be no black-out of peace in the US.'

Roosevelt remembered the First World War only too well – the war that was supposed to end all wars. The war to make the world safe for democracy, which ushered in Bolshevism and later fascism. He remembered his country's decisive rejection of the League of Nations, and the feeling which had grown through the Depression years of the Thirties that the First World War had been pointless, and American involvement a costly error. He was aware of the loss of American life in the Great War – more than a quarter of a million casualties – and the poem that children of that post-war generation still recited in school for those who had died on the battlefields of Europe:

> *In Flanders fields the poppies grow*
> *Between the crosses row on row.*

The President listened grimly to Charles Lindbergh, America's hero of the solo transatlantic flight, whip up emotion when he told nearly as large an audience as Roosevelt could hope to draw for his fireside chats that 'these wars in Europe are not wars in which our civilization is defending itself against some Asiatic invader. There is no Genghis Khan or

Xerxes marching against our Western nations . . . it is simply one more of those age-old struggles within our family of nations – a quarrel arising from the errors of the last war.' And who had made the errors? The 'victors of that war'. The President had read Robert McCormick, the editor of the influential *Chicago Tribune*, charge Winston Churchill with being ready to fight the war in Europe 'until the last American boy'. Meanwhile, the US ambassador to Britain, Joseph Kennedy, the father of the future President, had espoused Chamberlain's policy of appeasement, and his public pronouncements indicated that, in his view, there was no way that Britain could defeat Germany. Furthermore, he had intervened in Roosevelt's re-election campaign in November 1940 to insist that America had no valid reason for entering the war and to warn that if she did she might be compelled to transform herself into a totalitarian state in the way that Britain seemed to be doing with her emergency powers legislation. But above all the President was well aware of the isolationist sentiment in the country, expressed by a Baltimore woman who said, 'We went over there once and pulled England's chestnuts out of the fire. This time let them stew in their own juice.' In this climate, he had to move cautiously, whatever his own sober assessments of the future might be. The constituency of his country had no stomach for war.

But as well as listening to their President when he invited them to settle down in their armchairs by the fireside, the American public had become faithful listeners to Ed Murrow, the CBS correspondent who broadcast nightly from London during the Blitz – and, in the days before the familiarity of television, painted an eloquent verbal picture of Britain at war. His technique was to take a battery of microphones out into the streets of the capital at the height of the bombing, interspersing his serious, measured commentary with the sounds of sirens and bombs exploding, people screaming and crashing masonry. 'This is London,' he always began. 'This has been what might be called a routine night – air raids ever since about nine o'clock and intermittent bombing ever since.' 'You burned the city of London in our houses and we felt the flames that burned it,' the poet Archibald MacLeish, head of the newly created Office of Facts and Figures in Washington, wrote to Murrow: 'You laid the dead of London at our doors and we knew the dead were our dead – were all men's dead, were mankind's dead.'

But the American nation wanted no part of a war raging far away in Europe. In 1939 a poll had recorded that 67 per cent believed that America should remain neutral, with only 12 per cent prepared to give aid to Britain while remaining neutral, and a mere 2 per cent in favour of declaring war on Germany. And when the new ambassador to London, John G. Winant, set off for the Court of St James in February 1941 to replace Kennedy, he acknowledged that his job was to keep 'Winston Churchill and the British government patient while the American people assessed the issues which faced them'.

By the early months of 1941, Britain's tenuous lifeline to America seemed in danger of snapping altogether. The power of the Nazi U-boats and sea bombing raids were devastating shipping in the Atlantic. In order to maintain the war effort, Britain needed to import 43 million tons of supplies from the States, yet in the last five weeks of 1940, losses at sea had reached 420,300 tons. If this rate continued, it would be 'fatal to Britain', Churchill wrote. In addition, Britain had run out of money to pay for any American supplies on the 'cash and carry' basis by which Britain paid for all war matériel in full and hauled it across the Atlantic in her own ships.

At the end of December 1940, Churchill had sent Roosevelt a bleak assessment of the prospects for 1941. The British Prime Minister's most urgent appeal was for matériel – heavy bombers, in particular, on which 'we depend to shatter the foundation of German military power', and a safe delivery of goods across the submarine-infested Atlantic. Roosevelt knew that the question was not what should be done, but how it should be done. How could Britain's desperate situation be reconciled with America's formal neutrality and with the political climate of isolationism in Congress and in the country?

On 29 December 1940 Roosevelt had another fireside chat in which he announced his new policy of aid to Britain, which was to become known as Lend-Lease. The production of ships, tanks and other war supplies would be rapidly increased and they would no longer be sold to Britain but would be lent. Roosevelt used one of his homely analogies to explain the new policy: if your neighbour's house is on fire you lend him your hose and you don't ask for money – what you want is your hose back when the fire has been put out. The President explained his reasons starkly: 'If Britain should go down, all of us Americans would be living at the point of a gun, a gun loaded with explosive bullets, economic as well as military. We must produce arms and ships with every energy and resource we can command . . . We must be the great arsenal of democracy.' The isolationist Senator Taft saw the flaw immediately: 'Lending arms is like lending chewing-gum. You don't want it back.' He was right: neither Churchill nor Roosevelt ever imagined that the war supplies would be returned or paid for. One of Roosevelt's most consistent critics, Senator Burton Wheeler, of Montana, was vehement in his opposition: 'What hypocrisy! If it's our war we ought to have the courage to go over and fight it – but it isn't our war.' In fact, what Roosevelt was doing by the beginning of 1941 was precisely that: making it America's war – albeit an undeclared war, entered sideways.

In Britain the news of this bounty was received with jubilation in high places. To Churchill it 'transformed immediately the whole position, providing Great Britain with an almost unlimited and free supply of weapons needed to fight Hitler', while Harold Nicolson predicted that it 'was probably the decisive fact of the war'.

But not everyone was so convinced. The London correspondent of the *New Yorker* suspected that 'despite all the fine phrases something more than the tools was going to be needed before there could be a possibility of finishing the job.' And the much-heralded Atlantic Charter issued when Churchill and Roosevelt met off Newfoundland in August 1941 produced only a ponderous statement about long-term aims reminiscent of Woodrow Wilson's Fourteen Points in 1918, rather than the unequivocal declaration of war that had been hoped for by a British public now convinced of the need for the US to come into the war. *The Times* chided:

> The flood is raging and we are breasting it in an effort to save our drowning civilization. America throws out a line to us, and will give us dry clothes if we reach the shore. We understand her attitude, but . . . we think it would be no strain on her resources to wade in, at least up to her waist. We are frankly disappointed with the American contribution to the rescue.

In fact, the United States was already doing rather more than simply standing by with a towel. The country was increasingly being placed on a war footing – 'national defense', as it was euphemistically called. Throughout 1940 the strength of the Navy, Army, and

'Over here.' Private First Class Milburn H. Henke from Minnesota, officially the first GI to come ashore in the United Kingdom on 26 January 1942, poses for the photographers waiting on the quay at Belfast.

Army and Navy Air Corps (there was as yet no independent air force) was increased. The US equivalent of the Territorial Army, the volunteer National Guard, was rustled up for intensive training, and in September 1940 all men between twenty-one and thirty-five were compelled to register for military service. In the same month, the US transferred fifty over-age but reconditioned destroyers to the UK in exchange for the lease of bases in Newfoundland and the West Indies. In July 1941, the United States zone of influence increased when American troops landed in Iceland in order to release British troops for service elsewhere; it was announced that ships supplying the troops would be escorted by US warships, and that any submarine challenge would be regarded as hostile.

And there were already Americans engaged in war work 'over here' in the United Kingdom. At the end of June 1941, 362 civilian technicians arrived in Northern Ireland and more followed. Their task was to keep open the vital Atlantic sea lanes by building naval and air bases in Ulster to protect US convoys, as well as stations for refitting and re-fuelling US warships. To avoid compromising America's neutral status, they were nominally employees of the British government, which paid them. Although they were described as 'visitors' they worked ten hours a day six days a week, earning considerably higher wages than the local population working with them as unskilled labourers.

The Americans' experience in Ulster was a foretaste of things to come: 'They wandered around in the rain for days . . . the inclemency of the weather and lack of amusement drove a number of them to drink.' But when their materials finally arrived, they got down to work with 'a concentration of effort not familiar in this country', according to the official history of Northern Ireland in the Second World War.

WAR ON A FAR FRONT

*Already 'over here'. Members of the Eagle Squadron, Americans who volunteered
to fight with the RAF before the US came into the war, scramble
for their planes in March 1941.*

In addition, ever since the outbreak of war, individual American citizens, who were
determined to fight for the Allied cause, had crossed the border into Canada and joined
the armed forces. Some 10,000 Americans were enlisted in the Canadian Army and Royal
Canadian Air Force by mid-1942, when they were given the chance to transfer to their
own country's forces. And then there was the famous – or infamous – Eagle Squadron:
fliers with a reputation for wild and individualistic behaviour who, in the modest words of
one of them, had come to Britain 'because we were tired of hanging round the corner
drugstore at home – and we wanted to see what was going on. Didn't you ever hear of a
kid running away from home to join the circus?' They had heard that 'anyone who could
fly was welcomed in England at a time when her . . . men were being shot down like
birds out of the sky'. They had joined the RAF and were very soon flying missions
across occupied France, and though most of the 'eagles' were extremely young, they were
soon very experienced – unless, of course, they too were 'shot down like birds out of
the sky'.

General Raymond E. Lee, US military attaché and head of intelligence in London,
disapproved of Roosevelt's declaration that the US would give Britain all aid short of war.
'I wonder if it ever occurs to the people in Washington,' he wrote despairingly in his
diary, 'that they have no God-given right to declare war. They may wake up one day to
find that war has suddenly been declared on the United States.' But then, all of a sudden,
the terms of reference for 'the great debate' were radically changed.

That 'day of infamy', as Roosevelt dubbed it, came in the early morning of Sunday, 7
December 1941, when Japanese aircraft attacked the huge US naval base at Pearl Harbor

in the Pacific. Winston Churchill was dining with the American ambassador at the Prime Minister's official country house, Chequers, when news of Pearl Harbor came through. He was later to write:

> No American will think it wrong of me if I proclaim that to have the United States at our side was to me the greatest joy. I could not foretell the course of events. I do not pretend to have measured accurately the martial might of Japan, but now at this very moment I knew the United States was in the war, up to the neck and in to the death . . . So we had won . . . Britain would live . . . We should not be wiped out. Our history would not come to an end.

When Churchill telephoned the US President that same evening, Roosevelt confirmed the story: 'All of us are in the same boat and it's a ship which will not and cannot be sunk.'

> 'Pearl Harbor. Where's that?' demanded a British schoolboy, as did thousands throughout Britain and America. 'Place in Hawaii.' 'Where's that?' 'It's been bombed.' It didn't mean much to us kids . . . all it meant was that we went round yelling 'Praise the Lord and pass the ammunition.' It did bring America into the war, a thing that I feel, looking back, just about saved Britain's bacon.

'The forces endeavoring to enslave the whole world are moving towards our hemisphere,' President Roosevelt told his country. Four days after Pearl Harbor, Germany and Italy declared war on the United States. Within the space of a week America had been drawn into war on two fronts.

An infantry officer was watching polo at Fort Benning in Georgia on the day of Pearl Harbor. He recalls that

> the feel of the sun was pleasant, as was the sight of patterned movements of men, horses and mallets. Then the shock waves from the detonating bombs 6,000 miles away passed down the line of onlookers. The polo game went on to an unnoticed conclusion while we hovered around the car radios . . . By the close of that Sunday, we realized that any previous life plans were invalidated. Where we were now headed was too immense to grasp, so we students settled upon the comprehensible worry of whether Christmas leave would be cancelled.

CHAPTER TWO

SOLDIERS: GOVERNMENT ISSUE

'T HEN CAME PEARL HARBOR,' remembers Fred Huston, a student at the University of Oklahoma who'd signed up with the Army Air Corps along with some of his class mates when war seemed a distant prospect, 'and the phones were ringing all over town. They were for us. There was no time for the official letter calling us to arms; no time for the going-away party; no bobby soxers swooning in our arms and begging us to come back whole . . . just a lousy phone call telling us to report the following morning for induction and transportation. The following morning . . .'

Huston was one of the new recruits to the US Army – an army that needed as many new recruits as it could possibly get in 1941. General Dwight D. Eisenhower, who was to be Supreme Commander of the Allied Forces in Europe and would be in charge of the D-Day landings, pointed out that 'when the nation began, in 1939, [the] first steps towards strengthening its military establishment, it started from a position as close to zero as a great nation could conceivably allow itself to sink.' Isolationist policies and the effect of the Depression years when the social policies of the New Deal had taken priority, combined with a natural distrust of standing armies and the absence of a European tradition of military families, meant that the US Army was ranked seventeenth in the world – 'the army of a third-rate power', as one of its Chiefs of Staff described it. After a limited programme of expansion as the war clouds were darkening over Europe, the Army's strength was up to 185,000 men at the outbreak of war compared with Germany's six to eight million. None of its units had a full complement of men. No infantry division approached its combat strength. There was not a single armoured division: the total number of men in scattered tank units was less than 1,500, whilst the entire embryonic Army Air Corps consisted of 1,175 planes designed for combat and 17,000 men to service, maintain and fly them. The National Guard claimed to have almost as many soldiers as the regular army, but the units' equipment was often minimal and their training casual.

In June 1940, after the fall of France and as the Battle of Britain raged, a bill was introduced into the US Congress for military conscription – for the first time in the country's history in peacetime. There was considerable opposition. On Capitol Hill, a thousand demonstrators chanted 'Ain't going to study war no more,' while in the gallery of the Senate and then in the House of Representatives, six women wearing veils wept as they kept a silent vigil on behalf, they said, of the mothers of America. But, as one of the bill's supporters noticed, 'every time they bombed London, we gained a vote or two,' and the Selective Training and Services Act was finally passed in September 1940. Initially, the bill authorized the Army to take a maximum of 900,000 men between the ages of twenty-one and thirty-five – a modest trawl skimmed from a manpower pool estimated at some 17 million – and at first the term of service was limited to one year. Less than twelve months later, 'I'll be Home in a Year Little Darling', the country-and-western song popular amongst the draftees and those they left behind, was out of date. By a vote of 203 to 202, the House of Representatives extended the length of military service to two and a half years; a week after Pearl Harbor, Congress declared that the forces would serve for up to six months after the end of hostilities.

The great majority of the men mobilized went into the Army: when it reached its peak strength of 8,300,000 in 1945, over seven million of that number had been drafted, or 'selected' as the Army preferred to call it, and the age range had been broadened to span eighteen to sixty-five. The GI army that came to Britain was a mixture of draftees, regular servicemen and members of the National Guard – and most of them had been drafted.

With the expansion of military manpower after Pearl Harbor, the complicated lottery system whereby men had found their way into the Army was dropped: the criteria were now whether the men could be spared from essential civilian work and whether they met the standards of the armed forces. From 1942 the Navy and the Marines also took in men this way, though the Army Air Corps (renamed the Army Air Force in 1941) was always a service of volunteers.

Bachelors tended to be signed up first, though if a man was suspected of getting married just to escape the draft, he was less likely to get deferment from his local draft board which decided these matters, just as fathers of babies conceived after Pearl Harbor were regarded with some suspicion. Farmers were the least likely to be drafted: in 1942 only 15 per cent of the country's agricultural workforce had been inducted. Actors, on the other hand, were considered much more dispensable – more than half of America's 6,931 working actors were in the Army by mid-1942. Inevitably, physical and educational standards fell as the demand increased. A third of all those rejected in 1940 had correctible defects of teeth and eyes. By February 1942, if a man had 'sufficient teeth (natural or artificial) to subsist on army rations' he was in, and by 1945 one soldier in five was wearing glasses.

The troops trained in camps scattered across America. They included long-term regulars, and volunteers like Robert Burns who had visited his brother at Fort Knox back in 1940 when the situation in Europe was deteriorating and 'figured I might as well get into the Army without waiting for the going to get really tough', as well as the conscripts. The term 'GI' came to apply to them all – though it had originally been used as a derisive term for the new rookie, or 'jeep', as he was sometimes called. In the First World War the soldier had been a 'doughboy', a term that was still used, but to most people the enlisted men in the Second World War were GIs. GI meant 'government issue' – and covered anything from boots, blankets, soap, guns, rubbish bins and toilet paper to the soldier himself – all of them provided by the US government.

"Don't ask foolish questions. Th' schedule calls fer calisthenics. We'll start wid th' left eyelid."

Bill Mauldin's 'dogfaces' cross the Atlantic.

Bill Mauldin was a soldier who drew for *Stars and Stripes*, the US forces' newspaper which was distributed on a daily basis to all American forces in Britain after June 1942, just as it had been to the soldiers in France in the First World War; his cartoon 'dogfaces', Willie and Joe, became the most famous GIs of the war. Mauldin thought it 'faintly offensive' to label a man as 'government issue' but as one of his more robust colleagues pointed out, 'it sort of fitted.' The US government had taken in civilians and turned them out as soldiers, with two dog tags hanging on a chain round their necks giving their names and numbers.

Henry Giles had joined the Army when the Depression began to bite deep in Kentucky. He'd got 'sick and tired of the way we lived, hand to mouth, scrabbling along . . . you couldn't find a day's work in a month of Sundays.' To him – and to thousands like him in particularly depressed areas like the Appalachians and the dustbowl states – the Army meant 'security and pride and something fine and good . . . for the first time in my life I had clothes I wasn't ashamed of, for the first time in my life I was *somebody*. That uniform stood for something to me.' A weapons sergeant with the 291st Engineer Battalion, Henry Giles was none too pleased with the new recruits:

Shortly after Pearl Harbor . . . the first draftees began coming in. They came in bitching about this and that, regulations, the food, a cot instead of an inner spring mattress, barracks instead of private rooms. Sometimes I felt like wringing their necks. If they had gone as lean as I had, army food would have tasted good to them. If they had gone cold as often as I had, warm barracks would have felt wonderful. If they had slept on a cornshuck mattress in an attic where snow drifted in on your bed, they would have felt fine. I don't think that I was a particularly hard platoon sergeant, but they weren't there for fun and somebody had to begin making soldiers out of them.

Civilians had to be trained to be soldiers as soon as possible – America's small regular army needed reinforcements double-quick. It sometimes seemed to the new recruits that the whole object of the training was 'to make a man so mad that he wanted to get into combat to escape it'.

Raw recruits reported to Army reception centres across the country, and by the summer of 1942 14,000 a day were pouring into the reception centres and training camps. In the days before Pearl Harbor, men setting off from civilian life were often accorded a community send-off with bands and speeches, but after December 1941 the volume of departing troops built up so rapidly that Fred Huston remembers that there was 'no sense of occasion, no farewell speeches, no fluffy blondes waving goodbye. No damned nothing except our anxious faces pressed against the windows as we steamed slowly out . . .'

New soldiers were given a short physical examination of the 'drop your trousers' sort as a check for VD, and a lecture on morals and hygiene which often ended with the terse injunction 'Flies spread disease – keep yours buttoned.' After a lecture on the Articles of War, the Army's criminal code, they were kitted out in their new uniforms. To begin with, at least, they weren't always all that new: a GI might well receive a First World War kit, occasionally with a 1918 receipt still in the pocket. The First World War tin 'soup plate' helmets were soon to be replaced by the bucket-type helmet which was much more effective against shells, even if it did make the GIs look disquietingly like German soldiers. Some were even wearing puttees which, Bill Mauldin recalled, 'had to be coiled around your legs like anacondas; if you still had circulation in your feet you knew your leggings were too loose and would work their way down to your ankles like schoolgirl stockings.' If a man complained about his uniform to his sergeant, he was likely to get the unsympathetic reply that if it could be buttoned it wasn't too tight, and if it stayed with you when you moved forward, it wasn't too loose; and when a private from Oklahoma complained that his legs were six inches longer than the trousers with which he had been issued, his sergeant told him briskly that in the Army there were only two sizes of uniform – too big, or too small. But because an army marches on its feet, it was an altogether different matter when it came to boots. A soldier was often required to carry two buckets of sand to represent the weight of his pack while his boots were being fitted, and old veterans were full of tips for toughening up feet, such as soaking them in a bath of alum water.

From the reception centre, the new soldiers were sent to training camps to be turned into fighting men. All of them took the Army General Classification Test, which sorted them out into five categories of 'usable intelligence' or 'trainability', as the Army liked to call it, with a score of 110 and over (Class II) needed for entry to the Officers' Candidate School. A high score was also a plus in getting into the Army Air Force if that's where a draftee decided to apply. Then there were aptitude tests and a questionnaire to ascertain what a man's civilian work had been – or, if that wasn't too easy to translate into an appropriate military role, if he had any useful interests or hobbies which might help the assessors. The decisions were sometimes hard to fathom. A sailor explained its workings to an English writer:

> Take the cowboy from Texas. There is still cavalry in the Army and you might think that the authorities might be glad to have the cowboys ride their horses. That's where you would be wrong. The authorities choose clerks from New York offices to go into the cavalry, and they make the cowboys learn how to work a diesel engine. When a guy comes before the draft board and says 'I'm a cook,' they say to him, 'That's dandy, son, we'll make an engineer out of you. Don't worry. You'll never be a cook in Uncle Sam's army.'

He went on to explain that it was all to do with adaptability: 'Suppose the Army said to the chef of the Ritz-Carlton: "Here's a load of straw and a sack of cement. Now make some bread," what do you think the chef would say? He would answer: "It can't be done." But a truck driver from Brooklyn would say: "Well I guess if that's the way to make bread, it's OK by me." '

Airmen formed a class apart, but for everyone else training began to a programme designed to make soldiers out of the unpromising material presented by the average civilian. It included drilling, military discipline, fitness training, camouflage training, lessons in map reading and in reading aerial photographs, tent-pitching – and marching. A mandatory twenty-five miles with full equipment was prescribed by the War Department in 1943, but the enthusiasm of some officers meant that many infantry units in training exceeded this. After this course, which was common to all recruits, a soldier's training became more specific, designed to develop his own role and slot him into a particular unit. In 1942 the training of a division from scratch took exactly one year: forty-four weeks of individual and unit training followed by eight weeks of exercises and manoeuvres.

Most of the early equipment was strictly First World War stuff, including ancient tanks – though there were so few tanks available for training purposes that the soldiers sometimes had to use trucks with cardboard signs hung on their sides saying TANK, while saplings hacked from near the training ground served those for whom there weren't enough guns to go round.

Thomas Todd, who had been selected as a German interpreter and was training at Camp Reynolds in Pennsylvania, had to go through exactly the same assault course as an infantryman, though

> it was unlikely that we would ever tackle anything heavier than a typewriter or sharper than a pencil. We fired M1s, charged strawbags, bayonetted them, uttering ear-splitting yells as we did so. We crawled through ditches and under barbed wire with live ammunition zipping overhead and shells exploding in the

distance. There was little need for instructors to scream at us to keep our heads down. Mine almost became part of the landscape . . . But everything has a beginning, a middle and an end, and eventually we were released from the horrors of the course. We had, according to the Army, 'been toughened up' and most of us by that time had learned how to clean a latrine, scrub a garbage can until you can see your face in it, make your bed so tight a quarter can bounce on it, keep your barrack window sill so clean a white glove could wipe it and stay white, force your eyes to stay open during lectures on venereal disease and never, never, never volunteer.

And then, inevitably, the GI had to put into practice the first thing he'd learned in the Army – to 'hurry up and wait'.

For Robert Burns in 1941 'the scuttlebutt [gossip] had it that we were going to Europe, but no one seemed to have any idea for sure.' The troops' preparation for departure amused him: 'we had to remove all division signs from everything till in the end we started painting A. NONNIEMOUS on things.' At Camp Reynolds 'rumours were rife . . . the general opinion was that we would soon be leaving . . . and we kept hearing the name "Camp Kilmer", and though it was supposed to be hush hush, Kilmer meant overseas.'

Troops leaving America for Europe embarked from Boston or New York, from one of several camps built nearby. Camp Kilmer in New Jersey had been hastily erected: hundreds of thousands of troops were to pass through its barren confines over the next three years to feed the insatiable demands of the war in Europe.

Security measures at the camp were strict. All identifying marks of the division and its regiments were obliterated and replaced by shipping code numbers. Mail was censored by company officers, and men were forbidden to indicate in letters that they were outward bound. But despite this careful security, a number of wives and girlfriends were invariably waiting for the soldiers when they arrived at the camp, even though their destination was supposed to be top secret.

Troops were issued with a list of what should be in the two barrack bags they were to carry. Shoe polish was forbidden as a possible fire risk; so too were coat-hangers, though no one knew why. Their bags were packed and repacked, they were inspected, they cleaned their equipment, and, as preparation for overseas movement (POM), they were confined to camp which, given the attractions of nearby Manhattan, added to their sense of frustration – and to their apprehension about their final destination.

A ferry or train took the troops to the pier where their transport to war awaited them. The crossing was made in a merchant vessel, an ocean liner or a Liberty ship. In 1942 Churchill had offered Roosevelt the use of the two great *Queens*, *Mary* and *Elizabeth*, to speed the movement of US troops across the Atlantic, as well as whatever merchant shipping was available. General Marshall, the US Chief of Staff, had asked the British Prime Minister 'how many men we ought to put on board the *Queens*', given that 'boats [and] rafts could only be provided for about 8,000' – whereas if this precaution was disregarded, they could carry 16,000 men. 'I gave the following answer,' Churchill wrote later: 'I can only tell you what we should do. You must judge for yourself the risks you will run.' Soon the *Queens* were plying across the Atlantic, 'filled to the brim' with troops.

Into a war zone. A US infantryman has his first cup of British tea on his arrival in Northern Ireland in January 1942.

The shortage of commodious ocean liners meant that many of the Liberty ships, which had been developed as emergency freighters, built in sections and welded together, had to be pressed into service on the Atlantic run in 1943. They were more like tramp steamers, able to accommodate a maximum of 550 men and their equipment – and even then the decks were piled high. And whereas the *Queens* could race along at a cracking 28½ knots, often only taking five or six days to cross the Atlantic, on a Liberty ship the discomfort of a crowded and potentially hazardous sea trip lasted for much longer.

An infantryman with the 1st Armored Division was amazed when he saw the *Queen Mary* looming out of the fog in New York harbor: 'I'd never seen a ship like that, she was huge.' The troops were loaded from the riverside so that they could not be seen going aboard. The men clambered up the gangplank fully laden and fully equipped, including a helmet with a shipping number chalked on it, pack, rifle, cartridge belt, bayonet, canteen and gas mask – and lugging a couple of barrack bags or maybe a duffel bag. It was an ignominious departure. 'A few early rising civilians, New York City police and SOS [Services of Supply] soldiers stood at the gates of the dock and silently watched us as we moved along,' recalled an infantryman. 'Where was the traditional panoply of war that greeted the brave defenders of the republic departing for the front? No blaring bands, no cheering throngs and no pretty girls throwing roses! I reeled along under my suitcase which kept knocking my helmet sideways.'

Henry Giles had just met the woman he was later to marry when he got the order to embark. 'The last thing I wanted right then was to leave the States but maybe you're never ready to go to war . . .' He felt 'sick at my stomach' when he walked up the gangplank of the *Santa Elena* in Boston Harbor, and sicker yet

> when I watched the US fade out of sight . . . it seemed to me I was saying goodbye for ever to all that meant most to me and that I might never see again. There is something awfully final about going aboard a troop ship and sailing away from your own country. Like a one-way ticket to hell. But you live through it even if you think that you are not going to.

A group of GIs stood on the deck of the *Mauretania* and watched the New York skyline fade into the distance: 'We all wondered just how long it would be before we saw it again. For some of us it would be never . . .'

Crossing the Atlantic by ocean liner has the ring of Noël Coward to it, but the luxury liners were catering for a different kind of trade now. All of them had been totally refitted to carry the maximum number of troops in what sometimes seemed like the minimum degree of comfort, though some traces of former elegance remained in wood-panelled rooms with delicate marquetry.

The bunks were arranged in tiers of four, with the backs hinged on iron posts and the fronts supported by chains. There was usually just enough room to squeeze in between the bunks, but nowhere to sit down in the cabins. Often a double or even triple bunking system was in effect, with the men sleeping in shifts. Robert McCall had been in the advance party of his unit up the gangplank and he was 'lucky to get in a cabin on "C" deck', for without adequate ventilation, cabins deeper in the bowels of the ship soon became hot and dank. 'It was a twilight world of multi-tiered bunks . . . where the company had little room to move except in unison,' recalls an infantry officer, Charles Cawthon. It wasn't much better for the officers: 'a dozen of us were shoe-horned into double-tiered bunks in a richly panelled cabin originally designed for a privileged couple.' Helen Coops, who came over from Cincinnati in 1943 to take up an appointment with the American Red Cross, wrote to a friend about her crossing: 'I still marvel at the manner in which my twenty-nine cabin mates and I can live in a small cabin – without closet space, hooks for clothes, or even walking room. It is a combination of a child's jungle gym and a monkey cage. When I lie on my back, the space between my nose and the next bed measures just twelve inches.' But it was more than comfort that was at stake: 'If that ship had been hit,' wrote Henry Giles, 'we would have drowned like rats, we were packed in so close.'

On the *Mauretania* the latrines on the floor below the cabins were 'a strange sight. There were 15–20 pans all side by side and connected directly to a large conduit which ran below, through which ran a continuous supply of sea water.' It was impossible for the ship's evaporators to provide fresh water to all the men aboard, so fresh water was often only available for early morning shaving, and if you were very lucky, washing. Otherwise, it was bottled water to drink and sea water for washing. The troops were supplied with a specially developed soap which was supposed to lather in sea water, but no one seemed to be able to make any headway with it, and washing in sea water made the men itch all over so much that most gave up their ablutions for the duration of the voyage.

Mealtimes didn't win acclaim either. There never seemed enough food and the men complained that they were so hungry that they nearly started to eat the paint off the walls. What they did get was an introduction to a British wartime diet: watery, starchy and largely tasteless. For Thomas Todd, 'The food was just terrible. Each man received a hard-boiled egg that had been in pickle for so long that it had turned gray; along with this came two slices of toast, a spoonful of marmalade and a cup of hot tea.' Then a member of the crew made him count his blessings by telling him that on a previous trip they had 'dished out kippered herrings for breakfast'.

It wasn't long before the combination of cramped conditions and the Atlantic swell began to take its toll. Sergeant Giles noted that 'a day or two out and seasickness took care of the long chow lines.' Soon the stench of vomit permeated the already stuffy decks below. The lavatories were awash, and many of the queasy troops preferred to use their helmets as sick bags rather than venture into the washrooms.

William Schwinn, who had come to Britain with the 376th Air Service Group on a nine-day voyage in a converted cargo ship that 'looked as if it had been around since World War I', recalls some of his fellow GIs being so ill that

> they couldn't eat, they couldn't get out of bed, they just lay there and we had to lace the bunks because they'd laid there so long, the rope had stretched and the canvas had stretched. It was almost a daily chore to hoist them back up so that you could get into your own bed – not that that was a bed, just a bunk with your duffel bag on it.

William Barry, on his way to work in intelligence with the 8th Air Force, found the heat and stench below deck so stifling that 'I bought a straw mattress from a British member of the crew, and at night I used to lie it down in the little lobby outside the officers' quarters and sleep the night there. I gave it back when we reached Britain . . . I expect the seaman sold it again on the next crossing.'

During the day the men could take the air – and often the biting wind and rain – on deck. But at nightfall the ship's public address system boomed 'All troops lay below,' and it was back to the bowels of the ship, with the portholes blacked out.

Boredom was a constant companion – particularly when the seasickness subsided. All around the deck crap games were in progress, with the men sitting on blankets tossing dice. Small fortunes were made and lost on the voyage – it was rumoured on one ship that a man had won so much money that he had two of his companions act as bodyguards for the rest of the trip. Many ships' rules explicitly forbade gambling, but an infantryman from Arkansas with the 320th Infantry Regiment noticed that

> there were all kinds of card games from solitaire and two-handed gin rummy to as many as a dozen participants in a game of 'Black Jack'. To relieve the tedium of the voyage, many men made small bets on anything from the turn of a card to which side of the ship a seagull would fly while passing. When one submarine alert was over, they would bet on the time the next would occur.

The GIs might spend some time writing letters, perhaps – though that could be a thankless task since they were not allowed to tell the recipients of the letters where they were going, and in any case most didn't know themselves – or maybe reading one of the special wartime pocket-sized paperbacks printed on grey, wartime, economy-standard paper. *The Pocket Book of Verse*, edited by a professor of English, Morris E. Speare, proved remarkably popular when it first appeared in 1940 and was reprinted nine times before Pearl Harbor. Also much thumbed was the best-selling book of the war, *See Here, Private Hargrove*, an irreverent look at army life that every soldier came to recognize. Or there might be a session of penknife art, when GIs carved the name of their home towns, or their girlfriends, or occasionally a more elaborate design, on the teak deck rails. Time slowly passed in such diversions, interspersed with pacing the deck and lifeboat drill.

Lifeboat drill served to remind the troops of the danger from U-boats. Whenever the alert sounded, they had to fall out of their bunks and climb 'all those damned stairs' up to the deck bringing their full equipment with them. A soldier in Henry Giles's company 'got so sick of lugging his pack and rifle and stuff up and down and back and forth that the last time we were alerted, he just quietly dumped it all overboard – pack and rifle and everything! just fed it into the Atlantic. It threw us into convulsions, but it was what we all felt like doing.'

The GIs were often amazed when they realized that their ships were to travel without a convoy. The liners were usually escorted out of harbour from Boston or New York, and then met by British destroyers as they neared the United Kingdom, but many crossed the Atlantic alone. Although the *Mauretania* was one of the fastest ships in the British merchant marine, taking only six days to cross the Atlantic, the troops thought that sending them 'across the wild ocean on our own seemed utter folly'. A corporal from New York who had once worked in a shipyard and made the Atlantic crossing in 1944 wrote, 'it seems hard to conceive that there is but three quarters of an inch of steel now between me and the ocean: that the steel was made by man, and that other men in turn seek even now to break down that sheet and allow the sea to follow all.' The ships steered a zigzag course, changing direction between every four and seven minutes in an effort to outwit the U-boats' skippers; a convoy of troops arriving in Liverpool on the *Franconia* in early 1944 noticed that throughout the voyage, as a further precaution, the crew dumped garbage over the side only at night.

In the early autumn of 1942, Charles Cawthon was standing on the deck of the *Queen Mary* near to where the battalion's automatic rifleman had been positioned to supplement the anti-aircraft defences, for the Luftwaffe still posed a threat to Atlantic shipping, when he heard a thud, and a tremor shook the ship. A low-lying British cruiser, the *Curaçao*, had cut too close across the liner's bows: it was cleaved in half, and sank with the loss of 338 aboard. Cawthon was assembled with his fellow officers and warned that the news of the incident must not be leaked, since it would be damaging to troop morale.

In fact, the troop ships were rarely attacked and continued to travel without convoy protection on most voyages. In June 1945 it was estimated that of the 4,453,061 US soldiers sent to Europe, only 0.024 per cent had been lost at sea.

Drawn into the war, the men sailed into what was, quite literally, an unknown destination. The troops who sailed on the *Monterey* with Robert Arbib, a camouflage technician with the 820th Engineers, in August 1942 – the largest embarkation so far with

HAIL COLUMBIA!

The Saviour of Democracy; the Might of the Military; the Welcome of the People. A propagandist view of the arrival of the American forces in Britain. Punch, *1942.*

a company of 4,000 in a ship designed as a pleasure cruiser to carry 700 – were all convinced of a different destination. 'I'll bet it's the tropics. They gave us yellow fever shots, didn't they?' one man suggested, while according to another, 'They gave us mosquito nets, and headnets too. It's the west coast of Africa!' But the weather remained cold and stormy and, despite its zigzag path, it was obvious that the ship was steering a north-easterly course. The men then remembered that they were carrying their great-coats, overshoes, woollen clothing and heavy woollen socks, so they began to argue about whether it was Greenland or Iceland or Russia or, just possibly, Ireland. 'I still say England,' insisted Arbib, waving a tattered clipping from the *New York Times* reporting that 150 airfields for the American Army Air Force were needed in England and that American soldiers were to build them. . . . ' "Airfields in England." That's us!' And Arbib was right.

The GIs were on their way to Britain as the result of an agreement signed by Churchill and Roosevelt in Washington on New Year's Day, 1942. As soon as he heard of the bombing of Pearl Harbor, Churchill resolved to go to America: 'I have formed the conviction that it is my duty to visit Washington without delay,' he wrote to George VI: 'the whole Anglo–American defence and attack plan has to be concerted in the light of reality. We also have to be careful that our share of munitions and other aid which we are receiving from the United States, does not suffer more than is, I feel, inevitable . . .' Churchill was setting off across the Atlantic to ensure that the US would stick to their agreed 'Europe First' strategy, a commitment which he feared might be jeopardized by the Japanese attack.

HMS *Repulse* and the *Prince of Wales* (on which the Atlantic Charter had been signed) had been sunk by a torpedo attack off Malaya the week before – a grievous blow to both Britain and the United States. Hong Kong was to fall three days after Churchill's arrival in Washington and the Japanese were advancing at great speed on Singapore, the key British bastion in the Far East. US help was desperately needed, but Churchill was concerned that as a result of Pearl Harbor, the 'whole fury of the [American] nation would be turned against Japan'.

He was determined to act quickly to secure US troops on British soil both as protection against a German invasion – which still seemed a possibility at the time – and in preparation for an Allied attack on Europe.

Operation MAGNET, the code name given to the movement of US troops to Northern Ireland, was finally approved at this meeting. Churchill was delighted: 'I always felt that the arrival of sixty or seventy thousand American troops in Ulster would be an assertion of United States' resolve to intervene directly in Europe . . .'

But it was a rather different matter for the troops. John Downing, an 18th Infantry officer, recalled a very young GI sitting on his barracks bag on deck as the troop ship sailed out of New York harbour. He was stuffing his fists into his eyes trying not to cry. Downing looked away. 'I didn't want him to see me staring at him . . . there was no way out of this now. We were heading into something we didn't know anything about . . . and those that came back would have been through the greatest experience that our generation could hope to feel.'

CHAPTER THREE

THE GODDAMN YANKEE ARMY'S COME

WHEN CORPORAL TOM McPARTLAND ARRIVED in Northern Ireland in the spring of 1942, he cabled his parents in Cedar Rapids, Iowa: 'Arrived safely, beautiful country, don't wait up for me.' The US troops were well aware why they had crossed the Atlantic: as Pathé News explained in newsreels showing GIs arriving in Britain and marching over 'welcome' mats emblazoned with the familiar face of the Führer, 'the doughboys have come to stamp out Hitler and all his works.' But few of them had any idea in those early days how long it would be before they got anywhere near the Führer, or how long wives, mothers and girlfriends would have to wait up for them, and, as was the American custom, keep a banner hanging in the window of the family home with a star on it for every member serving in the armed forces.

By August 1942, when there were still only about 1,000 US troops to be seen in London, Mollie Panter-Downes, the London correspondent for the *New Yorker*, sensed 'the impatience of the American troops . . . most of whom talk as if they were somewhat doubtful of being able to give the town the quick once-over before leaving to keep a date with von Rundstedt [the German Commander-in-Chief in the west], which they seem to believe will be around Thursday week at the latest!'

In fact, it was to be two and a half years between the arrival of the first GIs in Northern Ireland and the cross-Channel assault on Europe. The 'peaceful invasion' from the US, which was to build up to nearly two million by May 1944, a month before D-Day, was to have an unforgettable effect on the British people – and on the American 'invaders' as well:

> *Dear old England's not the same,*
> *The dread invasion, well it came.*
> *But no, it's not the beastly Hun,*
> *The god-damn Yankee army's come . . .*

After the long and monotonous sea voyage it was a great relief to see land. 'We crowded the rails,' recalls Robert Arbib, 'looking with wonder at the strange shore as we drew nearer . . . it wasn't the ice-bound coast of Greenland or the bleak rock of Iceland, it was the incredibly green and trim landscape of Scotland – the Firth of Clyde.'

Arbib and his division had arrived at Greenock in Scotland – as had Ralph Martin, who watched Greenock come 'out of the misty dawn like a fuzzy painting in some museum, green and calm and lovely. The snugness of this Scottish port and the homes around its rim, all had the safe and settled look of complete peace. And for a second, the silence was overwhelming.' Greenock was the main port of entry for US troops, though many of the first troops came via Belfast, and later Liverpool, Plymouth and Avonmouth were to give other GIs their first impression of Britain.

Ernie McDonald Leo was a Californian, but he was also a thoroughgoing anglophile – his mother had spent a term at Oxford and had obviously told her son some attractive stories about Britain, and 'by the time the war came round, my whole family was involved in "Bundles for Britain" and used to listen to Ed Murrow's nightly broadcasts from London.' Leo was a medical orderly at a military base hospital in Ohio; when he heard that there might be a chance to go to England, he managed to pull a few strings, and soon he was 'on the list for overseas shipment – though they didn't actually say it was England – security reasons.' He arrived at Greenock in October 1943. Although part of the convoy in which he was travelling had disembarked at Liverpool,

> we had the added treat of the journey up the Irish sea to the Clyde. It was beautiful. The weather was mild and the autumn sun emerged as we cleared the coast and started up the Clyde. We anchored for the night past the famous John Brown's shipyard, where the *Queen Mary* had been built . . . I stood by the rail for the better part of that day just drinking in the sight of my beloved Britain. The bonnie banks of Loch Lomond were only a short way off to the north. When I saw Scotland that day, I loved what I saw.

Robert Arbib and his battalion, the 820th Engineers, were also impressed. 'Looks nice,' his buddy said – 'echoing my thoughts as we looked at the grey stone houses, the neat green hedges and at the green and brown hills above.' Henry Giles discovered that 'even the weight of a full pack and the crammed barracks bag didn't seem too heavy as we came ashore to be gloriously serenaded by a band of Scottish Highlanders playing shrill tunes on their ancient bagpipes, music which sounded like a one-night jam-session right out of the jazz din of Harlem.' Despite their heavy loads many of the soldiers went 'trucking on down to the railway station all laughing and excited and glad to set foot on something solid after bucking the ocean waves'.

Had William Schwinn's supply company been handed a document when they landed at Glasgow 'to say that we would stay there for the rest of our lives, they would probably have got a lot of signatures, because the green grass never looked better and we just wanted to get off that tug and we hoped we'd never see it again.'

When the 16th Infantry landed at Liverpool, Whitey, the company mascot came too – strictly against regulations. Somehow the mongrel, 'a good part of him bulldog', had escaped and was running up and down the platform barking and licking the shoes of everyone there. The assistant commander of the First Infantry Division, Brigadier-General Theodore Roosevelt Jnr, knew the dog well from route marches in Georgia, the Carolinas and Virginia, but he thought fast. 'Look at that English dog,' he said. 'He barks like an

'We'll Keep a Welcome in the Braes.' A bagpipe and drum roll for US troops arriving at Greenock on the Clyde in 1943.

English dog,' he insisted, quelling a naive soldier who had pointed out that it was Whitey: 'Somebody pick him up. We'll take him with us.' So the dog avoided British regulations, and whoever had smuggled him over the Atlantic avoided a charge.

When the first GIs arrived in the spring and summer of 1942, it was usually a collection of Englishwomen from the WVS (Women's Voluntary Service) or Red Cross who were waiting to welcome them on the quayside to serve them with cups of tea. 'We knew they wouldn't like our coffee,' a WVS worker predicted: 'we didn't like it much ourselves.' The booklet issued to the troops to introduce them to Britain had been blunt on the subject – 'the British don't know how to make a cup of coffee' – but had gone on to say evenhandedly that 'you don't know how to make a good cup of tea: it's an even swap.'

On embarkation back in New York or Boston, every GI had been handed a letter which looked as if had been personally written by the President on White House notepaper: 'You are a soldier in the United States Army,' it read: 'You have embarked for distant places where the war is being fought.' But where was the war? wondered Ralph Martin, who'd come to Britain as a combat reporter for *Stars and Stripes*. 'And then suddenly we saw it. Barrage balloons hanging ugly in the sky, spoiling the picture postcard.' 'We were in a war zone at last,' Robert Arbib realized:

We stared at our first barrage balloons, moored to barges in the river. We saw a freighter with a gaping torpedo hole at the waterline. We noticed little camouflaged naval craft and one large aircraft carrier moored at Greenock harbour . . . We looked for traces of war, and discussed the evidence of bomb damage that lay all around us . . . we hadn't heard that Glasgow had been bombed, and we were not certain that the occasional open space between buildings, a gutted building, was a sign of the Blitz. We soon discovered that they were indeed bomb damaged . . .

Bill Ong, arriving in April 1942 to help build an airfield in East Anglia, was appalled at what he saw: 'there is no way of describing to an audience who doesn't have the experience . . . I remember only too well how shocked we were when we disembarked at the sight of all the bomb damage. And if that wasn't enough, I guess it was the whole atmosphere of dirt and dinginess around the docks.'

As the *Queen Mary*, damaged in collision with the *Curaçao*, limped into Greenock and the troops transferred to tugs, Charles Cawthon heard for the first time an air-raid siren 'wailing for real', rising above the British army band which 'boomed and clanged' a welcome to the US troops, and saw the 'barrage balloons with dangling cables designed to keep off low attacks which swayed on the end of their tethers damp in the smoke'. The grimy dockside buildings were camouflaged with dirty green paint that to Arbib looked 'old and neglected, as if it had been hastily applied during the early days of the war and then had been found useless'.

For the GIs there was another poignant reminder, too, of the war they had sailed into. Rationing only began to take effect in the United States during the autumn of 1942, with restraints on the consumption of coffee and sugar. Food was still plentiful in America and as the boats pulled into British harbours, the troops would often toss apples, oranges and cigarettes down to those waiting on the quayside. Children, dock workers and even British soldiers scrabbled to pick up the bounty which the Americans had so insouciantly thrown. 'We didn't realise,' Arbib regretted, 'that those would be the last oranges we would see for more than a year.'

Almost before the *Queen Mary*'s anchor had been lowered as she drew into Greenock:

Little boats by ones and twos came rowing out from the banks. They were manned by sea urchins of the river fronts who had learned that newly arriving Yanks had money, cigarettes and candy in their pockets . . . Packs of cigarettes by the dozen whistled downwards, and not all of them landed in the little crafts. Paddles lashed furiously in the water trying to retrieve the cellophane-wrapped smokes from Yankee land. Hershey Bars . . . went overboard in great numbers . . . even dimes and quarters whizzed down.

So much was thrown down in the end that Ralph Martin heard the *Queen*'s loudspeaker system bellow 'Attention! Attention!' and the Commanding Officer informed the troops that nothing more was to be thrown overboard, and that such action would incur a court martial. But thirty minutes later, there was the occasional kerplunk in the water as packs of smokes sailed from portholes. No one troubled to find out from which portholes they came.

Eventually the gangplanks were lowered and the troops staggered ashore with their packs, rifles and equipment. As Arbib plodded along the cobblestones with his eighty-pound load, the string round a bundle of seven cartons of cigarettes broke, scattering them on the ground. Determined not to lose the 'last cigarettes and pipe tobacco I might see for many months', he broke ranks to pick them up. 'The next moments were high agony and low comedy' as he scrabbled on the ground gathering his scattered packages while 'trying to keep my rifle on one arm, my pack and blankets and overcoat and extra shoes on my back, my gas mask on my other arm, and my helmet on my head'. His commanding officer was not impressed: 'Fine lot of heroes we looked like . . . Arbib gathering cigarettes, like an old squaw woman in a field picking peas. The mighty American comes to Scotland. Goddamn poor performance.'

Bill Ong was excited to be in Britain – and in the war. He noticed the English troops on the quayside watching the GIs arrive, but it was only later that he learned that they'd turned out to see 'our loose-footed rolling gait after two weeks at sea! . . . the Yank marching style compared to the foot-stamping and exaggerated arm movements of the British soldiers must have made us look like something from the music halls.'

There were mixed reactions to the GIs' arrival. John Downing, a lieutenant with the 1st Infantry Division, noted a distinct lack of interest from the British when he arrived at Gourock: 'There was no fanfare or excitement. The railway employees and local civilians looked at us curiously and we in turn stared back at them, commenting among ourselves about the bobby with his characteristic helmet and the women working as freight handlers and car cleaners.'

By contrast Ralph Martin had

> never in all my life seen such a rich, warm and sincere welcome given to anyone. The Scottish civilians gathered all along the railroad banks to wave at us . . . the people yelled and threw thumbs up at us . . . and one old man leaned out of . . . a window and made a V for victory sign on both hands, whilst mothers leaned out of windows and waved towels and aprons at us.

As they came ashore, the troops were handed a tabloid newspaper proclaiming 'WEL-COME' in large capitals above a picture of Winston Churchill, smiling, looking confident and giving his famous V sign, while proclaiming that 'wherever you go in this country you will be among friends. Our fighting men look on you as comrades and brothers in arms.' But that still had to be put to the test.

As the *Duchess of Bedford* drew near to Liverpool, Brigadier-General Roosevelt Jnr called his men together to tell them that their destination was England and to give them a pep talk on Anglo–American relations and being ambassadors of goodwill and that sort of thing. 'Britain? Yuck!' was the consensus of Company E. Why were they going to Britain? The Limeys (so called since the eighteenth century, because, it was said, the British navy used to drink lime juice to ward off scurvy) were stuffed shirts – and they couldn't fight anyway. They'd run away at Dunkirk, hadn't they? Such jibes were commonplace: the Union Jack was sneered at as being 'red, white, blue – and yellow'; after Dunkirk the British soldiers were nicknamed the 'Dunkirk harriers', and a story went the rounds soon after the troops arrived of two US servicemen who, seeing a British soldier running for a train, bawled out after him, 'Is that the way you ran at Dunkirk?' The soldier had swung round: 'Yes,' he said, letting his train go, 'and when we ran out of ammunition we did this' – and he put up his fists and knocked the two Americans to the ground.

Ed Murrow, Britain's unofficial radio ambassador, admitted that he had been unimpressed with the country before the war: it was 'a small, pleasant, historical, but relatively unimportant island off the coast of Europe . . . a sort of museum piece – pleasant but small', and the people had appeared 'slow, indifferent and extremely complacent . . . I admired your history [but] doubted your future . . .'

The feeling that the war in Britain was not their war was deep-seated in many Americans. 'Perfidious Albion' was an imperial power, and the Americans had had to fight a war to be free of British control. If Charles Cawthon had not been so out of breath as he 'staggered along under the weight of rifles and baggage' when he came ashore at Greenock, he might have muttered, somewhat bitterly, 'George III, here we are.' The Americans had not forgotten Britain's non-payment of debts from the First World War, as citizens of a former colony they saw no great virtue in fighting to keep the British Empire intact, and they were not greatly in awe of the British political system: 'England isn't a democracy as I understand democracy,' complained a sergeant from Chicago. The author Phyllis Bentley, one of a number of British writers who tried to explain the two English-speaking nations to each other, recognized that American school textbooks 'often portray Britain as a blood-stained monster steeped in feudalism . . . I was often asked whether the war would "make England more democratic" – a legitimate and proper question: but once it was phrased "Will the war make England have representative institutions?" I pointed out with some heat that we had had a parliament since 1272.'

As *Fortune* magazine put it in 1942, for Americans 'the war was neither a threat nor a crusade, it was only a painful necessity.' In her conversations with many GIs who came to the American Red Cross Club where she worked in Norwich, Jean Lancaster Rennie recognized this reluctance:

> they gave us the tools – they sent us food parcels, they gave shelter to our children in their rich, wide country. But they didn't want a seat at the war any nearer than a seat at the cinema . . . they hadn't wanted to come, so it followed – did it not? – that their hearts were not with us in our hour of need . . . they were at home in Philadelphia, Tennessee, Boston, Connecticut . . .

The crux, as Harold Nicolson realized, was that 'whereas for us, Anglo–American co-operation means security, for them it suggests danger.'

Although on the whole the entry of the US into the war after Pearl Harbor was greeted with relief and gratitude in Britain, Mass Observation, the enthusiastic amateur sociologists who monitored public opinion during the war years, noted 'a malicious delight that at long last the Americans would have a taste of war' and contempt for a nation which 'went to war when they are directly threatened, after a year in which they seemed content to let other people do their fighting for democracy'. As a caustic Welsh soldier who settled in America after the war remarked,

> though many Britons seemed to hate and despise America, being vastly ignorant of American history, they still wondered loudly, indignantly and interminably, why the Yanks weren't already in the war, as if America was another dominion or

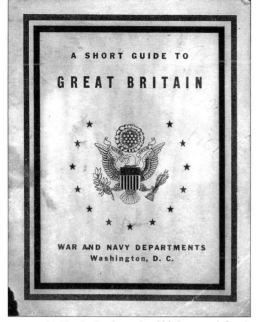

In "getting along" the first important thing to remember is that the British are like the Americans in many ways—but not in *all* ways. You will quickly discover differences that seem confusing and even wrong. Like driving on the left side of the road, and having money based on an "impossible" accounting system, and drinking warm beer. But once you get used to things like that, you will realize that they belong to England just as baseball and jazz and coca-cola belong to us.

The British Like Sports. The British of all classes are enthusiastic about sports, both as amateurs and as spectators of professional sports. They love to shoot, they love to play games, they ride horses and bet on horse races, they fish. (But be careful where you hunt or fish. Fishing and hunting rights are often private property.)

11

'A User's Guide to the Old Country.' On their journey over, all US troops were issued with this pocket introduction to British life.

latter-day Hessians at the beck and call of a latter-day King George. Many Britons went out of their way *ad nauseam* to tell me just what they thought was wrong with the Americans, who appeared to be a vicious, degraded and immoral lot, and I couldn't for the life of me understand why the British wanted such an unprincipled lot as allies . . .

'We were Johnny-come-latelies,' suggested the historian Laurence Lafore who had come from Washington to work with the US Information Service in London: 'that explained the peculiar form of self-defense against Americans that the British constantly presented to us: simultaneously to criticize us for not having arrived on the scene sooner while denouncing us for arriving at all.'

In March 1942, a commentator for Mass Observation pinpointed part of the reason for these ambivalent attitudes: 'Americans are often regarded as a rather eccentric kind of Englishman' and this 'comes out in people's feelings that the Americans ought really to have been helping us right through the early part of the war, just like the Canadians and Australians . . . America is not really regarded as a foreign country to be wooed with praise, but as a close relative to be freely chided for her shortcomings.'

Much serious thought had to be given to the problem of Anglo–American relations on the ground. Not only did winning the war depend on Allied co-operation: the post-war economic and political order did too, and good minds were set to the problem.

On their arrival in Britain, all American troops were issued with *A Short Guide to Great Britain*, a 38-page handbook written by Eric Knight, the American author of the best-selling war novel, *This Above All*. It emphasized the fact that

" They won't let on who the camp is for."

Considerable secrecy surrounded the arrival and dispositions of US troops in Britain during the early days of the 'invasion'. But they were hard to miss.

Since your ship left port, however, you have been in a war zone. You will find that all Britain is a war zone and has been since September 1939 . . . the British have been bombed, night after night . . . thousands of them have lost their houses, their possessions and their families . . . The British will welcome you as friends and allies. But remember that crossing the ocean doesn't automatically make you a hero . . . there are housewives in aprons and youngsters in knee pants who have lived through more high explosives in air raids than many soldiers saw in first-class barrages in the last war.

The booklet went on to make it clear why it was so important that the 'friendly invasion' should be just that:

You are going to Great Britain as part of an Allied offensive – to meet Hitler and beat him on his own ground . . . America and Britain are allies. Hitler knows that they are both powerful countries, tough and resourceful. He knows that they . . . mean his crushing defeat in the end. So it is only common sense to understand that the first and major duty Hitler has given his propaganda chiefs is to separate Britain and America and spread distrust. If he can do that, his chances of winning might return.

With the Japanese advance in the Far East and with German bombers less than seven minutes away this was 'no time to fight old wars over again and bring up old grievances . . . even if you come from an Irish–American family and think of the English as persecutors of the Irish, or you may think of them as enemy redcoats who fought against us in the American revolution and wars of 1812'. Hitler was the enemy now, and could only be defeated by an Allied force.

The anthropologist Margaret Mead was despatched to Britain in 1943 to 'study the relationships between American troops and the British'. The war in the Far East had put the Samoan islands out of court for field work and Mead brought her trained eye to the problems presented by the GI invasion of Britain, and in particular of translating the Americans' behaviour for their British hosts: 'Usually foreigners are described as being rather like ourselves but having a few funny customs, wearing different clothes, using odd expressions, eating some strange foods. Under such a method American soldiers would be regarded as very much like British soldiers with a few odd habits which would have to be forgiven or tolerated.'

Eric Knight recognized this paradox in his *Short Guide*: 'the most evident truth of all is that in their major ways of life the British and American people are much alike. They speak the same language. They both believe in representative government, in freedom of worship, in freedom of speech.' But, the booklet continued, 'Each country has minor national characteristics which differ . . . it is by causing misunderstandings over these minor differences that Hitler hopes to make his propaganda effective.'

Both Eric Knight and Margaret Mead agreed that 'you defeat enemy propaganda not by denying that these differences exist but by admitting them openly and then trying to understand them.' Margaret Mead expressed an anthropological view that was current at the time, which proved most useful in dealing with the fact that 16 million Americans were of German origin: 'It isn't race but the way in which people are brought up that makes them behave the way they do – who scolds them or praises them, for what and when; what they learn at play, at home and at school . . . these are the things which determine how people behave.' The *Short Guide* took a somewhat different tack, stressing a shared history: 'Our common speech, our common law and our ideals of religious freedom were all brought from Britain when the Pilgrims landed at Plymouth Rock. Our ideas about political liberties are also British and parts of our own Bill of Rights were borrowed from the great charters of British liberty.'

The British had their own version of the *Short Guide*. *Meet the US Army* was published in 1943 for use in schools, and was designed to give children and young people 'the opportunity for the ordinary people of the two great English-speaking nations to get to know each other in the mass . . . an opportunity never presented to the tourist traffic in peacetime.' Written by the poet Louis MacNeice, it stressed the temporary nature of the GI occupation and tried to forge a common experience between 'the average Tommy' and 'the average doughboy', neither of whom comes from 'a militaristic nation [which] thinks of war as an end in itself'.

Neither country might be military minded: but the two were vastly different, and all the *vade mecums* agreed that this went a long way to explain disparate attitudes between the British and the Americans. Louis MacNeice pointed out that: 'the USA is practically a continent, its area being over 3 million square miles, as against 59,000 square miles of Great Britain', which meant that 'in the USA, you can get in a car – a high-powered car at that – and drive for a week or more in a comparatively straight line without running into the sea.'

Similarly, the guide book issued to the disembarking GIs brought home the dinkiness of Britain to the Americans: 'You will find out right away that England is a small country, smaller than North Carolina or Iowa. The whole of Great Britain – that is England and Scotland and Wales together – is hardly bigger than Minnesota. England's longest river, the Thames (pronounced "Tems"), is not even as big as the Mississippi when it leaves Minnesota.' And Louis MacNeice advised: 'remember what Texans remember [and, he might have added, rarely hesitated to mention] – that it is the largest state in the US – three times the size of England and Scotland combined.'

Britain not only seemed small to the GIs as they clambered into the trains that would take them to their first postings: it seemed cold and drab and dirty as well. And they were going to have to get used to it: the common response to any complaint was 'Don't you know there's a war on?' As their handbook told them:

> Britain may look a little shopworn and grimy to you. The British people are anxious to have you know that you are not seeing their country at its best. There's been a war on since 1939. The houses haven't been painted because factories are not making paint – they're making planes. The famous English gardens and parks are either unkempt because there are no men to take care of them, or they are being used to grow needed vegetables. Britain's taxis look antique because Britain makes tanks for herself and Russia and hasn't the time to make cars [and, it could have added, there's no petrol to drive them]. If British civilians look dowdy or badly dressed it is not because they do not like good clothes or know how to wear them. All clothes are rationed and the British know that they help war production by wearing an old suit or dress until it cannot be patched any longer. Old clothes are 'good form'.

Or, as Robert Raymond, an American who had joined the RAF on the outbreak of war, saw it, 'the English people have never cared much for their personal appearance and this peacetime liability has proved a tremendous wartime asset.'

The US soldier's guide continued:

> For many months the British have been doing without things which the Americans take for granted . . . You are coming to Britain from a country where your home is still safe, food is still plentiful, and the lights are still burning. So it is doubly important for you to remember that British soldiers and civilians have been under tremendous strain. Sixty thousand British civilians – men, women and children – have died under bombs and yet the morale of the British is unbreakable and high. A nation doesn't come through if it doesn't have plain common guts – you won't be able to tell the British much about 'taking it'. They

'Don't you know there's a war on?' A traditional British greeting
to a visiting GI.

are not particularly interested in taking it anymore. They are far more interested in getting together a solid friendship with us so we can all start dishing it out to Hitler.

That was the crux of it. The US troops had come to Britain to help win the war, and they knew that they weren't going to get home again until they'd done it. So their anxieties about the incompetence of the British war machine and the passivity of the British people had to be dispelled: 'The British are tough, strong people, and good allies. Don't be misled by the British tendency to be soft-spoken and polite. If they need to be they can be pretty tough. The English language didn't spread across the oceans and over the mountains and jungles and swamps of the world because these men were panty-waists' – or cissies in English-speak.

But despite all this sound advice, a British journalist writing for an American audience had to admit that 'when American soldiers landed in Great Britain we made the mistake of thinking that because they spoke English they were just like ourselves. The attitude of the American soldiers was naturally the same. They expected a home from home and what they found was, to all intents and purposes, a foreign country.'

CHAPTER FOUR

'WHERE THE HELL AM I?'

'THIS, YOU SAY TO YOURSELF as you look out of the train window, is England,' thought Private William Hogan from San Francisco, 'and you find yourself repeating that fact all during the long train ride through the Midlands from a west coast port, and later too, when you bivouac temporarily in a grove of tall trees in an immense meadow with a thatched-roof farmhouse nearby . . . and you keep saying to yourself, "Look: this is England." '

Most US troops got their first impressions of Britain from the railway carriages – which they found odd enough, with their small, six-seater compartments and corridors – that took them from their ports of embarkation and distributed them all over the United Kingdom to the camps and bases where they were to be stationed.

When Colonel Ross, Chief of Transportation in the European Theater of Operations (ETO), took his first look at the facilities available in Britain in 1942, he reported that the country was 'so cramped and small, the railroad equipment so tiny, the roads so small and crooked, and methods so entirely different' that the entire plan for transporting troops and equipment from America would have to be rethought. But the troops were generally quite impressed: 'the English railroads are neatly laid out with very few side crossings. The roads either go under or over the tracks, which is a good idea. The freight cars are not much bigger than some of our trucks; the British call them goods wagons. They have only four wheels and carry at the most about twenty tons.' Although on many occasions the railways were to prove less than adequate for the vast amount of supplies and troops which were moved around Britain, and a quantity of US rolling stock had to be shipped over, by the summer of 1942 the railways were already running an additional 5,000 special trains for American requirements.

An infantry officer on his way to Hampshire was struck by the small scale of Britain, too: 'all night we clattered through a countryside of what seemed miniature houses and cottages. Occasionally, the train ground to a halt at station platforms, dimly lit by blackout lamps, where ladies in dark uniform poked trays of vaguely sweet buns and mugs of hot tea at us.'

As Ralph Hammond's train steamed south from Glasgow 'through the green patches of farm land', he was particularly struck 'by the field after field of turnips. "Jeepers," a GI cried, "they must eat turnips for bread." Later I found out that they were fed to stock [cattle] during winter.' To anyone from the East Coast the English countryside appeared much like Connecticut, but with one difference: 'England has no timber land to speak of.'

The greenness of the English countryside impressed many of the Americans. 'Why is it so green?' a GI asked a Shropshire girl: 'What do you put on it?' – to which she replied, 'It's our climate, it's always raining.' He said that in America 'it's a sort of grey colour, you know, sort of sage colour. It's not like here.'

There were women in the US Army who came to Britain, usually as administrative assistants, cryptographers, censors or as interpreters of reconnaissance photographs, but the volunteer WACs came to the UK in droplets rather than the flood of the men. By December 1943 there were only 1,200 and on the eve of D-Day only 4,715 who were briefly in Britain on their way to the continent. One was Camilla Mays Frank, who arrived on the dockside at Liverpool in April 1944 and 'stood around, wondering just what this England was all about . . . So far it seemed cold, raw and forgettable.' The women boarded a train to take them to Lichfield, and as they sat

> in the tiny compartments of this fussy little English train watching the country-side amble by, one could have been forgiven for asking where the war was. Certainly it had not reached here. Herds of cattle grazed in the patchwork of fields all around. I was fascinated by the hedgerows bordering the tiny fields. Those in turn gave way to such beautiful villages and small towns that looked like pages from the history of England. I couldn't believe, when confronted by so much beauty, so much peace, so much history, that this country had been fighting for its life against the Germans since 1939.

But her reverie was soon disturbed

> by the roar of engines. Across this same landscape flew four enormous bombers with British markings to the front and rear, escorted by tiny fighters displaying their RAF roundels . . . I realized that the war was here, all around us. I just had not been looking for it . . . We were alone with our thoughts. Most of us were wondering what the next few months held in store for us in this tiny island fortress, anchored off the coast of France.

John Downing had just settled down in his railway carriage with his fellow officers to play poker when one of his colleagues, who had been detailed as a mess officer, enlisted his help in distributing food – K-rations – to the troops. These cartons of survival fare had originally been issued only to parachute troops, but proved useful for any troops on the move. At first they were a novelty. Downing felt himself lucky to have received a dinner ration which was

> the most edible of the three types of meal. It tasted more like food than like a mess of canned vitamin complexes. It was almost a game to fish out the soya bean meal crackers, the stick of gum, the three Chelsea cigarettes, the synthetic lemon powder, the lumps of sugar (which were wrapped in paper advertising Joe's Steak House or Moroni's Spaghetti Palace), the candy, and finally the *pièce de résistance* – the small can of processed American cheese.

'The whole thing was a triumph for American ingenuity,' concluded a satisfied soldier. But after a few months of K-rations one GI had decided that the only way to get a bit of variety was to eat the box they came in as well.

As night drew in, the centre compartment lights were dimmed and the black-out blinds pulled down, for in 1942 troop trains were a favourite target for strafing by the Luftwaffe. The troops slouched down in their seats and tried to sleep. Every time the train jolted to a halt at a station, several GIs would poke their heads out of the window to find out where they were. It wasn't easy. All station signs had been removed or painted over to baffle any German parachutists who might land and when the GIs did manage to call out to a station employee the name they were told didn't usually mean anything anyway. So they went back to sleep, cramped and uncomfortable and not a little apprehensive about what they would find when they finally reached their destination.

By May 1944, on the eve of D-Day, American uniforms were evident all over Britain. US ammunition and supplies and equipment were stacked along every road and US troops occupied 100,000 buildings, either newly built or requisitioned, ranging from small Nissen huts, cottages and bell tents to sprawling hangars, workshops and assembly plants in more than 1,100 cities, towns and villages. It was a dramatic process – and it had its problems. In June 1942, when the ETO was established, there were fewer than 60,000 US troops in the British Isles, most of them in Northern Ireland: by May 1944, an invasion force of 1,526,965 combat and service troops (including air and ground forces) was stationed in an already overcrowded island, with a population of just over 48 million in an area smaller than the state of Oregon.

This operation – the reception, accommodation and maintenance of the US troops in Britain in accordance with the requirements for the invasion of Europe – was code-named BOLERO: like Ravel's music, it was intended to build up to a climax – and that climax would be D-Day. The story of those two and a half years is that of a stop-go policy in which Operation BOLERO began to look more like Operation SQUARE DANCE, as estimates of troops were revised and re-revised in the light of the requirement of US troops for the Far East and for the Allied offensive in North Africa, Operation TORCH in November 1942, shipping difficulties, and the problems involved in the rapid assembly and training of a US army and air force for war, not to mention military and political disputes over objectives, strategies, tactics, command networks and responsibilities.

Accommodation needed to be found – or built – for the BOLERO forces, depot space located for storage and services, and hospitals, airfields and assault training courses constructed. It was, said Dwight D. Eisenhower, Commander of the ETO, 'an appalling task'; and it was these facilities that the first contingents of GIs had come to prepare.

At first, the problems of housing the GIs and of storing their supplies and equipment were dealt with by taking over and adapting accommodation from the British Army and Royal Air Force and erecting Nissen huts and bell tents around airfields and supply depots. Although officers more often lived in private houses, billeting with families was regarded as an emergency measure for enlisted men, though this happened with increasing frequency as troop numbers increased. (Though a Bridgwater woman remembers a policeman telling her father that he had the greatest difficulty arranging billets for US Military Policemen in the town at first. 'Anyone would think I was expecting them to take in a German.') Plans were therefore made for the gradual replacement of British troops from the Southern Command area; US ground troops also took over such depots as Burtonwood in Lancashire and Ashchurch near Cheltenham. Former warehouses were often ill-suited for the purpose; a depot in Liverpool, used in peacetime for brewery

LIFE IN A NISSEN HUT
'You don't know what you're missin'
Until you've heard the raindrops kissin'
On the roof top of your Nissen.'

US engineers building Nissen huts in the mud of East Anglia.

GIs stationed in Northern Ireland marching through their camp.

Kit inspection in a Nissen hut . . .

. . . and back to life as usual.

storage, still relied on dray horses to convey supplies. And existing facilities only went a small way to providing the anticipated hospital requirements for US troops.

Given the scale of the task facing the US authorities, it was agreed that the process of displacement would be gradual, and British services would provide daily maintenance and supplies until US supply staff could take over – including the NAAFI facilities which continued to run canteens until the US PXs (post exchanges) were stocked and fully functional.

Ironically, the headquarters of the supplies division itself, established at Cheltenham, had a problem. Barracks for the enlisted men were non-existent, and they had to be quartered in tented camps around the town, and on Prestbury Park race course, where some of the more fortunate commandeered the grandstand, stables and other buildings on the track as billets. As one GI pointed out to his 'stable mate', if the commodious stall they occupied was good enough for a £10,000 thoroughbred horse, a $10,000 GI shouldn't complain.

The fact that the GIs were in Britain to launch a cross-Channel invasion influenced their movements from the start. The general plan was that US troops would be landed on the western section of the French coastline, British and Canadian troops towards the east of the designated invasion area. The US troops would therefore embark from the ports of south-western England when the invasion was launched. The troops and cargo had disembarked at ports along the west coast of Britain – the Clyde, Mersey and the Bristol Channel – and it was clearly logical that they should be quartered in the areas between these points of entry and the anticipated ports of departure. The British Isles were divided up into base sections for supply, with a western section running from the Bristol Channel up the west coast to Scotland. This was the area that received and processed the thousands of troops that were to pour into the UK (most of the troops bound for North Africa in the autumn of 1942 went through Northern Ireland). And when the forces for the Allied invasion of Europe started to build up in late 1943, this region handled the huge quantities of cargo and operated as supply and distribution depots. The eastern base section covered East Anglia and up the east coast to the Scottish borders; and the whole of East Anglia, with its flat terrain and proximity to Germany, became a chequerboard of air force bases for the British RAF and the US 8th Air Force. The southern base section, which encompassed extensive moorland and the rocky shores of Devon and Cornwall, provided a perfect area for training. As D-Day approached, this coastline was also used for amphibious training, as was that of western Scotland, and the whole area eventually became the springboard for the cross-Channel invasion.

Although the ARCADIA conference held in Washington after Pearl Harbor envisaged a cross-Channel assault in the spring of 1943, the timing remained a contentious political matter among the Allies, Britain, the US and the USSR, and before long it became accepted by the US military planners that it would be difficult to contemplate mounting a continental invasion before spring 1944. But as soon as the airfields were there to accommodate them, and the difficulties of transport across the Atlantic had been resolved, the United States Army Air Force (USAAF) could bring across a vanguard of its heavy bombers – the B-17 'Flying Fortresses' and the B-24 'Liberators' – to join the RAF in what would become virtually round-the-clock bombing of occupied Europe and Germany. At the outset it was hoped that it might be possible to win the war by technological

What! No coal?

superiority from the air, so avoiding a repetition of the spectre which haunted British and American strategists alike – the slaughter of the ground troops fighting in France in the First World War. Building or taking over a planned 127 airfields, along with workshops, depot facilities, and accommodation for aircrews and ground staff, was a top priority for the first contingents of US troops arriving in Britain.

As the GIs stumbled off the trains at their destinations, most had no idea where they were. Robert Arbib and his contingent of the 820th Engineers had been sent to build an airstrip near Debach in east Suffolk, probably not more than 200 miles from the nearest German aerodrome. As a camouflage expert himself, Arbib was impressed by the 'maze' which was to be the group's home for several weeks. The tents and their guy ropes turned it into an obstacle course 'with a path that was fairly practicable during daylight hours when you could stop and duck under branches or step over ropes without running the danger of being garotted or tripped too often'. But at night, when the troops were ordered not to shine bright objects or wear white clothing, and forbidden to light even a match, 'the maze became almost impassable . . . a walk from one end of the camp to the latrine bucket at the other became a daring adventure.' He invariably 'got trapped, tripped or lost': as did his companions, whose shouts of 'Where the hell am I?' echoed through the night – and could have been asking a more fundamental question.

John Downing and his 1st Infantry Division had arrived at 7.00 a.m. at the station 'which was our destination'. After some verbal bullying, the platoon was shaped into a marching formation and with a 'washed-out, sleepy, early morning look' marched off to the old British cavalry barracks at Tidworth on Salisbury Plain – a British Army garrison town to which Charles Cawthon's 29th Infantry Division was heading as well. They found it 'dismal' with 'the disconsolate look of age, not raw newness. Its architecture dated from the Victorian height of empire and was built for the ages: brick, iron, slate, concrete and asphalt, all constantly damp or drenched, for rain and mist dominated the weather on Salisbury Plain.'

Maurice Commanday from Yonkers, New York, was an engineer attached to a depot group with the RAF. He landed in England in August 1942 and by September he was quartered in a former RAF post, 'one of the most palatial palaces I have ever seen . . . our quarters are in a tremendous building complete with stratospheric ceilings, dining hall, billiard room, parlor (and what a parlor), card room and oh just lovely.' But Commanday and his friends were not overawed by their surroundings:

> It is the custom here, when the evening's entertainment is at its height, to pile tables and chairs on top of one another in our spacious anteroom (parlor). If the persons so engaged are sufficiently sober to accomplish this task with reasonable precision, some brave drunk or foolhardy individual climbs this tower of Babel armed with pencil or pen or be-sooted naked feet and inscribes his name or footprints on the ceiling. Our anteroom ceiling is so vast, so stratospheric that its inscriptions are usually overlooked by landsmen. It takes an old airman, long experienced at scanning the heights, to notice them himself. For obvious reasons I hope they never clear it off. The names of heroes long dead are up there, alongside of ours.

Bill French, an artillery officer, hit lucky too: he was first 'quartered in an old English country manor. It has sixty-four rooms and at the last count I found six bathrooms! Oh yes, there is an enormous fireplace in every bedroom!' However, his men were

> located in Nissen huts which are scattered around among the trees, and the living conditions in them are pretty rugged. The only heating they have are little coke heaters about three feet high. As they are strictly rationed with coal and coke, the tricks they turn to get just that little bit more are really something but nobody complains because we all expected to be sleeping on the ground . . .

Later, he was billeted in the cottage of a caretaker and his family in the grounds of a ducal estate. 'The manor house was still inhabited by this duke and he sure was very hospitable. He would allow us to be taken on guided tours around this ancestral pile and he also very generously allowed the use of the main hall for dances and parties.'

But in some of these grand billets, remembers Bill French

> there was a good deal of vandalism: unthinking vandalism perhaps, but the damage was there nonetheless. The general feeling among some troops was that 'Uncle Sam will pay'. Indeed, I understand that the British aristocratic families did put in heavy claims after the war when they returned to their homes to find, in some cases, whole panelled walls stripped and burned for firewood. Even window frames. And in one case that I heard about, a whole hand-wrought staircase, probably hundreds of years old, had been demolished.

Snug in his luxury accommodation, Commanday had to 'laugh when I think of myself setting off to war with a complete kit of field equipment, including pup tent, sleeping-bag etc and winding up living like this.' But the majority of GIs lived in barracks, in hastily erected Nissen or Quonset huts, or exposed to the weathers in tents.

A radio operator with Fighter Command of the 8th Air Force arrived at High Wycombe, the headquarters of the RAF's Bomber Command, to be directed to rows of tents: 'All of the mattresses were in one of the tents . . . no lights were allowed, so I spent my first night in England using my overcoat as a mattress. Then the rains came. The tent leaked every place the gush touched it so I had very little sleep that first night.'

As Bill Ong, who'd come to Ipswich to build an airfield, explained:

> thousands of tent cities sprang up to house the increasing hordes of GIs. It was impossible for the British to build enough solid shelters for everyone. We luckless engineers mostly had a hard life, but the tents were looked on with special disfavor. You couldn't stay dry in them, and on a rainy night the trick was to avoid touching the sides. If you did, you were lucky to get any sleep because the water would form a pool on the ground-sheet and before you knew it the place would be swamped.

F Company of the 18th Infantry Regiment had a particularly tough time when they were posted near Glasgow for training. The golf course on the Pollick estates 'had been converted to a military camp by the simple method of erecting tents on it. These tents were the British type, conical and small, the walls reaching up only a foot from the ground before the cone began. You slept in them with your feet toward the center and your head toward the circumference . . . three officers or eight enlisted men to a tent.' The officers' tents were at the foot of a small hill and the rain

> which came down steadily drained off into the area and the mud was calf-deep. There were small duckboards in the tents which helped to keep the bedding out of the mud . . . the washrooms were open sheds with large metal troughs for basins. Cold-water faucets were placed at intervals along these troughs. The latrine was a sheet iron shed divided into a series of doorless stalls with heavy iron buckets under the holes in the board seats. The mess was a large hospital tent surrounded by soapy mud and furnished with long wooden tables and no lights. The whole camp looked so miserable and depressing that we were sure we were going to spend quite a little time there!

When he arrived at Tidworth, Lieutenant Downing was directed to the officers' quarters, 'called the Kandahar barracks after some obscure Indian frontier battle'. He found a dejected group of officers sitting around: 'our advance details had failed to function properly and quarters had not been assigned.' Because of some other administrative difficulty, there was no lunch for the weary platoon. Downing went off and found a table in a side room, lay down on it and went to sleep. Finally, next day, he was able to move into 'Quarter Master House', near the main barracks, which had been turned over to the 18th Infantry Regiment for its officers' quarters. Downing and a colleague laid claim to the living room for themselves: 'it was bare of furniture, but it had a fireplace and panelled walls. We moved our belongings in and set up housekeeping.'

Charles Cawthon and his fellow officers were assigned a two-storey section of the red-brick barracks at Tidworth. Each floor consisted of a long, cavernous room and each room was heated by a single fireplace. 'Lining the walls were double-deck bunks covered by stained, sectional mattresses called "biscuits" by the British – straw-stuffed sacks pretending to be mattresses.' His company soon began to feel nostalgic for their training camp, Camp Meade in Maryland, which they had so disliked at the time, but now referred to as 'Meade Country Club'. But dour as the quarters were, the Stonewallers (the name by which the 116th Regiment had been known from the days of the Civil War) came to prefer them to 'marching and training in what seemed like continuous rain'. Much of their equipment had not yet arrived and some of their 81mm mortar guns had been lost in transit, so while they waited their seven-day-a-week training schedule involved endless road marches – 'the standard one being a 30-miler that at its halfway point circled the prehistoric monument of Stonehenge.' Cawthon recalls that the soldiers expressed very little curiosity about the origin or purpose of the enormous slabs of stone 'or how they had been transported and erected at a time so far back beyond the dawn of history . . . we were more concerned with getting back the fifteen miles to Tidworth and out of the damp.'

But for most people it was the endless rows of Nissen and Quonset huts caterpillaring over the countryside round airfields and supply bases – 'tin billets' – that particularly evoked the GI occupation. Whereas the Quonset hut, an American construction, was octagonal and had a flat roof, the more familiar Nissen hut was made of curved corrugated-iron plates bolted together, with a concrete floor, a brick wall at either end and a few small windows – 'iceboxes open at both ends'.

'It looked like a metal pipe that had been sawed in half and set on a concrete base,' remembers William Ruck who was serving with the 448th Bomb Group at Seething near Norwich.

> There was very little space inside . . . it had six double-decker bunks with very little room for personal effects and a small metal bar connected to the wall by each bunk for hanging clothes. Each bar was only about a foot long, so not many clothes could be hung. There were two crews, twelve enlisted men assigned to that hut – and on the door the number 13 was painted in large, white letters which didn't add much to our peace of mind.

But the men soon improved the look of the place with pin-ups on the wall, and they made lockers for themselves out of the crates in which 500lb incendiary bomb clusters had been shipped, and foot lockers from the boxes which had contained flares for the bombers – and since these were already hinged, it was an easy conversion job.

The huts were heated – usually barely heated – by a coke-burning stove in the centre, called a 'tortoise' by the British. If it was glowing red soldiers could keep warm by standing within five feet of it, but because a week's coke ration would only keep them warm for about one evening, it didn't glow red very often. To the hut dwellers, the barracks' heroes weren't men who had distinguished themselves in combat, but those who had managed to pilfer some extra coke or coal from the camp's stockpile, which was supposed to be guarded round the clock. The coal dump was next to the mess hall at Seething, and though coal was only supposed to be burned in the mess and the hospital, it

The interior
decorator

provided much more heat than the coke which was issued for the barracks. So Benjamin Everett and his fellow crewmen used to 'go to evening chow wearing our steel helmets and after eating we would stop at the coal pile and fill our helmet with coal, which we kept in a foot locker under our bunks – it was never found.' Other men purloined metal drums which had contained fuel and fashioned from them woodburning stoves which they fed with wood lying around the construction site or gathered from the nearby woods. A navigator stationed at Shipdham USAAF base in Norfolk went to even greater lengths to keep warm. The crew's belly gunner had managed to pick up a five-gallon wooden barrel of whisky when the crew had stopped down in Brazil. It was lethal to drink, but as good as petrol for starting a fire: 'it must have been 500 per cent proof – it was sheer rotgut.' 'People were forever tossing CO-2 cartridges into our stoves,' remembers a pilot, 'you'd be backed up to it on a cold day when all of a sudden it would just blow up and hot coals would fly all over the place and scare everybody.'

An 8th Air Force gunner recalls that 'the huts were dark, their concrete floors were usually littered with tracked-in mud, and their mingled odors of cigarettes and cigars both past and present, damp woollen clothing and socks too long unlaundered gave them the heady aroma of a goat barn.'

Enlisted men slept in bunks, usually double-tiered, while the officers had small beds or 'cots'. Narrow and made of two frames of iron, these were 'sheer torture . . . the frames were about three feet long and the iron crossbars where they joined would cut you right about the hips.' The mattresses consisted of three separate, unforgiving little biscuits stuffed with excelsior [packing material] and they tended to separate in the night, and at 2 a.m., Everett recalls, 'you would be woken with a cold draft coming from below . . . in the end most of the crews sewed their mattresses together and that was much better.' The troops slept without sheets, covered only by thin blankets which were scratchy to the skin and often drifted in the night; flying crews who could wear their warm sheepskin-lined jackets day and night in the long, damp, chill British winter were much envied.

Philip Haberman, a New York lawyer who came to Britain as an intelligence officer with a bomb group, had a theory that when the British discovered early in the war that dispersal was the key to safety from air attack, they extended the principle to include the plumbing department: 'you bathe, wash, shave and go *wo der Kaiser zu Fuss geht* in four separate and distinct places, usually from a block to half a mile apart.' Haberman was lucky: his batman brought him hot water in a bucket to shave with and in lieu of a mirror he used the bottom of a peanut tin, though it provided a 'somewhat distorted vision' of his face. But when he wanted to partake of the 'officers' ablutions' facilities, he found

> washing almost impossible . . . small tin tubs stand on a brick and concrete pedestal. They are filled from a leaky spout which drizzles cold water or drenches you by turns. To empty, you simply dump the contents onto the pedestal which has a trough down the center. If two dump at once, the pedestal overflows and both get their feet wet. The room is also unheated.

But the baths were better: 'there are tubs, nice long English ones. There is hot water a-plenty . . . however there are two drawbacks: first it is miles from anywhere, and second if you accidentally touch your bare foot on the floor after bathing, you have to bathe again.' But Haberman concluded that

> the result of all this is good: it saves water as bathing and washing are kept to a minimum . . . the British are bears on saving water which has to be pumped at the expense of fuel. A little jingle says: 'Switched-on lights and turned-on taps Make happy Huns and joyful Japs'. So a complete toilet is spread over quite an area and when the cold wind doth blow, a shower is easily discouraged.

But in many bases it was rare to have hot water in the bathrooms: the men used to heat water in their canteens on the top of the stove, and use their ever-useful steel helmets to have a sponge bath. When they had really had enough of barracks hygiene, they would take a bus into the nearest town and go to the Red Cross Club for a hot shower, and then take the bus back to base.

The primitive sanitation at these early camps meant that 'honey buckets' dogged the lives of the GIs – particularly the problem of disposing of the contents, which were often 'put over a fire and cooked until only ash remained', remembers a member of the 364th Engineers stationed near Hereford. This operation was carried out 'within about 400 feet of the mess tent where mutton was usually cooking. The combination of odors caused many a Yank to pass up his meal.' A GI in the Signal Corps was amazed when he saw his first honey wagon: 'It had arrived to empty the troops' latrines. I really had no idea that the inside plumbing found in the US was not available in the rest of the world.'

As an officer, Haberman was rather more fortunate. He had a 'privy', but even this caused embarrassment: 'it is well provided with [lavatory paper] each page of which bears the stern legend "Government Property" . . . I felt I was desecrating Magna Carta on each occasion,' he wrote to his wife. To a nation which still had a high proportion of houses without bathrooms, the GIs' determined efforts at cleanliness were impressive: they showered in the freezing cold, punched holes in water pipes to provide a makeshift shower and even wrote an ode about it in *Stars and Stripes*:

> *Oh GI soap of thee I sing*
> *You're chemically an awesome thing*
> *Concerning you my thoughts are rife*
> *You dominate my GI life.*
>
> *You take the grime from barrack floors*
> *You shrink my long grey woollen drawers*
> *You peel the grease from pots and pans*
> *You chew the skin right off my hands.*
>
> *Your powers of destruction seem*
> *The answer to a chemical dream*
> *You look as though you're meant to be*
> *Just soap. Inside you're TNT.*
>
> *The War Department isn't wise*
> *To waste time on inventive guys:*
> *All GI soldiers have the dope*
> *OUR secret weapon's GI soap.*

CHAPTER FIVE

GETTING TO KNOW THE INVADERS

'THE YANKS HAVE ARRIVED. There are seven of them in The Dog right now.' The word spread round the small Suffolk village of Grundisburgh one August evening in 1942. As a handful of the 820th Engineers who had arrived in the district a few days earlier to start building an airfield for the 8th Air Force sat rather self-consciously in the snug bar of the village pub,

> people came from all the farms and cottages and they filled the old public house with a carnival spirit. By eight o'clock there was standing room only and by nine o'clock even the dark, narrow hall between the rooms was full and you could hardly turn round. The smoke was thick and the conversation excited. The Yanks have arrived!

And it wasn't only in rural villages that the GIs quickened the pace of life that spring and summer of 1942. Robert Henrey and his wife, Madeleine, lived in Shepherd Market in Mayfair – which, to them, was still a village full of shops and people they knew.

> The Americans came to our village in the chilly fogs of March. They wore battle dress and forage caps and hailed from anywhere and everywhere between Oregon and Maine and North Dakota and Texas. After dark they moved like shadows along Piccadilly straining their eyes, unaccustomed to the blackout, for a feminine shadow to engage in conversation. They stood in little groups . . . humming tunes we Londoners didn't recognize. They talked in low tones, as if fearful to break the silence of the night, and their accent lingered in our ears.

Within months, Mayfair came to be known as 'Little America'. Grosvenor Square was nicknamed 'Eisenhowerplatz', since Number 20 was the headquarters of the European Theater of Operations United States of America (ETOUSA), while the elegant and spacious Georgian houses all around were commandeered as offices, housing and recreation facilities for US administrative staff, and many of the grand hotels along with such institutions as the English Speaking Union were turned into clubs for US officers and men. Soon, it was no longer a case of 'A Nightingale Sang in Berkeley Square': an equally remarkable event would now be 'an Englishman spoke in Grosvenor Square'. And 'Little America' began to colonize Piccadilly too: Rainbow Corner, the largest and most popular of the clubs the American Red Cross ran for the troops, was housed in what had been Del Monico's on the corner of Piccadilly Circus and Shaftesbury Avenue.

As one GI put it succinctly: 'there was scarcely a corner of this already overcrowded island which we did not overcrowd the more.' As this 'peaceful invasion' spread throughout the country, the British at first treated the Americans as curiosities. A Post Office employee who had volunteered for the ATS (Auxiliary Territorial Service) on the outbreak of war recalls going into the NAAFI canteen, where she was astounded to see American soldiers.

> This was really incredible . . . somehow one did not expect to see them in Wales. To find Americans happily ensconced, and apparently very much at home in our NAAFI canteen was something quite remarkable . . .[for] whereas Americans and all their manners and habits are familiar to anyone with a television set today, it was not quite the same thing in 1942. There had been American films for years of course; the type of film I had usually chosen to see pre-war had been the gay, happy ones or else those of the domestic comedy type with such actors as William Powell and Myrna Loy, or costume films. I had, of course, seen many gangster films . . . but there were very few films depicting the normal, everyday life of the average American. It was something of a shock, therefore, to be so unexpectedly confronted with the real thing.

But to a Birmingham schoolboy, also reared on Hollywood films, the 'real thing' turned out to be something of a disappointment: 'we found that they didn't walk like John Wayne, talk like Spencer Tracy, dance like Fred Astaire or look like Clark Gable. They turned out to be ordinary fellows with a variety of accents.'

Many of the girls were determined to be impressed: 'they seemed to have left the ugly ones at home' was the consensus. A nurse from Lancashire recalls that 'they *all* seemed to be handsome six-footers with friendly grins and toothpaste advert teeth. The impression was of frustrated vitality . . . they told us they had just got to England by sea from the States . . . we must have been among the first English girls they had seen.' A WVS worker remembers the buzz of excitement when she and her colleagues heard news of

> the friendly invasion of some 1,000 American troops, our new allies . . . ideas as to what would best make them happy were conflicting . . . this was our first opportunity of repaying the US's fabulous generosity, and we seemed to be anxious to the point of hysteria for them to like us.

'They were as good as a tonic' was a common reaction from British people, for whom the war seemed endless, and sometimes hopeless. For a woman Red Cross worker in Norwich, the GIs 'brought with them colour, romance, warmth – and a tremendous hospitality to our dark, shadowed island'.

When the first GIs arrived in Northern Ireland 'the war was in its third dreary year, the fall of Singapore seemed imminent [it capitulated on 15 February 1942], the butter ration was down to two ounces a week', and it was the coldest winter a Belfast woman could remember. '[We] were in the throes of a depression,' emphasized Mrs Robert Henrey,

> and we welcomed this friendly invasion from across the Atlantic as a breath of much-needed hope. Singapore had fallen, Ceylon was being evacuated, India and

Australia were threatened . . . mothers wept silently for their sons last heard of in lands over-run by the Japanese; to those who had no ties and who lacked sensibility, the shortage of tea and rice in the village stores came as a vague, misty foreboding of worse things to come.

Not everyone was as enthusiastic and welcoming. 'We were a wartime necessity,' thought an American infantryman, 'just like rationing.' 'We might have been needed,' recalls the historian Laurence Lafore, 'but we certainly weren't wanted.' The urbane Harold Nicolson pondered the question at the request of a visiting American academic intent on

> strategic research . . . which means that he travels the country reporting on British morale and the attitude of ordinary Englishmen to the US. Not, I should imagine, a very enlivening enquiry . . . I said that such prejudice as existed (really there is not much) should be divided into an upper and a lower level. (He was thrilled at this.) The upper level were afraid that America would insist on imposing idealism on Europe and then would withdraw to a self-righteous shell. The lower level didn't care for American boasting much, disliked their being richer than our men and thought all their Hemingway he-men were soft, hating cold, shuddering at the slightest draught and starting to limp if asked to walk more than two miles . . .

'Oh my God,' Nicolson winced, 'he wrote all this down in a really horrible pocket book bound in crocodile skin.'

Not many people encountered GIs at work in Britain. Contact was usually made at a social level, in pubs, dance halls, clubs or cinemas – and when the British invited the Americans into their own homes. When they saw US troops in the street, it was usually because they were on a night out or on leave. US bases were closed environments, off limits for outsiders as a rule. Maurice Gorham, acting Assistant Controller of the BBC Overseas Service, who visited the United States several times during the war, was sensitive to the problem:

> To my mind their troops, especially those who were here for a long time, were too much insulated from the British people. They already had almost everything laid on in their camps – their own daily newspaper, their own movies, their own food, and every sort of American amenity stocked in the PX . . . Coming from an environment so scrupulously American, they had nothing in common with the people they met there; they had not eaten the same food, read the same news or even heard the same radio; they had no common ground.

This was one reason, Gorham conjectured, why the US troops seemed to treat Britain like an occupied country rather than an ally – an attitude which was encouraged by 'high American officers whose line was "These men are fighters. They are being conditioned for combat. They don't have to know whether they are in Britain or New Britain; it makes no difference to them." '

In London, the only US troops the British ever saw were either administrative personnel or GIs on leave, hell-bent on packing as much of a good time as they could into their few days' furlough: 'We never saw an American soldier *doing* anything or even carrying his own bag.' When Gorham finally got to a combat zone 'and saw how the Americans could look when they were on the job, I longed to bring a handful of them back to London and say to the people in Piccadilly "Look, these are Americans too." '

This goes some way to explaining the different attitudes towards the 'peaceful invasion'. Although strenuous efforts were made to ensure that the Press always portrayed the GIs as ambassadors of goodwill, the British as grateful and welcoming hosts and the whole exercise as a triumph for Allied co-operation, things were not always good-natured. The problems might have been anticipated. As Gorham observed:

> Soldiers do not usually get on with civilians anywhere. You would not normally choose to send as ambassadors a couple of million men who did not particularly want to come, and you would be careful who you sent from a country with the world's highest standard of living to a comparatively backward country like Britain which had been stripped down to almost primitive austerity by three or four years of hard war.

The impact of the US troops was enormous. As the GI William Bostick wrote:

> to the British our mass arrival, however necessary, must have been a constant inconvenience. Most of us did not stop to realize this. At least, not often. We were in the main young, bumptious, good-natured, though demanding, dough-heavy, homesick, hitherto untravelled and in every way hungry. We presented an acute problem in supplies, no less than space and hospitality.

The impact that the GIs made on the British population obviously depended partly on their behaviour. Some of the Americans were charming, and everyone liked them. Some of the Americans were badly behaved, and no one liked them. Predictably, it was in areas where there was a relatively static GI population that relations between the Americans and the local communities were best. The majority of air bases were situated in rural areas: although there was a frequent turn-round of aircrew, many of the ground crew and supply workers remained on the same bases for almost the entire duration of the war, and often forged close links with the villagers of the area. Even so, the average number of Americans on one of these bases at any one time was between three and four thousand and the impact of such a concentration on the resources of the surrounding rural area is explanation enough for many of the tensions.

For women with sons, husbands or boyfriends at war, the anxious times could be lightened with the society that the GIs offered. For young women there could be parties and dances, glamour, treats and luxuries, the possibility of romance, and certainly some fun at a time of loneliness and drab austerity and danger. For the older women, there might be a substitute son, or at least a hope that by welcoming a foreign soldier into their home, somewhere else in the world someone might do the same for their son.

For younger men, whether civilians or in uniform, the stakes were different. The GIs were a threat: the oft-repeated saw, 'overfed, overpaid, oversexed and over here' (to which the GIs would respond 'underfed, underpaid, undersexed and under Eisenhower' – which was at least three-quarters true), had the ring of truth. Wartime rationing in Britain meant that the population never felt replete and often felt hungry. A high proportion of the GIs' food was shipped in from the States. Rumour had it that a British family could live for a month on what was scraped into the garbage can of any American base after a single meal. GIs could buy things at their PXs (mostly at subsidized prices) which could not easily be had for coupons or money in Britain: cigarettes, chocolate, tinned fruit, tinned ham, razor blades. And the privates and corporals in the American army were paid nearly five times more than their British counterparts. As the writer and journalist George Orwell reflected:

> I rarely see American and British soldiers together. Quite obviously the major cause of this is difference in pay. You can't have really close and friendly relations with someone whose income is five times your own. Financially the whole American army is in the middle class. In the field this might not matter, but in the training period it makes it almost impossible for the British and American soldiers to fraternise.

GIs had the appeal of the exotic for many British women, particularly when they talked in glowing and not always strictly accurate terms about life back stateside, and the Texas ranch or Manhattan penthouse – an appeal underlined by a liveliness and generosity with food, drinks, candy, nylons, lipstick, scent, invitations to dances and the thrill of learning to jitterbug to Glenn Miller or another big band sound. 'We didn't stand a chance when the Yanks turned up at a dance,' was the disconsolate view of the few youngish British men who weren't in the forces or away doing essential war work. And for those in the forces, there was always the danger that while they were away, their wives or sweethearts might have their heads turned by a Yank and 'drift', as the current terminology had it.

An Allied offensive – which was why the GIs were 'over here' – meant British and US troops fighting together. And that was not a prospect which reassured either side in 1942. Apart from the jibes about 'running away at Dunkirk', to which was soon added the jibe about 'running away at Tobruk', there was the sort of incident, recalled by a Sutton Coldfield office worker, whereby whenever the popular song 'There'll Always Be an England' was played on the radio, the Americans in her office would intone 'as long as we're here to defend it for you'.

The Times introduced an historical perspective by explaining that the GIs viewed the British not as 'the heroes of Trafalgar, Blenheim and Waterloo, but as the descendants of the men who blundered at New Orleans and Saratoga. The doughboys come to Britain, it is apparent, with little faith in British military prowess.' And an infantryman from Chicago explained in March 1943 that though he felt very sorry for the English,

> they've taken an awful beating. And yet, nothing happens, day after day. If New York had been bombed the way that London has been, every man, woman and child would be working day and night to whack whoever'd done it. I don't say that America takes the war more seriously than England does, but if that had happened in America, we wouldn't have taken it so quietly, we'd be yelling for their blood AND GETTING IT. The English have got so passive, I don't know how it is.

If the Americans were wary, in those early days, about British prowess in the field, the feeling was mutual. It was felt that the Americans had been 'caught napping' at Pearl Harbor. As Laurence Lafore discovered,

'The Goddamn Yankee Army's here.' US troops training in the summer of 1942 invade the English countryside.

the fact of being bombed generates a certain condescension towards people who haven't. To this kind of condescension [the British] could add the pride of having Stood Alone plus their fully justified assurance that they knew a great deal more about the technical business of fighting a war than we did. We were automatically tenderfeet and due humility was expected of us.

And to the jibes that the Americans threw at the British after Dunkirk, could be added the one the British taunted the Americans with, particularly after the battle of the Kasserine Pass in Tunisia in February 1943, 'how green was my ally . . .'

Newly arrived American soldiers didn't do much to reassure some onlookers, who saw them as 'soft . . . degenerate . . . too damned wealthy . . . the hardship and conflict of war will do them a lot of good.' The GIs, 'unbloodied by conflict', appeared to be 'slovenly soldiers'. A middle-aged countrywoman was censorious: 'every time I see an American soldier slouching along, hands in pockets, shoulders hunched, chewing gum, I'm glad I'm not an American.' Those who had watched the GIs disembark had been particularly struck by the way 'the troops marched off in a curious silence on their rubber-soled shoes – it was more like a soft-shoed shuffle than marching.' A Lancashire girl was startled to see a GI break ranks to pick some poppies by the roadside before rejoining his column and a British soldier thought that 'their marching, by our standards, was very loose, though maybe none the worse for that, Americans seem to spend just as much time on spit and polish as we do, but their standard of results is lower.' It was especially shocking to the older generation: 'My father had been a sergeant in the 1914–18 war,' recalls an East Anglian woman, 'and he was *very* disparaging when he saw them marching through our village street: "What a shower! They can't march to save their lives." '

Jean Lancaster Rennie, who observed GIs at close quarters in the American Red Cross Club where she worked in Norwich, thought that it was precisely this attitude which gave rise to misapprehensions:

> they had come, heaven knows how many miles, to help our sore-pressed island. To assist in man's ultimate lunacy – the comic opera of war. And we thought: they're too happy . . . The British soldier always looks serious in his uniform: he knows only too well what it all stands for. After all we'd been invaded before: the whole of the Empire had been built on war. So it doesn't seem to us that these carefree, talkative, wolf-whistling GIs are going to be much use against the mad arrogance of Adolf Hitler.

Margaret Mead realized that

> no one had bothered to tell the British people that Americans don't set the same store that the British do on standing upright, and see no harm in taking the weight off their feet by leaning against the nearest wall in sight, they will judge the Americans whom they see leaning against a wall as undisciplined, spineless, low-grade people . . . but they would be wrong, because leaning against a wall doesn't mean the same thing to the average young American as it does to the corresponding young man in Britain.

And the booklet *Meet the US Army*, referring to the average GI, recognized that while 'some of the British eyewitnesses, indeed, are somewhat shocked by his informality,' it should be remembered that

> in action the US army is noted for its stern discipline . . . this army has a victorious history [which] has been unduly ignored in our schools, possibly because many of its victories have been won at our expense. . . . both the British and American armies are exceedingly tough . . . and when you meet a Doughboy, don't be misled by his easy line of talk, his wisecracks . . . into thinking that he has any illusions about what he is here for. He regards your island as a halfway house to the front – and he knows what the front will be like.

The easy-going 'Hiya sarge' attitude of the US Army was a revelation to the class- and rank-conscious British. 'They were all buddies,' recalls a woman from Dorset, 'it didn't matter what rank they were, they were always friends. A private would go up to an officer and say "Hi Bud, can I borrow your Cadillac?" and the officer would immediately hand over the keys to his Jeep.'

A Cambridge newspaper, responding to the discovery by some local soldiers that their admiration for the Americans' smart uniform had led them to 'salute men of a rank similar to, or lower than their own', published 'A Guide to American Uniforms: Some Insignia Hints' which began: 'Both officers and men wear well-cut uniforms, very similar in appearance . . . how, then, are we to tell them apart?'

To one correspondent these attitudes were likely to have serious consequences: 'we were inclined to be patronizing . . . the GIs were cheerful, chatty, not over-disciplined – which we thought, morosely, would be a bad thing. Fancy going to war and treating your officers as "buddies".'

By contrast, Robert Edberg, a radar expert attached to a Royal Corps of Signals unit, who was stationed for a time with his battery outside Aberdeen, lived

> with several British officers and loved every minute of it. I thought I had practically reached heaven. In the British Army, officers are treated more deferentially than in the US Army. I . . . was served by a batman who woke me in the morning with a large cup of hot tea and whilst I slowly woke he finished shining my shoes and uniform leather belt and he laid out my uniform for the day. I don't know how he did it but they were kept spotless and creased to a knife edge . . . What a way to fight a war.

Time spent in Britain might begin to erode some US prejudices: it might disabuse the GIs of their perception that 'England is still ruled by Burke's peerage', and make them realize that there were Englishmen who were 'neither aristocrats nor Cockneys'. Or, as J.L. Hodson put it in a radio broadcast, 'there are people in England apart from those who live in Park Lane and costers who push barrows.' Even so, the British class system remained the despair of many Americans.

In the view of Robert Raymond, a US pilot who had joined the RAF on the outbreak of war, 'the power of the old school in this great stronghold of democracy' was a dangerous matter:

> I sometimes feel that England does not deserve to win this war. Never have I seen such class distinctions drawn and maintained in the face of a desperate effort to preserve a democracy. With powers of regulation and control invariably centered in the hands of the few, and abuse and preservation of the old school tie is stronger than ever on every side . . . it has been well and truly said that General Rommel of the German army's Afrika Korps would never have risen above the rank of NCO in the British Army. The nation seems inexplicably proud of the defects in its national character.

The US soldier's attitude to rank was grounded in his attitude to class and authority. Anthony Cotterell, who, as a soldier-journalist, was detailed to spend time with the US Army, recognized it

> as an expression of the [GI's] constant determination to resist being ordered about. Englishmen, of all ranks, take orders with far less question. The ignominies of K.P. (fatigues to us) are much less keenly felt . . . Americans look on the army more as a nine-to-six job. Their loyalty is more akin to the pride of a businessman employed by a first-rate firm, whereas the British soldier's loyalty is based on the feeling that he won't let the old place down, plus personal attachment to officers, which I think that Americans are too independent to develop to the same extent unless their officer is an acknowledged hero.

As a Ministry of Information pamphlet explained, 'Unlike the German, in particular, who runs his "civvy life" as if he were in the army . . . the American soldier's mind is still in "civvies" even when his body is in uniform.'

As far as some of the British were concerned, there was another side to this sort of soldiering. An additional charge was sometimes tagged on to the 'overpaid' epithet:

THE MONEY OVER THERE
'British money is in pounds, shillings and
pence. The British are used to this system
and they like it, and all your arguments that
the American decimal system is better won't
convince them.'
LEFT 'They won't be pleased to hear you
calling it "funny money" either.'
BELOW 'Playing poker's the fastest way to
learn about British money and to
lose it, too.'

'over-medalled'. A soldier in the Queen's Own Royal West Kent Regiment thought the GIs' uniforms superb – 'and they even had a few medals for merely coming over; rumour had it they got them for using the jakes and for catching the pox (and, others claimed, for eating Brussels sprouts) . . . but they were certainly *not* soldiers. More goes into soldiering than wearing a fancy uniform: it is discipline and endurance among other things.'

Jokes were made on the subject – 'Heard the one about the Yanks who went to a war film? One fainted and the other got a medal for carrying him out' – and a verse taunted

Alas they haven't fought the Hun
No glorious battles have they won
That pretty ribbon just denotes
They've crossed the sea –
Brave men in boats.

There were also jibes from the US troops themselves: the European and African Theater of War medal was known as the 'Spam' medal. Yet when, in March 1944, the US authorities issued figures to show that medals weren't 'handed out with the rations', they were able to point to the fact that the ETO was the 'toughest in the world for fliers' and that of the 126,526 medals awarded by then, Air Medals and Distinguished Flying Crosses accounted for eight out of every nine – and that these had to be approved at the highest level while Washington's agreement was required for the award of the Congressional Medal of Honor and the Distinguished Service Medal – though the US forces still managed to be much more decorated than the British.

Perhaps it was the confidence that this positive thinking gave the Yanks that most irked the British soldier in his first contacts with his American counterpart. 'On my recent journey about Britain,' Margaret Mead reported, 'I was asked in one form or another, over and over again, why Americans talked so big.' One member of the ATS complained that 'the trouble with Americans is that when they are good at something they say so.' And in June 1942 *Yank*, the serviceman's Sunday magazine, cautioned: 'Don't brag. Don't tell an Englishman we came over and won the last war for them. We didn't. England lost a million men; we only lost 60,000.' Intelligence officers warned that the tendency of Americans to brag about the superiority of US arms and equipment could be dangerous for security. German officers who interrogated American POWs would ask them: ' "Do you really think you can beat us Germans" to which the prisoner tended to reply "Damn right we can" . . . and go on to tell the German how.'

In a survey conducted by Mass Observation just after the arrival of the first US troops, the characteristic that 48 per cent of those polled most disliked about the Americans was their 'boastfulness'. When Americans said that they'd arrived from the training camp at Fort Bragg in North Carolina, the British response was likely to be: 'That figures.' 'Of course they always had something bigger and better than we had,' recalls a Shropshire woman. 'I remember one coming up to me one day and saying "Can you tell me where Market Street is?" So I said, "Yes, it's this turn here," and he said, "I don't call that a road, I call it a gap." '

Before landing, US troops were advised: 'Don't show off or brag or bluster – "swank" as the British say. If somebody looks in your direction and says "He's chucking his weight about" you can be pretty sure you're off base. That's the time to pull in your ears.'

Some Britons were tolerant. One Lancashire woman didn't 'think that the Americans . . . intended to indulge in one-upmanship. In fact they were always very friendly, but having come from a country with big money, big cars and huge towering buildings, they naturally talked big . . . it was just their way.'

Nor did Ted Hill, who encountered US troops in his home city of Bristol, think the Americans' style was entirely to be deplored: 'the American character is more flamboyant than the British . . . an American is like a large dog trying to be friendly with everyone in the room, whilst wrecking everything with its tail wagging.'

The particular irritant of American superiority was recognized in the soldiers' handbook, *The Short Guide*:

> the British dislike bragging and showing-off. American wages and soldiers' pay are the highest in the world. When pay day comes it would be sound practice to learn to spend your money in accordance to British standards. They consider you highly paid. They won't think any better of you for throwing your money around: they are more likely to feel that you haven't learned the common-sense virtues of thrift. The British 'Tommy' is apt to be specially touchy about the differences between his money and yours. Keep this in mind.

The Northern Irish reaction to the first wave of GIs had been of a people 'talking high wide and handsome and spending high wide and handsome'. But for their part the GIs often found the image of the 'rich American' hard to bear. Many of them had come from areas which had been hit hard by the Depression, and the common British assumption, voiced by Robert Raymond, that 'the majority of the rank and file are millionaires because 6 out of 10 owned motor cars in civilian life' rankled.

The discrepancy in pay was real enough: in June 1942 a private in the British Army was paid 14 shillings a week, whereas a private in the US Army received £3 8s 9d, nearly five times as much; a British sergeant was paid £2 2s a week, compared with his US equivalent who got £5 7s 2d. But the gap narrowed considerably towards the upper end of the scale: a US general pocketed £179 4s 3d a month: his British counterpart £247 12s 11d. And at the very top, a field marshal commanded £275 5s a month compared with a US general of the Army's £281 14s 10d a month. As Norman Longmate points out, these are only rough comparisons, since there were various allowances and deductions on both sides, though no British soldier received an overseas allowance.

As *Stars and Stripes* reminded the US forces:

> This war's soldier is a rich man compared to his father in World War One. In 1917 the pay ran from $30 for a private to less than $100 for a master-sergeant, plus a 10 per cent bonus for service overseas. At present, a master-sergeant can draw, with his longevity allowance, overseas pay and service bonus, more than $200 a month. With his food, clothing and lodging taken into consideration, that puts him into a high salary bracket.

With almost 'all found' – unlike his British counterpart – and a subsidized PX, the GI had a considerable disposable income, though married men had a proportion docked for their families. And while the US government was always urging the troops to 'put some in war bonds', many managed to resist the blandishments.

GETTING TO KNOW THE INVADERS

It was among privates, corporals and sergeants that the inequality between American and British rates of pay was felt the most. 'They're too well paid and they flash their money about. What chance has a poor Tommy with a couple of bob jingling in his pocket?' was a common reaction, given that the GI's spending power meant that he had first call on food, drink and female companionship. The 'profligacy' of the US troops was regarded as having a deleterious effect on the British way of life, with GIs tipping taxi drivers so lavishly that they drove past British fares if there was a Yank in prospect, while a Cambridge don complained that the amount that the Americans were prepared to pay the local women to do their laundry meant that his college was losing its best workers.

The troops' introductory booklet explained that

> English money is in pounds, shillings and pence . . . the British are used to this system and all your arguments that the American decimal system is better, won't convince them . . . They sweat hard to get it (wages are much lower in Britain) and they won't think you smart or funny for mocking at it.

Despite the handy table at the back of their *Guide*, most Americans found English money meaningless 'monopoly money'. They were irritated by the size of the £5 notes which they termed 'wallpaper money', and baffled by the complexity and the nomenclature of British currency. 'Half a crown equals two shillings, sixpence. About four bits. Remember? . . . A pound – 16 ounces at home but 240 pence or 20 shillings (about $4) over here,' explained *Stars and Stripes*.

The GI, Robert Arbib, noted,

> ridicules the monetary system the first time he changes a pound and finds himself with a slight list to starboard as his pocket is filled with weighty half crowns and enormous pennies. The pounds, shillings and pence, and above all the apparently superfluous guinea, seem unnecessarily and aggravatingly complex, and he solves the matter by offering a note in payment for every purchase, accepting the change without question. But after his first poker game, when he must make lightning and intricate transactions with the coins, he has no more trouble. Before long he is talking about 'bobs', 'florins', and 'quids' like the natives.

But this wasn't always so: 'We played poker and it would get expensive,' said an 8th Air Force airman, 'because we weren't really used to English money. The pound note was really a five-dollar bill, but it said "one" on it, and when you bet a pound in your mind you were betting a dollar. A pot could get to $200–$300 without anybody realizing it, and when you were making $150 a month plus flight pay, that was a lot of money.'

The GIs' confusion about English money led them to behave like tourists. Often in shops they would proffer a handful of coins and invite the vendor to help himself: in pubs they would make a pile of coins on the bar and indicate that the landlord should take for their drinks out of that. For the most part, the British were honest, but the reaction of one GI was not uncommon: 'I sure do admire your taxi drivers – they drive – my can they drive! But they chisel. As soon as they see our uniforms, up go the prices.' And when the Americans left their change on the bar after buying a round of drinks, it would add to the feeling that they were 'overpaid' and fair game for fleecing: 'The Americans are rich: let's rook 'em all we know.'

CHAPTER SIX

THE BATTLE OF THE MUD

THE ASSERTION MADE BY SOME GIs that 'We've come over to win the war for you' may not have made them popular, but it was what a lot of the British fervently hoped – including the regulars at The Dog in Suffolk: 'The work on our aerodrome is about to begin at last! It has begun already! Right here in changeless old Grunsbra we are going to have a great new bomber aerodrome, and thousands of American soldiers and airmen! And bombers flying right over Berlin to pay those Jerries back! Surely the tide of the war is turning today!'

The first priority of the US Army Air Force in Britain was to join in the fighting in order to demonstrate the American commitment to the Allied war effort, to assuage criticism of Americans being armchair soldiers and, in particular, to put to the test US theories of the efficacy of daylight precision bombing – in attempting to knock out the industrial base of the German war machine they hoped to avoid having to throw their troops into ground combat. The RAF's strategy was completely different: its bombers flew night-time saturation raids aimed at destroying German cities and sapping the morale of the people. The British – who had applauded the RAF's successes in the Battle of Britain and seen its actions as a response to what the Luftwaffe had wrought on London during the Blitz – tended to be sceptical about the policies of their new allies, 'Johnny-come-latelies' in the battle of the air. Brigadier-General Ira C. Eaker, Bomber Commander of the 8th Air Force, was well aware of the reservations of the British – including Churchill – when he told a British audience shortly after his arrival in March 1942 that 'We won't do much talking until we've done more fighting. When we leave I hope you'll be glad we came.'

On the outbreak of war, the entire US Army Air Force – the USAAF was not to become an independent force until 1946 – comprised less than 20,000 men: by the spring of 1944, it had grown to 2,383,000, of whom 185,000 officers and enlisted men, with 4,000 aircraft, were with the 8th Air Force in Britain. 'The 'Mighty Eighth' had been activated in Georgia in 1942; its headquarters were housed in sprawling huts at Bushey Park in Middlesex, under the command of General Carl 'Tooey' Spaatz, while Bomber Command under Brigadier-General Eaker was stationed near its British opposite number under Sir Arthur 'Bomber' Harris, at Daw's Hill Lodge, High Wycombe in Buckinghamshire. In peacetime the lodge had been the home of a well-known girls' school, Wycombe Abbey, and Bomber HQ staff were heartened to find notices above their beds informing them 'If you require a mistress in the night, ring the bell'.

One urgent task facing the Allies in 1942 was to prepare the flatlands of East Anglia as a launch pad for the planes of the 8th Air Force into occupied Europe and Germany. By May 1942 plans were afoot for the building or transfer from the RAF of 75 airfields – later increased to 127 – to the 8th Air Force in a broad sweep of eastern England reaching from Norfolk and Suffolk through Cambridgeshire and parts of Essex and Huntingdonshire into the borders of Northamptonshire and as far west as Bedfordshire. In addition, operational headquarters, combat crew replacement centres, gunnery schools, quartermaster's depots and supply and maintenance depots (at Warton near Liverpool, Burtonwood near Warrington in Lancashire and Langford Lodge in Northern Ireland) had to be built or converted.

The heavy US bombers – B-17 Flying Fortresses and B-24 Liberators – would have sunk into the mud on a grass airstrip, so old RAF fields had to be concreted to accommodate the 'big birds'. During 1942, £6.5 million was spent on new and rehabilitated airfields – a job that involved immense quantities of material and large numbers of men. The British were responsible for the construction, and to begin with the RAF worked with civilian contractors, but within three months of Pearl Harbor US engineer battalions, with their more sophisticated equipment, had joined a British workforce, which included men brought over from Ireland and local women.

'Across the green fields of England, from before dawn to late at night, US engineers are pouring concrete and steel and sweat into one of the most gigantic building projects ever undertaken anywhere,' reported Bud Hutton, a correspondent for *Stars and Stripes*:

> They're building the bases from which the 8th someday will bomb Adolf Hitler and his satellites into space. It's a job that takes three or four overlapping shifts of men every 24 hours, tearing into the job before it's completely daylight and staying long into the evenings. The engineers who are doing the job are living in tents and working in rain and shine. Great ribbons of concrete and steel go stretching across what short months ago were fields of new wheat or barley or potatoes. These are the runways from which the Flying Fortresses and other big bombers will take off, bearing their loads of bombs for Germany and the occupied countries.

An airfield usually took some thousand workers about seven months to complete. The airfield at Thorpe Abbots in Norfolk gives some idea of the scale of the task. It stretched over a total area of 500 acres and had three runways. The main runway was 6,300 feet, one of the longest in Britain; there were three and a half miles of perimeter track and hard-standing, 300 individual buildings, three and a half miles of sewers, five miles of water mains and fourteen and a half miles of drains. Its construction involved the pouring of 49,000 square yards of concrete, the laying of four million bricks and the excavation of 330,000 cubic yards of earth. It cost one million pounds to build, and when finished it accommodated four bombardment squadrons, with up to 3,500 men on base.

Hard-standing for the planes and the box-like concrete control tower were set alongside the perimeter track, along which the aircraft would taxi to the main runway for take-off. The administrative offices, maintenance huts and accommodation for the crews sprawled across the countryside, dispersed in an effort to minimize damage in the event of an enemy attack – and an inducement for the men to buy themselves an English bike.

READY FOR THE 'MIGHTY EIGHTH'

*Building airfields in East Anglia. The impact of US machinery
transformed the speed at which the English countryside could be ploughed up
for runways.*

" O.K., sir—if you insist that we leave your residence where it is
we'll have to rebuild the runway like this."

The enormous hangars were built to house the largest planes, some of which were as much as 240 foot long and 150 foot wide; they were also used for servicing and repairing planes. A plane damaged on a mission 'beyond economical repair' would be towed in to become a 'hangar queen', cannabalized for spare parts. The runways often seemed short to the pilots of the Flying Fortresses, heavy planes which had been developed to defend the shores of America. It took skill and strength to manoeuvre them along a runway which could be as short as 4,000 feet, and since a loaded B-17 carried more than 20,000 pounds of bombs and fuel, a crew that failed to get off the ground before reaching the end of the runway would be spoken of in the past tense.

By the end of 1942 8th Air Force bases began to litter the East Anglian countryside – an area best known to the more historically minded GIs as the principal place of origin of the seventeenth-century Puritan settlers of New England. The names of their bases read like an idyllic litany of Domesday England – Thorpe Abbots, Tibenham, Kimbolton, Chelveston, Thurleigh, Podington, Seething, Horsham St Faith, Snetterton Heath, Bungay, Wattisham, Wendling, Steeple Morden. By 1944, there was on average an airfield every eight miles throughout East Anglia. A pilot with the 92nd Bomb Group recalls:

> there was always a runway somewhere in the neighborhood. If you were coming back from a raid in trouble and needed a field in a hurry, or if you were in soupy weather and couldn't find one, you'd just fly a circle while giving your code and call letter on the radio. Then this English voice would come on and say 'Hello, Yank!' and in thirty seconds he'd have you on the radar and in two minutes more, he'd have you right over a field.

And a pilot with the 91st Bomb Group recalls: 'If you had some kind of trouble, an engine failure or something, why, all you had to do was hop over a hedge and set down on one. We had bases in every direction around there.' A plane would make for its own airfield whenever possible, but if damaged or short of fuel would put down anywhere – another USAAF or RAF airfield, or one of the specially constructed runways like those at Manston in Kent and Woodbridge in Suffolk: 'just one massive runway, [on which] a plane could land at any angle', these provided a safe haven for crippled aircraft that had only just managed to limp back across the Channel after a raid.

The local population may have been enthusiastic about the contribution that the 8th Air Force was making to winning the war, but they were less so about the effects that the airfield construction programme was having on the countryside. Extensive tracts of high-yield farmland were commandeered for these bases – 100,000 acres in Norfolk alone – and frequently the Air Ministry seemed cavalier in its demands. The National Farmers' Union complained in October 1942 that in one area in East Anglia hedges had been cut down, ditches cleared and runways drained for two years, only to have the site suddenly abandoned and six farmers served with notice to surrender 400 acres of highly cultivable land only a stone's throw away. In response to their protests, the Ministry simply repeated that the initial site 'no longer suited its original requirement'.

In Suffolk, Robert Arbib watched with regret as the countryside he found so beautiful slowly disappeared

> as a result of our relentless handiwork. As each new field was invaded by our crushing machines, as each new hedgerow was smashed and uprooted and shattered, as each great oak succumbed before axe and dynamite and bulldozer, we felt a pang. For there is nothing quite as final, quite as levelling, as an aerodrome. Each growing stick was beaten down and uprooted. Every patch of cover for rabbits and partridges was flattened. Every graceful contour softened and smoothed by centuries of wear by little brooks and by wind and rain, was hacked and shovelled and levelled . . . whatever had stood there before was lost

... the war wrecked these ... farmers' monuments just as surely as the bombs wrecked the monuments of architects and stonemasons when they exploded beautiful churches in London.

A soldier with the 862nd Engineers recognized that his unit wasn't 'really popular with the local population. They didn't take kindly to us Americans moving in and tearing up their countryside ... our "brass" decided it would be an indoctrination for us all if we went on a hike around the local area. It was a disaster! As we marched round our new "home" we got catcalls and "Go home Yanks!" ' But he

> didn't blame the people for feeling the way that they did. They knew that we were there to ruin their land – and when we had ruined it we would then fly hundreds of aeroplanes from this base ... low over their homes and there would always be the danger of a crash landing.

He was realistic, too, about the long-term prospects: the government had promised the owners that as soon as the war was over, the land would be returned to agricultural use. 'Hogwash! We knew it would take years to reconstitute the land after the war, if it could ever be rescued at all ... but that wasn't our problem ...'

'We never wanted to do this,' was all Arbib felt he could say to dispossessed and sometimes bitter farmers: 'a power greater than any one of us has brought us here – and this destruction we wrought helped in a small way to save you.'

Building the airfields was considered dangerous work. As a camouflage expert, Arbib was concerned that the scale of the work meant that there was neither the time nor the manpower to hide each night the hundreds of pieces of heavy equipment and vehicles which 'scarred and marred the Suffolk countryside'. The 820th Engineers were constructing an airfield only a few miles from the east coast, 'probably not more than a hundred miles from the nearest German aerodrome', and they considered themselves 'an ideal target' for the Luftwaffe. 'Don't worry,' counselled one of their number, 'the Germans already know we're here. I wouldn't be surprised if they came around tonight and dropped cards saying "Welcome 820th Engineers. Hope you get your aerodrome built soon. We'll wait until it's completed before we bomb it." ' When the men went to work on the field, they took their rifles with them; while they worked, anti-aircraft batteries and .50-calibre machine guns were set up and manned, and an anti-aircraft tank travelled with the construction crew. 'It is giving away no military secret,' *Stars and Stripes* confided, 'that the average airfield construction battalion of American engineers carries with it more fire power than an entire brigade of infantry in World War I.'

It was hard work, too, 'with the weather and the cold and the mud – well, fighting the Germans would have been child's play compared with this.' The 'battle of the mud', which figures so prominently in almost every GI's memories of his time in Britain, was waged most heavily by the engineers building airfields. The land in East Anglia was predominantly flat and low, and the combination of what seemed like continual rain and heavy vehicles churning up the ground produced a sea of mud. Bill Ong, with the 862nd Engineers, recalls that

> the mud was everywhere. It bedded down trucks. Bicycles fell into the stuff, never to be seen again. Even bulldozers became bogged down in the filthy stuff

and it got worse and worse as the rains came. We wondered how the hell we were ever going to pour concrete . . . the land in this area was only a few feet above sea level and the continuing rain made drainage almost impossible. We had mechanical diggers, but a fat lot of good they were; mostly we had to dig by hand. Mud, mud and still more mud.

This *nostalgie de la boue* became an important feature of the GIs' lives. The mud seeped into their tents, was trodden into the floors of their huts, caked their trousers, weighed down their boots and even, some claimed, like sand, got into their food. The engineers joked that they were building an underwater runway for seaplanes and that a periscope had been sighted a few fields away. Indeed, the whole enterprise was rumoured to be a decoy to provoke the Luftwaffe into dropping its bombs harmlessly in a sea of mud.

But there was mud, and there was mud. The 384th Bomb Group soon renamed Grafton Underwood in Northamptonshire, Grafton Undermud, and at Corkerhill Camp in Scotland, the endless rain made the area a morass, almost calf-deep in mud. This mud was reckoned to be particularly unpleasant, for

being a golf course, the top soil was sod and was lacking in any gravel to give it firmness. The grass slowly disappeared. The soil had been tended for years by sheep which grazed the grass short and fertilized it all in one cycle. The nauseous odor of generations of sheep droppings arose from the churned-up mud and gave the camp its distinctive smell.

The men of the 1st Ranger Battalion who were stationed there had to adopt drastic measures to make themselves presentable on evenings out. To preserve some semblance of a shine on their shoes, they would pull an extra pair of wool socks over them, walk through the mud and, on reaching the tarmac road, discard the socks and make their way into town. The exit from the camp soon became a supply sergeant's nightmare, strewn with brand-new muddy socks.

The British weather – the rain, the endless grey damp and the fog – left an indelible imprint on all GIs, particularly those from 'sunshine states' such as California, Florida, Arizona and New Mexico. As a despairing member of the WACs wrote home to a friend, 'You can believe everything you read or see in movies about English mist and fog and rain – none of it can be exaggerated.' Another WAC wrote of a rare sunny day when 'thousands sat around absorbing the sunshine, which is truly one of the rationed items in London.' In similar vein, Charles Cawthon noted on his arrival that 'Britain at this moment of its finest hour, was usually gray by day with rare interludes of sunshine. It was universally stygian by night (in the black-out) except for the weak hooded lamps marking main road intersections.'

In the autumn of 1942, the University of Cambridge, anxious to do its bit for Anglo–American relations, endowed a professorship in United States history. What the university was looking for in the man who would fill the post was 'an American who had American mud between his toes and grass burrs in his heels' – it didn't matter whether the incumbent 'took up the tariff question or the chewing-gum question'. When the second appointee, J. Frank Dobie from Austin, Texas, arrived at Emmanuel College (because this had been John Harvard's college, it has always been particularly hospitable towards American university men) he was as struck by the inclement British weather as any of his more physically engaged fellow countrymen. 'The air is no colder than the air of central Texas on a cold winter day,' Dobie observed and

> it is no damper than the air at the mouth of the Hudson River on a foggy day; but the peculiar chemical combination . . . is colder and more bone-chilling than the bottom of a cellar in January, is wetter than a soaked saddle blanket and more dampening than the sweat of death . . .

For Dobie, winter in Cambridge dispelled some cherished myths, among them the notion that Englishmen are 'effete': 'Few woollen-clad Americans who have shivered through an English winter and watched Englishmen pull up their socks over bare legs, and Englishwomen sometimes wear no stockings at all, any longer entertain the idea.'

The British weather posed particular problems for the USAAF, which, unlike the RAF, flew by day. Besides the rain and the almost perpetual low cloud which so often aborted missions, the rapid changes in weather could pose a real hazard. Sometimes a plane would begin its take-off and the cloud would close in on the far end of the runway before it could get off the ground. One lieutenant confessed that he was anxious to get home, not so much because he was homesick but 'to fly in a little Texas weather for a change'. Although air combat crews were much envied for their sheepskin flying jackets, one of them maintained that he had never been so cold as he was the winter he spent in England – and 'I come from Iowa, where it can get to 20 degrees below.'

When George VI paid his first visit to a US air base in November 1942, he asked a sergeant how he liked the British weather. 'I don't like it, sir, it's too damp,' he replied; and when mildly reprimanded by his superiors, countered with 'You wouldn't want me to lie to royalty, would you?'

It wasn't just the climate outside that the GIs found daunting; it was the fact that it was often hardly warmer inside that depressed them. 'I can't understand,' an infantryman from Illinois puzzled, 'why you British weren't the pioneers in central heating, the way

Eleanor Roosevelt, wife of the US President, on a visit to the troops stationed near Hungerford in Berkshire in November 1942.

your climate is. You need it far more than we do back home.' A GI stationed near Runcorn was just as perplexed at the way the English family he got to know 'would sit in front of the fire with all their clothes on, and then go upstairs to a stone cold bedroom to take them off'.

In November 1942, Eleanor Roosevelt, the wife of the President, came on a visit to the American bases and camps in Britain to 'report to the folks back home on how their boys were settling in' and to boost the troops' morale. She toured the country asking questions, and her heavy schedule impressed at least one Briton who, when asked by a BBC reporter on a live broadcast if he had seen Mrs Roosevelt, replied: 'No, but I understand that her chief purpose in coming here is to have intercourse with the American troops.'

When she returned to the States, the President's wife gave the families an accurate picture of their men's lives 'over there' in a radio broadcast:

Most of your boys were landed in . . . the late autumn, and late autumn and winter are gloomier than anything you can imagine in the US. There is a great deal of rain. The temperature isn't so low, but the cold is penetrating. There is a great deal of mud around the camps – endless mud. The sun rarely shines and everything seems unusual. One drives on the left-hand side of the road for instance, and eats at different hours, tea is the natural drink, not coffee. One is in a country which is prepared for invasion, which came close to invasion when they were not prepared and therefore is extremely conscious of the danger . . . For the first few days the men [or 'boys', as Mrs Roosevelt was prone to call them in her maternal way] eat British Army rations and British war bread, which is much darker than ours but very good and healthful. Our boys do not like it. They are accustomed to white bread. They do not like the mess much either because they are not accustomed to it. They get colds and may be in hospital for a few days . . . in spite of all this, it is an adventure and the first ones to feel the excitement are the young ones. The older men, who are married and who have left a pattern of life which they made for themselves at home, are more homesick and are the ones who pray nightly that the war will end and they can go back to those whom they love. The younger ones, though they might grumble, are filled with curiosity about this new life.

America's first lady, who by now must have plunged her attentive audience back home into a gloom to equal the British weather, then drew her broadcast to a close by entreating those who were listening 'to hold up their fingers in the V sign' and to translate 'that symbol into tangible work and sacrifice – for till we have our victory, our boys won't come home.'

When she spoke to the troops in Britain, the President's wife had struck a less inspirational, but more practical note. 'I have already found out that you want thicker socks because your feet are cold. And when I get back, I'm going to see if something can't be done about that. However you know how long it takes for the Army to change anything.' But despite rumours to the contrary, she must have had the ear of the President, for on 1 December 1942, a matter of days after Mrs Roosevelt's return, an order was issued: 'Soldiers in the ETO are entitled to one more pair of wool socks.'

CHAPTER SEVEN

WARM BEER AND BRUSSELS SPROUTS

BY THE END OF MARCH 1943, a twenty-year-old infantryman from Connecticut had decided what he didn't like about his posting to Britain: 'the climate and the beer and the cigarettes and the way the pubs shut just when you want another drink.' It was only surprising that he didn't include 'the food' on his list, since it jostled the weather for first place in most GIs' laments about life 'over here'.

To Charles Cawthon the 'taste [of Britain] was of Brussels sprouts, old mutton, Spam, powdered eggs, dehydrated potatoes and strong tea.' An infantryman from Michigan, who had to wait all day for a meal when he arrived at Tidworth Barracks, found when it finally came that it was 'the regular British ration . . . predominantly mutton, cabbage, Brussels sprouts, boiled potatoes and heavy dark bread and tea'. A sergeant in the 8th Air Force remembers: 'I never cared for mutton, and we had a whole lot of it. First they'd serve it as chops, then a couple of days later, it'd come back at you as stew, and by the time it got to be stew you could smell it a quarter of a mile away.' A radio operator stationed in RAF quarters in Wales found the food – 'bad – thick globs of grease which someone claimed to be mutton, whole cold potatoes and lukewarm tea. I quickly located the Salvation Army hall where I lived on hot tea and biscuits.'

The Brussels sprout – which in the absence of fresh fruit was a good source of vitamins, and was in the front line of Britain's 'Dig for Victory' campaign – came in for special vilification, still more so since the concept of the *al dente* vegetable was not yet a familiar one in most British kitchens, and boiled still implied a thoroughgoing process. Indeed, the Ministry of Food became so concerned about vitamins being boiled away that it urged women to abandon their habit of leaving cabbage for the evening meal to simmer on the stove all day while they were out at work. *Stars and Stripes* observed:

> Americans over here are short of many things. They miss maple syrup and tomato catsup, cigarettes, T-bone steaks. Sometimes it can be hard to find razor blades and pipe cleaners. But it can be stated without contradiction that they have never been short of either cabbage or Brussels sprouts . . . the British a few hundred years ago made the two vegetables standard fare to the exclusion of practically everything else which grows. The tradition has flourished without, as far as the average American can see, any serious challenge. And the 1942 season which began in October and ran to May has been the most flourishing in the mortal memory of man.

The group commander of a bomb group stationed in Suffolk instructed his men: 'If you must make a forced landing, do it in a Brussels sprout patch.' And an ode penned by Technical Sergeant Tom Reeves in *Stars and Stripes* put the sentiment even more forcefully:

Sure I can stand corn willies
Or army beans and grin.
Wheatless bread and chicory
Or goldfish from a tin.
But when I get back home
The guy will get thrown out
Who takes me out to dinner
And serves a brussel sprout.

Thoughts of home, mixed up with thoughts of food, took up a lot of a GI's waking hours and were reflected in the pages of the newspapers and magazines produced for him. Concerned at the US troops' distaste for the ubiquitous powdered egg – 'leathery and sulphurous', it would, claimed a pilot, 'make a buzzard gag' – *Stars and Stripes* called for a genius who could invent a way 'to take those powdered eggs we're getting over here and make them sunnyside up'. But an airman with the 448th Bomb Group could have told them that although 'the book' called for powdered eggs to be cooked in a steamer, 'they weren't good at all. Our cook learned to scramble them in bacon fat on top of the stove and then they were fine.' In April 1943, a bomb group stationed in Norfolk announced that they were going to copy the traditional 'Easter Egg rolling competition' held each year on the lawn of the White House but in their case 'all eggs will be powdered and rolled in the can.'

Throughout the autumn of 1942 there was a long and anguished debate about the provision of turkeys for the US troops' traditional Thanksgiving dinner in late November. This involved treading a fine line between wanting to keep up American morale without offending the sensibilities of the British, who were rationed to thirteen pennies' worth of scarce meat a week. The dilemma was finally resolved by donating the 50,000 turkeys that had been shipped to Britain to local hospitals and providing the GIs with a Thanksgiving dinner of roast pork and apple sauce – a meal the British might also have coveted.

Ironically, one of the 'locally produced' items that many GIs *did* like was denied to them. They were forbidden to drink fresh British milk, for the US authorities regarded unpasteurized milk as a serious health hazard; many were the stories of GIs slinking up to farmhouse doors and dairy milking-sheds with a can for illicit milk, either to drink on the spot or to take back to their barracks for hot chocolate or cocoa.

When the Americans first arrived, they could be insensitive to British shortages. A technical sergeant explained in a letter home in April 1942 from Northern Ireland:

Dear Mom – at first we got a big kick out of going into a restaurant and asking for a big T-bone steak, with fresh green beans, celery, mashed potatoes and apple pie and all the trimmings. We knew darn well the chances were pretty good that we wouldn't get it, but we wanted everyone to know that's what we were used to before. Well, Mom we don't do things like that now . . . nobody told us to stop doing those nasty little things. We just came round to it gradually!

'You cawn't *miss it.'* One-hundred-year-old Mrs Hamblin of Bishop's Cleeve near Cheltenham directs GIs to a local beauty spot.

Nevertheless, when a GI allowed his thoughts to wander, it seemed that they often ran to chocolate milk shakes, apple pie, blueberry pie, ice cream, Coke and steaks 'as big as a plate' – symptomatic of missing home and all it stood for. The British were sometimes less than sympathetic to the Yanks' apple-pie-deprivation syndrome: a sixty-year-old London woman snorted, 'President Roosevelt seems to think that Brussels sprouts are the last word in wartime hardship.' But the US authorities were concerned that the morale of their troops – let alone their digestions – was being seriously undermined by a wartime British diet. A catering adviser to the 8th Air Force suggested that the excessive starch being served to aircrews could generate gas in the intestines which could prove agonizing at 30,000 feet and advised that what was needed was spinach and hamburgers rather than sprouts and mutton. Soon valuable shipping space was bringing the GIs food from home. 68 per cent of their food was still purchased locally but the other 32 per cent made the difference. A technical sergeant stationed at Wendling near Norwich was dramatic: 'I think the first shipment of peanut butter saved our lives!' It made a welcome difference to British lives too, as alerted by the authorities to the severity of British rationing, many GIs who were invited into British homes would arrive with cans of peaches, packets of sugar, tins of luncheon meat or other delicacies unobtainable in wartime.

The culture shock of food was not all one way, however. The Americans' penchant for mixing sweet and savoury food was a source of horrified fascination. An Exeter woman looked on in wonderment as three GIs whom she and her daughter had invited to tea heaped pilchards, chocolate pinwheels and fruit jelly on to the same plate and then wolfed them down altogether. A GI mesmerized a Smethwick family by dipping his stick of celery into the raspberry jam and then eating it with gusto. A woman in Saltash sat next to a GI in a restaurant and watched in disbelief as he spread strawberry jam and Cornish cream on his breakfast bacon and eggs. And a journalist invited to a US Army camp noted 'the odd mixture of apricot jam and sultana cake and fresh lettuce'. 'I can't remember,' a Shrewsbury woman reflects – 'they either had custard on chips or gravy on fruit pies, and I know it was a joke for a long time.' An American infantryman, who had dined one evening next to a snobbish and frosty British officer, took a perverse delight at breakfast the next morning in pouring marmalade over his porridge and stirring it in under the officer's horrified gaze. When an ATS girl and her friend were invited for a meal at an American base in Wales, she noticed that

> every man had a queer mixture of food on one plate . . . tinned peaches and jam were indiscriminately mixed up with slices of veal and ham and sauteed potatoes and vegetables. A kindly orderly handed us two plates . . . saying 'I know you Limeys don't like to mix food on a plate like we do' . . . we were very grateful because I doubt if we could have eaten the delicious meal the way everyone else was doing.

There was one British custom 'that wasn't long in developing' at Tidworth –

> that of going to the NAAFI hut . . . about 10 a.m. for tea and cakes. British troops had a rest period at that hour every morning, so we adopted the custom. All officers and enlisted men who could arrange it drifted up there and enjoyed a mid-morning snack. It called for a slight stretching of the ten-minute break in drill, but nobody minded until the battalion commander happened by one morning for his cup of tea. He found a large proportion of his battalion sitting around the room in a country club atmosphere. That afternoon a battalion order was issued putting the hut 'off limits' during hours.

Eating, as usual, reinforced national stereotypes. If the British thought that the Americans got medals for eating Brussels sprouts, the Americans thought that the British might be rather better placed to win the war if they cut down on their tea breaks. Faced with a problem the British soldier's attitude seemed to be to 'brew up'. 'Because they did stop for tea at what appeared to be most inopportune times, the thought developed among us that they might not go as far or as fast as they might have,' reflected an infantry officer from Arkansas. An infantryman attached to a mechanical division remembers watching a farmer ploughing round the base: 'it seems as if he went up and down the little lane to the house about fifty times a day. I suppose he had to go home and drink some tea. It would seem as if that is all they did here.' As an American pilot flying with the RAF wrote to the woman he was to marry at the end of the war:

> I'd like to show you England
> The England that I know
> Of rain and fog and tweeds and tea
> A place where time is slow . . .

The one item in the British culinary desert that did seem to find favour with the GIs was fish and chips. 'There is a national dish over here called "fish 'n chips",' explained a US colonel in a letter home: 'It is fried fish and fried potatoes which are cut into long, thin cubes before frying. I don't think they are very good, but they are popular.'

Soon GIs became accustomed to saying, 'Fish 'n chips with a dash of vinegar and plenty of salt,' rather than 'Hot dog, please.' In every city and town throughout Britain there seemed to be a fish and chip shop (fish was never rationed in the war, though some varieties became scarce and the Ministry of Food encouraged people to try the 'more unusual varieties' – whalemeat for example), and fish and chip shops were often the only place to get any food in the evening. It was a bit confusing because 'chips' were what Yanks called 'French fries', and in England a 'potato chip' was a 'crisp'.

It was often at the fish and chip shop that a GI had his first experience of another British phenomenon – the queue. 'Over here,' the observant colonel reported, 'the people are very orderly. They stand in line for everything – it is called queuing. It is pronounced "cue" and you do this for a bus, for a shave and for practically any merchandise and food.' 'It didn't take the GIs long to fall hand-in-glove with the fish and chips queue . . . you stood in line for buses, at the movies . . . and of course, the chow line,' explained an infantryman from Georgia who often thought 'it would be a good policy to take back to America', especially when he remembered 'how we used to scramble to get on the buses in front of Rich's in Atlanta'. An infantry officer learned the etiquette of queuing when he and a couple of friends took their first furlough (leave) in London. They saw a queue for taxis and it occurred to them that if they went down the street a little they could hail a cab before it reached the queue. But when they tried this tactic

> the cabbie protested 'You cawn't get in 'ere. You have to stand in a queue' . . . and drove off. Resignedly we went back to the queue and waited our turn. We were beginning to see that what was a smart trick in the States was frowned on in England . . . the ideal of 'fair play' and the right to refuse trade if they wanted to, coupled with a respect for their police, seemed more important than making an extra shilling.

Pubs were another local institution which most GIs embraced wholeheartedly. For many troops stationed in rural areas, the pub was the only place to go in the evening if they wanted to get off the base – it wasn't all that different in towns and cities, particularly in the early days before the American Red Cross set up clubs for the US troops.

Pubs accustomed to a couple of farmers and a sheepdog in the corner had fresh life injected into them with the arrival of American forces in the area. And the troops had already been briefed on pub behaviour by their handbook: it was described as a 'poor man's club where the men have come to see their friends not strangers . . . if you want to join a darts game, let them ask you first (they probably will).' In fact it wasn't just a 'poor man's club'; GIs were surprised to see that men and women often went to the pub together, something that was rarely seen in the States at that time, where in any case some states were still enforcing prohibition.

The pubs provided companionship, often darts, cribbage or shove ha'penny – and weak, warm and watery beer. It was explained to the GIs that British beer is 'not an imitation of German beer like our beer is, but ale (though they usually call it beer). The British are

Noontime serenade. US troops at ease in London.

beer drinkers – and can hold it. The beer is now below peacetime strength' – as Robert Arbib found out when he tried the mild and then asked for something stronger: 'We tried the bitter. It was weak and sweet and warm. We tried the brown ale. We tried the stout. We tasted the Guinness. We ended up by drinking the light ale, which was the only variety that seemed strong enough to put a foam on the glass!' Later he came to like, or at least become accustomed to, ' 'arf and 'arf'.

'I think your beer's an acquired taste, and somehow I can't get round to acquiring it,' regretted a GI from St Louis, while another thought the beer tasted as if it had been 'boiled, and then boiled again'.

The Yanks shocked many locals by adding shots of whisky to their beer to give it strength, or salt to give it taste. One was even seen stirring in an egg – to give it body, perhaps? – and it was rumoured that some GIs sprinkled cigarette ash in their beer, allegedly to increase its potency.

Troops stationed in the West Country had another choice – cider. An Englishman, then a schoolboy in Bristol, remembers 'Kingston Black, a speciality of The Ostrich pub on the quayside which catered for seamen, dockers and people who liked their drink strong'. This 'fed cider', in which a lump of meat – rabbit or hare – had been suspended, made a drink compared to which

> the rotgut served up by the Al Capone mob during prohibition seemed like distilled water . . . The average, hard-drinking Yank would walk in yelling 'Cider, Bud.' This was gleefully provided and, once the first drink had gone, another soon took its place, often paid for by some hard-bitten docker in the interests of Anglo–American relations and a good laugh. After an evening of harmony, the Yank rose to his feet to get back to his base – that was the moment he discovered he'd mislaid his feet. While he was looking for them he also made the curious discovery that the previously still room had started to rotate. Willing hands helped him outside. The Ostrich stood on an open waterfront. If he was lucky he collapsed on the dockside and was hauled into a Jeep by the MPs [Military Police]. If not, a few staggering steps, a shout, a splash! The ultimate indignity, hauled out on the end of a boathook by a grinning river policeman, his ears full of water and the ribald laughter of his drinking companions.

Although this may have been an amusing spectacle, other Britons could be shocked at the habit of some Americans of drinking to excess in public – and did not always stop to think of the paucity of alternative entertainment for young men far from home, with little else to spend their money on.

A woman from Shropshire noticed that when she was waiting for a train, the majority of GIs were drunk and the majority had found themselves girls:

> Because a lot of them were drunk, one or more Jeeps would do a round of the pubs to make sure that the helpless ones got on the train. They got them into the Jeeps from out of the pubs . . . others who were more capable of walking and had found themselves girls were very preoccupied with them in the waiting room so that we couldn't go into the waiting room because there wasn't room because they were all horizontal, and as others were drunk, I usually used to travel in the

guard's van . . . they were never objectionable . . . never abusive. They were jovial . . . if I'd been a single girl, I might even have found them attractive.

A woman who married a GI from Oklahoma after the war recalls a young man stationed at Thurleigh airfield in Bedford who was very taken with a particular pub in the locality, some four or five miles from the base. On his evenings off, Hank would walk to the pub pushing his bike. 'After a convivial evening . . . and fortified by an unspecified number of pints . . . he would mount his bike and take off.' He made over a hundred such trips back to the base unharmed, 'but try as he might, he simply could not ride that bike when he was sober.'

When tensions between GIs and British soldiers flared up, it was usually over girls, money or 'too much beer'; and often the three came together in dance halls or pubs. In December 1942, a report on British attitudes towards the US troops noted: 'people complain that the Americans have money to burn, pub owners are encouraged to take advantage of them and overcharge. And Americans are alleged not to pick up the small change when paying for a drink, which has a bad effect on British soldiers in the pub who have to count their pennies.' 'I wish I could *afford* to get drunk,' a British soldier said wistfully as he watched two legless GIs being evicted from a dance hall in Bedford.

'They were incredibly generous at all times,' remembers a Dorset man, 'but in a pub they were really crazy the way they threw their cash around. I don't know whether it was just to be big, or if they thought the money wasn't going to be of any use to them much longer.'

'We did all right out of the Americans,' a Dorset pub-owner recalled, 'that's how the missus got this place. Them bloody Yanks were crazy for whisky. The missus used to nearly fill a bottle with cold tea and then add a tot of whisky. Then she'd shake it all up and sell it to the Yanks for a couple of quid.' Another pub-keeper was more generous: 'Whisky was always scarce and more than once I was offered as much as £10 for a bottle, but I always said that to sell it would only please one person. By selling it behind the bar, I brought pleasure to a lot of people.'

The Ministry of Information, which was particularly concerned with what today would be thought of as the public relations aspect of the 'peaceful invasion', reported in the late autumn of 1942 that there was a vast amount of drunkenness among the American troops, especially in Manchester and Liverpool (where there were considerable concentrations of troops connected with the supply bases), but predicted that 'the position will no doubt improve when the Red Cross clubs and hostels are functioning.'

It was hardly surprising that some local tensions developed. With free evenings and a lack of other entertainment, the GIs would head for the pubs as soon as they opened and would soon consume the limited stock available, with the result that 'the agricultural workers, who, because they are working long hours and cannot get to the public houses as early as the American troops, find on their arrival that there is no beer left for them. This is causing very considerable resentment.' It was by no means unusual for the GIs to drink a pub dry halfway through the evening, or even all the pubs in the town, as the 820th Engineers did: 'On Tuesday night, The Dog went dry – and [the landlord] hung out a sad little sign on his door – "No Beer" – and closed his inn for the evening – the first time in the 450 years of The Dog's history. The Yanks had come to England.'

WARM BEER AND BRUSSELS SPROUTS

A volunteer with the Royal Observer Corps found Bournemouth 'brimful of Yanks . . . They monopolized the girls and guzzled the beer in record time. With a shortage of beer and glasses, their method of getting more than their share, with six glasses each, being filled in relays, was not appreciated.' When glasses ran short, there was a trade in jam jars, and if the response to the perennial children's request 'Got any gum, chum?' wasn't 'If you've gotta sister, mister', it was an offer to swop the chewing-gum for jam jars so the drinking could go on.

But for many GIs it was companionship rather than alcohol they were looking for in the pubs. A lieutenant with the supply services made a foray into town the first evening he arrived at Gourock:

> I soon discovered one word that wasn't in the official advice given us. It was 'black-out'. In the velvety darkness, I stumbled around and amazingly found a pub just where I was told it would be. I was made to feel welcome in its smoky fug and although I wasn't a beer drinker, I happily settled for the cider that was on offer . . . after a few rounds the conversation flowed and we relaxed. I talked about my home and family.

A soldier with the 289th Infantry did much the same when he arrived in Swansea.

> One evening seventeen of us took over the bar of the local Hare and Hounds. It was our first time out of camp . . . It soon developed into a great party and we all sang all the old songs. At the end of the evening I saw my first sergeant sitting on the floor unconscious. He was what the locals called 'pissed'. That was quite a night for me because it wasn't the sort of thing I would do normally. But we weren't living in normal times.

The Americans would never get used to the complexities of pub opening hours – a cartoon in *Stars and Stripes* showed a parachutist bailing out of an aeroplane with the caption 'Say, I just hope I come down near a pub that's open'. Equally bewildering were the social gradations involved in the design of some pubs – places they called 'taverns' back home. An infantryman remembers a pub round the corner from Grosvenor Square in London, where there were 'separate doors for family bar, saloon bar, public bar, ladies' bar etc . . . a person had to be really sober when he went in . . .'

But the GIs were almost universally taken with the phrase beloved of British publicans, 'Time, gentlemen, please'. This and 'You *cawn't* miss it' – the standard response whenever they asked for directions – became the most mimicked sentences of their time in Britain.

'It's a pity,' mused a sixty-nine-year-old woman, 'they speak our language. If their language was a foreign one, we could make excuses for them and expect them to be different.' For the GIs did – and didn't – speak English.

As a leaflet handed out by the American Red Cross warned, 'Perfectly harmless American "slanguage" sometimes has a very embarrassing meaning to English ears, so watch out for these expressions when you are in a British home.'

Conversely, the GI who found a pub to relax in on the evening he arrived in Britain was told by a British woman 'You're very homely.' She clearly meant it as a compliment and 'she couldn't have known that it meant "You are downright ugly." '

The GI's *Short Guide* was helpful:

A PUB WITH WEAK BEER

'The beer is now below peacetime strength,' regretted the GIs' Short Guide, *'but it can still make a man's tongue wag at both ends.'*

Almost before you meet the people, you will hear them speaking 'English'. At first you may not understand what they are talking about and they may not understand what you say. The accent will be different from what you are used to and many of the words will be strange or wrongly used. But you will get used to it . . . In England, the 'upper crust' speak pretty much alike. You will hear the news broadcaster for the BBC . . . He is a good example, because he has been trained to talk with a 'cultured' accent. He will drop the letter 'r' (as people do in some sections of our own country) and will say 'hyah' instead of 'here'. He will use the broad *a* pronouncing all the 'a' in banana like the 'a' in father. However funny you may think this is, you will be able to understand people who talk this way and they will be able to understand you . . . you will have more difficulty with some of the local dialects. It may comfort you to know that a farmer or villager from Cornwall very often can't understand a farmer or villager in Yorkshire or Lancashire

– though it could have added that a GI from the Bronx might claim that he had difficulty in catching on to what a compatriot from Tennessee was saying.

A Shropshire woman remembers that 'they used to make fun of the way we pronounced our words. They would say they spoke English and we would say, No you don't, and some of the dialects got them a bit foxed. I don't think some of them could understand the broad Shropshire.'

Standing on York station, an American was puzzled by the voice over the speaker repeating 'Canoe, Canoe' at the start of each announcement until a British commando on the platform explained that what was being said was 'Hello, Hello'.

The advice given to the British was blunt:

Some Americans consider that our English accent is affected when it is 'standard' and repulsive when it is 'dialect'. There are also Britons who resent all American accents and American phraseology on the grounds that they are a sign of vulgarity, pretentiousness etc. Some people in these islands even believe the Americans 'put on' their accents in order to emulate the movies . . . It would be helpful, however, if Britons today would acquaint themselves with some of the more common differences between American and British phraseology, especially such differences as may lead to practical misunderstandings – eg when an American speaks of the hood of a car, he means what we call the bonnet; when he says vest he means waistcoat, and when he says undershirt he means vest; when he says crackers, he means biscuits and when he says biscuits he means scones.

The *Short Guide* for GIs elaborated on this: 'automobile lingo is just as different. A light truck is a lorry. The top of a car is a hood. The fenders are wings (and bumpers too). A wrench is a spanner. Gas is petrol – if there is any.'

The list Louis MacNeice came up with in his guide to the Americans anticipated a more discursive interchange, substituting 'apartment' for 'flat', 'graduate' (verb) for 'to leave school', 'preparatory school' for 'public school' and 'alumni' for 'old boys', but coming back to a vital difference: what are 'suspenders' to Americans are 'braces' to the British – though he omitted to translate what the British call 'suspenders' into US-speak.

The Americans were also advised how not to offend with the unintentional *faux pas*:

> The British have phrases and colloquialisms of their own that may sound funny to you . . . it isn't a good idea, for instance, to say 'bloody' in mixed company in Britain. It is one of their worst swear words. To say 'I look like a bum', is offensive to their ears, for to the British this means that you are trying to look like your own backside; it isn't important, just a tip if you are trying to shine in polite society . . .

Despite all this advice there were still misunderstandings. 'Keep your pecker up', meaning 'Keep cheerful', struck the Americans as a somewhat frank suggestion; a 'fanny' was an altogether different part of the American anatomy from the British; the innocent question 'Shall I knock you up with a cup of tea?' asked by landladies the length and breadth of the land, caused hilarity, since to the British it meant 'wake up', to the Americans 'make a girl pregnant'; and typists working on US bases soon learnt not to ask for a 'rubber' when what they wanted was an 'eraser'.

Not all British girls were unaware of the linguistic traps: an ATS posted in Norfolk recalls a friend who declined to pose for a GI's camera. 'He wanted me to stand under a noticeboard which read NAVIGATION ON THIS BROAD IS FREE,' she explained.

One GI went into a chemist in Birmingham: 'wanting a torch, I asked for a flashlight, and was sold a fly swat.' But the language difference which seems to have caused almost the greatest ire was when Americans used British phones. Infuriated by the inefficient system at the best of times – 'it's like lifting the receiver at home and asking for the wrong number please,' reported *Stars and Stripes* – it drove a GI to distraction to be told 'you're through' when he hadn't even started to speak, when at home it would have been crystal clear: 'you're connected,' the operator would have informed him.

CHAPTER EIGHT

FURLOUGHS AND PASSES

'ON OUR FIRST WEEKEND IN ENGLAND officers and men were given permission to go to London . . . we skipped the noon meal and thought we'd get an early start. Fourteen thousand of the fifteen thousand men in the division had the same idea,' remembers an infantry officer stationed at Tidworth Barracks. London was a magnet to the GIs, the place where they headed to spend their furloughs.

'Wartime London was special,' recalled a nineteen-year-old from Oklahoma:

> It is difficult to describe it now, but . . . it became a mecca for just about all members of the nations in the war, except Germans and Italians. Although I did hear that one of the big newspapers at the time dressed a couple of guys as Germans and they walked around the town all day with nobody taking any notice. That would be typical of the times though – just about everybody there was in some uniform or other.

According to one GI at the time,

> The conviviality of London in wartime is unimaginable – unless you have actually experienced it. I have seen people who literally hadn't seen each other five minutes earlier become comrades. Romantic attachments are formed on the spot, sometimes with no more than a searching look! In the UK just about everyone has been drafted . . . you could reckon on striking up a conversation in about five minutes of getting off the train. Everyone was real friendly, and the girls were simply wonderful . . . Language? no real barrier either. It usually took a Pole about ten seconds to tell a girl he wanted her. It took us a little longer.

'Battered and dirty, worn and scarred, the city swarmed with scores of different uniforms and it spoke in a hundred different tongues,' one veteran relates: 'No matter where you were going in the UK you had to go through London and no matter how long you stayed, you never saw it all. London was the Babel, the Metropolis, the Mecca. London was IT.'

London was the nerve centre of US Army activity in Britain: 'it had a higher concentration of important personnel, a greater variety of installations and probably more problems per square foot than any other area in Britain . . . and in addition it was the principal leave centre in the UK, ministering to the wants of a transient population half as large as its assigned strength.' Whereas in April 1942 US troops occupied 10,000 feet of office space, along with an officers' mess, sales store, garage and various billets, by D-Day

" Hey—taxi ! "

there were 33 officers' billets (including 24 hotels) and 300 buildings in use for troop accommodation, while 2½ million more square feet had been taken over in offices, depots, garages, shops and various other places to house such American facilities as PXs, messes, a detention barracks, the Military Police headquarters in Piccadilly, and a gymnasium, as well as clinics and dispensaries. The grandest of the US installations was undoubtedly the officers' mess at Grosvenor House in Park Lane which had taken over the hotel's spacious and elegant ballroom. Opened in 1943, it was nicknamed 'Willow Run' after the car assembly line in Detroit; eventually it was able to serve between 6,000 and 7,000 meals a day – but only after the services of its original French chef had been dispensed with when it became apparent that his Gallic spirits 'were crushed by the prospects of serving the contents of the "C"-ration can'.

The US Embassy was at 20 Grosvenor Square. The ambassador, John G. Winant, described it as located in 'an old section of London. The architecture is predominantly Georgian. It is a place of early American tradition – the house occupied by John Adams on his mission to Great Britain still stands there . . . the square marked out a bit of America in the war.' It seemed rather more than a 'bit of America' to some. As Mrs Henrey reported from Shepherd Market in late 1943:

> my village in Piccadilly had changed little during the last six months except that more and more Americans were to be seen in the streets. They called to each other with strange Red Indian cries and organized baseball games in Green Park . . . their hostels and clubs were augmenting in number, especially between Grosvenor Square and Piccadilly, and it was a long cry from the days when, before the United States entered the war, a small bunch of American marines was sent here to serve as fire guards at the US Embassy with orders to change into civilian dress when off duty. The first uniformed troops were housed in two Piccadilly buildings, the former Hotel Splendide and the Badminton Club. Others were billeted near the Embassy in Grosvenor Square. Then began a pincer movement converging on our market. South Audley Street became a miniature Fifth Avenue [with its own PX where GIs could buy seven packs of cigarettes a week, two bars of chocolate, two razor blades and a can of fruit juice. In addition

they could buy soap, toothpaste, shaving cream, handkerchiefs, fountain pens, and dozens of other little things], the late Sir Philip Sassoon's mansion facing Stanhope Gate became a senior US officers' club and the Washington Hotel in Curzon Street blossomed out as a Red Cross Club for doughboys. Meanwhile Half Moon Street and Clarges Street, famous in the old days for aristocratic bachelor lodgings, became an American dormitory. There was not a tailor, a shoemaker, a laundry or a French cleaner in our market that did not start working overtime to cope with this invasion. Whereas eighteen months earlier during the night raids, these little tradespeople had carried on stoically with an order here and there and a narrow margin of profit, prosperity now burst upon them. They hammered and served, they washed all day and far into the night.

On his second visit to wartime London in 1943, Ernie Pyle, an American journalist, was struck by the extent to which the city

was crawling with Americans, both Army and civilian. All headquarter cities were alike in their overcrowding, their exaggerated discipline and what appeared to be military overstaffing. There were those who said that London was as bad as Washington. Others said it was worse. Certainly the section where American offices were most highly concentrated was a funny sight at lunchtime or in the late afternoon. Floods of American uniforms poured out of buildings. On some streets, an Englishman stood out as incongruously as he would in North Platte, Nebraska. . . . There were all kinds of cracks about the way Americans had flooded the island and nearly crowded the English off . . . One said to another, 'the English are beginning to act as if this country belonged to them.'

One American habit proved particularly hazardous in London:

the American Army was very strict about saluting. Everyone had to salute. Second lieutenants saluted other second lieutenants. Arms flailed up and down by the thousands as though everyone was crazy. People jabbed each other in the eye saluting. On one short street much travelled by Americans, they had to make sidewalk traffic one-way, presumably to prevent salute casualties.

But there was more space for pedestrians in London streets as petrol rationing meant that many private cars were laid up for the duration of the war. At weekends traffic was so light in the city's streets that one Sunday

a green dray cart filled with American soldiers and their girlfriends and drawn by two white shire horses clattered at full speed past Hatchard's. The driver's whip was garlanded and everyone was singing 'Idaho', the melancholy strains of which were wafted away on the breeze,

while in nearby Hyde Park, US troops joined British servicemen in listening to the harangues of the speakers, and in Green Park, British visitors – and the sheep who grazed there as part of the 'produce more food' wartime campaign and occasionally escaped into Piccadilly itself – watched the Yanks play hectic and noisy games of baseball and softball in the shadow of the anti-aircraft rocket batteries.

But it wasn't only the streets that became 'a bit of America'. The Washington Club in Curzon Street held regular dances and Robert Henrey and his wife, who lived nearly opposite, were invited along:

> the swing doors led from the heart of London into another life. One had the impression of crossing, within the space of a few seconds, the broad Atlantic. American accents, from the New York twang to the drawls of southern states, replaced the warm, slow talk of the London streets. There was a faint, but appetizing smell of apple tart and cream, roast pork and Camel cigarettes. The newspaper racks were filled with journals from every state of the union and the familiar red post-box was replaced by a US Army mail bag. An entire wall was covered with posters of the New York Central and Southern Pacific railroads, inviting one to spend a vacation in Texas or Mexico. One expected to hear from without the chiming bell and plaintive whistle of an American locomotive . . . from the end of the corridor came the sound of jazz . . . men and women stood on benches and tables behind arclights watching others dance the boogie woogie, the conga and the samba, and in a corner silver machines were turning out scores of doughnuts spread with powdered sugar.

To complete this vista of 'little America', 'a US sailor . . . was opening bottles of Coca-Cola with swift flicks of his supple wrist. He handed them to dancers as they passed, who drank from the necks of the bottles. At 10 p.m. the orchestra played "God Save the King" and "The Star-Spangled Banner".'

'The gigantic bigness of London never ceased to overwhelm GIs. Nobody can ever again tell them that New York is the biggest city in the world,' mused the *Stars and Stripes* correspondent, Ralph Martin.

But with the deluge of GIs converging nightly on the capital, hell-bent on having a good time, one group of Americans who had to get acquainted with the byways of the capital were the Military Policemen. 'We had to learn our London fast,' recalls Clarence Roesler. A Wisconsin farmboy before the war, Roesler was posted with the 32nd Military Police with his billet at 101 Piccadilly:

> We did it the hard way: we pounded the streets day in day out. It wasn't easy. There were so many short and crooked streets that not only changed direction but changed names as well all in the space of one block. But I think that after a while we knew it better than the London bobbies. They only had to learn one block square intimately, we had to know the whole town – and MPs were soon to be seen directing British visitors around their own capital.

The MPs were distinctive in other ways, too. At Eisenhower's directive they began to wear white helmets, white belts, white gaiters and carry long white truncheons: 'we felt like something out of a road show.' The idea, no doubt, was that the MPs would show up in the black-out, but as well as being visible to those GIs who needed help or directions, they proved equally obvious to those GIs who were AWOL (absent without leave).

The GIs called MPs 'snowdrops' – 'not that the Military Police drooped their heads, but coincidence made them blossom out in white when the first snowdrops of the year were to be found in the more sheltered corners of Hyde Park,' so Mrs Henrey whimsically but somewhat improbably explained. They drove around in Jeeps 'which could turn on a dime', and their two-way radios were great crowd-pullers – though the natives 'soon learned to leave the antennae alone when we were transmitting. They got one hell of a shock if they held on.'

> *To know one thing I've often yearned*
> *One fact I would discover*
> *I'll never rest until I've learned*
> *Do MPs have a mother?*

queried one US private.

'MPs didn't endear themselves to soldiers at all,' a former policeman confirmed: 'Tough titty. When a soldier came to London he conformed both in behavior and in dress, or else we put him behind bars . . . That's what we did, we either helped them, or put them away.' The unpopularity of the MPs was not confined to London nor to their fellow countrymen. Many British people were shocked at the alacrity – and sometimes violence – with which the MPs kept order, rounding up GIs into their paddy-wagons, often with liberal use of their truncheons, as soon as trouble threatened, particularly if black GIs were involved – and in many onlookers' opinion often mistaking noisy high spirits for criminally rowdy behaviour, thereby dangerously escalating situations which more conciliatory action might well have defused.

The United States (Visiting Forces) Act, rushed through Parliament in August 1942, made all US troops in Britain subject to disciplinary action under US law if only Americans were involved in the incident. A number of Britons found this provision disquieting in its secrecy, and something which set the US troops further apart from their British hosts. Exaggerated stories circulated of trials where the defendant was found guilty and promptly hanged, and the apparent anxiety of the MPs to hush up any possible trouble at all costs did nothing to allay this unease.

However, the Military Police faced a formidable challenge in London's streets. Some GIs on furlough 'would go from one pub to another, drinking just about anything on offer . . . we would awaken the next morning in a stranger's arms in a stranger's bed. To go with breakfast would be a splitting headache and a conscience full of remorse. We usually promised ourselves "never again". But like most promises we broke them again and again,' one infantryman ruefully recalls. Charles Cawthon saw the melancholy in the situation, too:

> The trips by special train to London for the two days off each month had the supercharged aspect to be expected, given the pent-up – not to put too fine a point on it – social and physical energies, and the unspent pay, of healthy young men. Some used their energy on the British Museum, and some burned it on a non-stop binge, but for the most it was just a continuation of the lonely sense of being strangers in a strange land.

Along with the drink and the carousing went the traditional taking-in of the sights. The GIs crammed into taxis – they greatly admired the London cabbie's ability to get around in the black-out – and it was a commonplace that no Londoner could get a taxi to stop since the drivers preferred to take the generous-tipping Yanks instead. This was

A YANK IN LONDON

ABOVE *'You* cawn't *miss it.' Military Police on patrol in London direct a GI on leave.*
Their Jeep 'could turn on a dime'.
RIGHT *Shoe shine for city shoes.*

something that GIs occasionally resented: 'I like your taxi drivers very much. I admire the way they drive. But I don't like their way of asking for a tip when you're paying them. We'd tip them anyway, but we don't like their asking for it.' They also travelled by the Underground, which on the whole impressed them, or simply wandered the streets, craning their necks to see the sights – and the devastation of bomb damage.

> We all did it. Sometimes five or six of us would hire a taxi and ride round town calling after girls, using up our nation's goodwill with London bobbies, and now and again stopping to photograph Big Ben or the Mother of Parliaments . . . we saw Pall Mall, Buckingham Palace, Leicester Square, the Tower of London.

A WAC from Illinois spent her first leave in London.

> I didn't miss much, with the exception of sleep – which we didn't much, period . . . there's nothing I can tell you about these beloved old historic places which you haven't read over and over . . . but inside the places were simply breathtaking and one only needs to see it once to understand why London has pride in

age and tradition. I stood spellbound in front of the Tower of London, trying to realize that it was built one thousand years ago . . . I couldn't believe my eyes in Westminster Abbey – the stained-glass windows are something out of this world and I found myself, as I listened to the old guide's voice – choking up – just as I did when I first saw Washington DC and New York. I think I must have expected a New York grown old with age and each time I looked up I was surprised to find no building more than five or six storeys high.

Some GIs had the opportunity to take a closer look at the traditions of the 'old country'. Harold Nicolson 'had an appointment to conduct some doughboys round the Palace of Westminster'. As usual, he was pessimistic: 'in they slouched, conscious of their inferiority in training, equipment, breeding, experience and history, determined in no circumstances to be either interested or impressed.' When the Lord Chancellor offered to show the American visitors 'the Great Seal', Nicolson assumed that they were 'expecting to be shown a large wet animal such as they had seen so often at the aquarium in San Francisco. But not at all. All they were shown were two cylinders of steel with a pattern inside.' Given such attempts at entertainment, it is not surprising perhaps that a woman who worked at the Milestone Club in Kensington remembers that 'it was not . . . to Downing Street, nor even to *Bucking-ham* Palace that most of them wished to go. It was to Madame Tussaud's – "the wax museum", as they called it. When questioned about this preference, the reply invariably given was, "My buddy says don't miss it." "But why?" I persevered. "It's different." '

She also recalls a 'particularly fed-up GI' who came up to her one day at the information desk complaining, 'Say, lady, I've seen everything in this town – old buildings, new buildings, everything. Shucks. You can see them any place. We have 'em all back home – what have you got that we ain't got?' She thought for a moment before replying. 'We've got one thing you haven't got back home.' 'What's that, huh?' 'Bombs,' she replied. He saw the point immediately and apologized.

The US authorities were anxious to discourage troops on furlough from all converging at once to savour the temptations of the metropolis. 'If you've already been to London a couple of times, on your next leave get well off the beaten tourist track and see some of *real* England,' encouraged *Stars and Stripes*. They particularly recommended Sulgrave Manor in Northamptonshire, the birthplace of George Washington:

> It's a warm, friendly village . . . and the village highspot is the manor which was bought from Henry VIII in 1539 by the great-great-great-great-great-great-great-grandfather of George Washington. In 1914 school kids, farmers and store keepers contributed pennies and pounds to restore the house and dedicate it as a monument to the 100 years' peace between England and America.

The most popular leave towns for GIs, once they'd torn themselves away from the delights of London, were Stratford-upon-Avon and Canterbury, though Edinburgh had its aficionados. Charles Taylor, who came from Ohio, found the Scottish people much more cheerful and friendly than the English. He also liked the habit of taking a hot water bottle to bed, and he was uneasily thrilled during a guided tour of the Castle by the sight of 'the room where one of Mary Queen of Scots' suitors, a Count Rizzio, was murdered. The

Private First Class Pieszchala salutes an officer in Salisbury High Street in August 1942.

legend says that fifty-odd stab wounds were found in his body. Gruesome, eh? The whole place was gruesome.' But the highlight of the trip was a visit to a court session. Taylor was intrigued 'with all the robes and wigs', and the way that the judge was addressed as 'his lordship'; but despite this he summed up his feelings on the ancient ceremonial with 'I thought that all these Gilbert and Sullivan scenes were passé.'

Troops who visited Canterbury were amazed at the antiquity of the city as they strolled along and saw the signs hanging out reading 'Sun Hotel, founded 1505'; there were streets that 'we'd almost call back alleys, and many antique shops lined the way where people coming on pilgrimages could purchase relics and souvenirs.'

Robert Arbib found 'barrage balloons over the Close at Canterbury and the city badly damaged by a Baedeker raid [so called after the German reprisal raids in 1942 on English cathedral cities starred in the Baedeker guide book] . . . but the Cathedral itself was still a thing of beauty.' He also went to Windsor and had lunch in a little tea room that called itself Nell Gwynne House ('there are as many Nell Gwynne houses in England as "George Washington slept here" houses in America').

In the afternoon he walked across the river to Eton, where he was disappointed by his first glimpse of the famous school, and contemptuous of the outlandish garb of the students, which

Easy riders. US airmen found bicycles essential transport for getting around their bases —
and down to the pub in the evening.

seemed to be swallow-tailed coats, badly in need of cleaning, long scarves which almost dragged the ground, dirty, unpressed grey flannel trousers, top hats and tennis sneakers. Here, it seemed, tradition has gone a little off the deep end. Character-building, self-immolation, or not, there is no need for those scarves in summertime and there seemed little point in dressing these future rulers of the realm like refugees from a travelling circus.

A *Stars and Stripes* correspondent was sent to Stratford-upon-Avon to do a story about GIs on furlough. He 'found the place overflowing with soldiers', and the Red Cross director told him it was like that all year round. His explanation was that 'in most English towns you found a few medieval-looking houses with crooked walls of brick and wooden timbers, but here in Stratford, they were nearly all that way. The place reeked with antiquity.' He sat on 'the same wrinkled bench where Anne Hathaway, [the woman] the young Bill Shakespeare wooed and won . . . did their courting in front of an open hearth'.

Cambridge was another favourite 'liberty town' for GIs – especially airmen and soldiers stationed in East Anglia. But a don at Trinity College was not entirely welcoming to the parties of American airmen he encountered being shown round the college 'and photographing their buddies, or cuties (if I have the term correctly) in front of the fountain or sundial . . . these objects must be pretty familiar in the States.' He asked the head porter whether he had taken much in tips but 'somewhat to my surprise he said that though plentifully rewarded with American cigarettes, no money had come his way.'

It didn't take the GIs long to realize that the best way to explore the English countryside – and get to the pub in the evening – was to employ what to them was a novel form of transport: the bicycle. Many claimed never to have ridden a bike before they came to England, and coming from a land of automobiles, they tended to regard them as 'kid's transport'; but they soon learnt to wobble along the East Anglian lanes – sometimes remembering that the English drive on the left.

A soldier stationed at Tidworth vividly remembers 'snitching a bike from the orderly room one afternoon. I wasn't used to handling bar brakes and all went well until I started down a long, steep hill. I applied the brakes. The front ones locked and the back ones didn't. I described a beautiful arc over a tall hedge into a field. I spreadeagled right into an impromptu ball diamond . . . I fairly well broke up the game.'

The GIs soon found that saluting on a bicycle was none too easy: a major ended up in a bramble hedgerow as he returned a stream of salutes while cycling along a Suffolk lane, and a WAC sergeant from New York wrote home explaining that 'learning to ride a bike, which is a must in England, has been both embarrassing and almost "fatal". Running down colonels, majors, GIs and cats by the WACs brought out a circular which forbids us to salute whilst riding a bike.'

The GIs' need for transport – any transport – gave a great boost to the local economy. Bikes were dug out of cobwebbed, rusty retirement in sheds and barns as reports spread that there were Yanks who were prepared to hand over as much as £20 for a boneshaker for which its owner would have been glad to get thirty shillings before the war. A Bedford farmer's daughter remembers her father taking a ninety-year-old neighbour's bike from his shed on the grounds that 'he won't be riding it anymore', painting it black and selling it for ten shillings to a GI who had asked him to look out for a bike for him. 'He gave my mum five shillings so she didn't say anything . . .'

CHAPTER NINE

ISLANDS OF LITTLE AMERICA

'I T'S A PRETTY COUNTRY – when the sun's shining . . . on the whole I like the people,' reflected a twenty-five-year-old soldier from Missouri, 'but it's the life that's slow. There's not enough amusement over here.' 'A graveyard with stoplights' was a US sergeant's description of his local Midlands town. And GIs in Northern Ireland summed up their feelings: 'Gee, Rostrevor's a swell little place but why the hell don't they bury their dead?'

As the influx of the American troops grew ever larger, and thousands and thousands of energetic young men – and some women – flooded into Britain, drafted for war but needing relaxation and hoping for some fun, British facilities, limited at the best of times, were entirely unable to rise to the demand.

The American Red Cross was charged with the task of providing recreational facilities for American troops on leave – most troops had an eight-day furlough every six or seven months, while weekend passes were issued more frequently – and this meant clubs and hostels to save the troops who flooded into the cities from having to sleep on the floor of railway stations, as earlier many had been obliged to do.

The first club was opened in Londonderry in May 1942 – four months after the first GIs arrived in the province. There had been a club for Americans in London since 1940, the Eagle Club. This was taken over by the Red Cross in April 1942, and in June the Washington Hotel in Curzon Street, which had been damaged in the Blitz, was acquired. The charges were 50 cents (2s 6d) for bed and breakfast and 20 cents (1s) for dinner. Within months, the Milestone Club in Kensington – with its motto that 'Nothing Is Too Good for Our Boys' – opened. Soon, enlisted men could disport themselves at the Mostyn in Portman Street, the Columbia and the Victory in Seymour Street near Marble Arch, and the Hans Crescent Club near Harrods in Knightsbridge. Officers could patronize the Princes Garden and Vandyke Club in Kensington, and the Jules Club and Reindeer Club in Mayfair; the WACs had two women-only clubs in Charles Street, Mayfair (one of which was for officers); and black GIs were eventually catered for at the Duchess Club near Oxford Circus. Just as the troops were leaving for the Normandy landings, the Stage Door Canteen, modelled on its namesake in New York, opened in a blaze of publicity, with Bing Crosby photographed serving waffles.

But far and away the most famous of all the clubs was Rainbow Corner. The British government had commandeered two famous London eating places – the Del Monico restaurant on the corner of Shaftesbury Avenue and Piccadilly and part of the adjoining

Lyon's Corner House, and there the American Red Cross had deliberately set about recreating a 'little America' for homesick GIs.

When the club was opened in November 1942, the key was thrown away in a symbolic gesture to indicate that so long as US troops were fighting the war in Europe, Rainbow Corner would keep its doors open twenty-four hours a day – which it did. In the thirty-eight months it was open, hundreds of thousands of soldiers, sailors on shore leave and airmen passed through the club's doors. But it was not an assured success from the start. One of the staff looked back to the earliest days of Rainbow Corner:

> those khaki, .50-caliber and Garand rifle days when Eisenhower was still a brigadier general, when GI brides were GI maidens, when Claridge's Hotel looked like the billeting office of the 8th Air Force . . . In a grim red-brick Victorian building which had once housed restaurants, there was a great unhappiness. The lights were burning in a somewhat austerely decorated lobby. A restaurant on the ground floor was almost as foggy as the streets – English fog having remarkable powers of penetration. Blue-uniformed young women lined up in the lobby and white-frocked women, young and old, stood lined up before the steam tables of the empty restaurant, waiting. The scene was reminiscent of the household staff of some vast English manor waiting for the movie-style return of the master. No guests arrived. Finally several of the blue-uniformed young women barged disconsolately out into the fog, grabbed passers-by by the arms to identify them in the thick fog, and on finding American soldiers, dragged them behind the rather grim façade . . . They got hold of ten slightly bedraggled, fog-ridden individuals and – as legend has it – brought them in, fed them coffee and the inevitable doughnuts and Rainbow Corner was officially opened.

The club had recreation rooms where the GIs could do things they liked to do at home – play craps, shoot pool, massage the pinball machines, listen to the juke box pumping out favourites like, 'Deep in the Heart of Texas', 'Chattanooga-Choo-Choo' or the poignant 'Don't Sit Under the Apple Tree' (with anyone else but me). But the GIs liked to come to Rainbow Corner to eat, too. There were two dining-rooms which could seat 2,000 men and served meals at 25 cents, and in the basement was a snack bar, which stayed open long after the surrounding establishments had closed their doors at around nine or ten o'clock in the evening, serving waffles, hamburgers, American-type sandwiches, hash browns, doughnuts, coffee and endless bottles of Coke. For Rainbow Corner, like all American Red Cross Clubs, was not licensed; it aimed to create the atmosphere, if hardly the surroundings, of a corner drugstore.

In the large recreation room films were shown and visiting speakers like Lord Woolton (of pie fame), Ed Murrow (the CBS correspondent) and Lady Astor (American born, Nancy Astor had been the first woman to take a seat in the House of Commons) talked to the GIs about what being in Britain was all about. Boxing and wrestling matches were held, and so were dances – five times a week. The club had an approved list of partners – and a blacklist, too, of those girls who would *not* be admitted. GIs found that with a little encouragement British girls could jitterbug with as much enthusiasm and disregard for injury as those back home in Flatbush or Little Rock – and when he toured Britain in 1944, Glenn Miller and his band gave four performances at Rainbow Corner.

'OVER HERE'

RAINBOW CORNER
BELOW *A home from home right here in Piccadilly.*
BOTTOM *Coffee and Coke. English volunteers served all-American food in the club's cafeteria to GIs on leave.*

98

BELOW *Sewing and Sympathy. Irene Whittaker chats to a sergeant from Chicago as she sews stripes on his uniform.*
BOTTOM *A WAC from Michigan, a soldier from Massachusetts and Adèle Astaire (left) join Irving Berlin at the piano to sing 'Always' at Rainbow Corner in 1943.*

GIs could get their shoes shined, their hair cut in approved Yankee style, and their cigarette-lighters filled at Rainbow Corner. There was a first aid room and an adjoining 'Where am I?' room which was used to accommodate GIs whose excessive pub-crawling led them there to sleep it off, and ask that question when they woke up. There were hot showers. There was an arts and crafts room where servicemen could use charcoals and paints, sculpt and model or have their portrait sketched and sent off home free of charge. Tickets for the theatre were arranged, as were sightseeing tours for which a GI paid one dollar twenty cents 'and got in a taxi and let the sights roll by', or borrowed one of the club's bikes, each of which was named after an American state. 'Alabama's gone, Connecticut too, but I can book Minnesota for you for 7 a.m.' During the time the US forces were in the UK, 142,206 free theatre tickets were issued from the club and 309,832 troops were taken on conducted tours of London.

In the recreation room was a wall-sized map of the USA with the legend, 'Is there someone here from your home town? Watch the flags'. The map was dotted with tiny red flags and when he paid the club an official pre-D-Day visit, General Eisenhower had a problem finding space to stick a flag on his home town of Abilene, Kansas.

In the lobby there was one arrow pointing in the direction of Leicester Square, only yards away; another pointing towards the reason for the GIs' presence in the UK – 'Berlin 600 miles'; and a third which reminded the GIs, if reminder they needed, that New York was 3,271 miles away.

Like other Red Cross Clubs throughout Britain, Rainbow Corner was directed by Americans with some staff from the US helped both by paid British employees and hundreds of mainly British volunteers. At the peak of the programme, there were more than 2,000 American Red Cross workers on duty in 265 service clubs, assisted by nearly 13,000 volunteers and close to 10,000 paid local employees.

'We answered questions of something like 70,000 men a month at the information desk,' recalls Blossom Brown, daughter of the xylophonist 'Teddy' Brown, who worked as a receptionist at Rainbow Corner. 'For months before D-Day we literally did not see the floor here, it was so packed tight with questioners.' A British volunteer, Lady Irene Whittaker, set up a sewing table in the corner of the basement snack bar when the club first opened, and worked round the clock darning socks, mending tears and sewing stripes and insignia on to the uniforms of the GIs, and under each shoulder patch she would tuck a 'flying robin', a farthing coin for luck, or a silver half crown under the patches of pilots in the US Army Air Force. Like many of the women who worked in Red Cross Clubs, Irene Whittaker became a great confidante for hundreds of the troops, providing an element of motherly interest for young soldiers, sailors and airmen incarcerated for long periods in an almost entirely male environment far from home. They would write to her from postings abroad, and she sent news home to their families; and a plane, the 'Lady Irene' was named after her.

Another woman with a famous name, Lady Charles Cavendish, was also a volunteer at Rainbow Corner. Better known as Adèle Astaire, the sister and former dancing partner of the more famous Fred, she wrote letters home for the GIs at their dictation, or at her gentle prompting.

Letters from home were an important part of the GIs' lives overseas – the arrival and distribution of the mail was eagerly awaited, and with an official ban on the keeping of diaries and journals, the letters the troops sent home may be the only record of their wartime years. But though every GI was avid to receive letters, writing them was sometimes a different matter. Anona Moser, who came to Britain from running a Girl Scout club in Richmond, Virginia, to be programme director of the Red Cross Club in Bedford, remembers encouraging young GIs to write home to their mothers: 'Don't tell me she hasn't been looking out in the mail for a letter from you every day.' Volunteer stenographers worked at some of the clubs to help the troops get their sentiments down on paper, while *Stars and Stripes* came up with a versifier's reproach:

> *How long since you wrote to your mother?*
> *For you the hours may fly*
> *But these hours are years to your mother*
> *When the mailman passes her by.*
>
> *How long since you wrote to your mother?*
> *Better get that letter done*
> *For mothers fade like flowers*
> *When they miss their wandering son.*

The volume of transatlantic mail grew to huge proportions: by 1943 it was estimated that on average, each GI in the UK received fourteen letters a week from home, in return for an average of three and a half letters home. In order to save shipping space, V-Mail was introduced to supplement the ordinary mail. Letters were written on a special form, then photographed on microfilm which reduced them in size; on receipt the film was printed. V-Mail letters were free to US troops, and would get across the Atlantic faster than sea mail, but somewhat slower than air mail. It was called 'V-Mail' for 'victory mail' – though one GI asking for a 'V-Mail' affronted the receptionist at a Red Cross Club who thought that he was soliciting for a 'female'. Since a ton of ordinary letters recorded on negative this way only weighed 25 lbs this saved space for freighting war matériel.

All mail from the United Kingdom to the United States was censored 'in order to prevent military and naval information from falling into the hands of the enemy and to retain good relations with the Allies and neutrals'. Letters from enlisted men were first censored by their company or detachment commanders, but officers censored their own mail. Then, before final despatch, all letters went to the office of the Chief Field Censor, who, in theory, passed them within three or four days providing that the letters did not violate censorship regulations.

The troops were given guidance:

> the censor will not pass mail that contains secret or confidential military information of any nature, rumors of operations, details of weather conditions, unverified reports of atrocities, details of convoy journeys and criticisms or statements which tend to bring our forces or those of our allies into disrepute. It's not against the rules to say: 'I have been promoted to sergeant and transferred to a signal battalion'. It is against the rules to say, 'I have been promoted to sergeant and transferred to the 999th signal battalion where I'll be a photographer with a unit that's going to fly over to Utopia and take pictures of munitions factories'. It's not against the rules to say 'I'm stationed near enough to Belfast to

make a trip over the weekend'. It is against the rules to say 'I'm stationed in an old castle about three miles outside Pumpkin center and only 18 miles from Belfast'.

But the GIs were ingenious: in a bid to outwit the censor, an Iowa airman sent his wife a sprig of forsythia from the hedgerow in his first letter home from Northern Ireland 'as a way of telling her where I was – it didn't'. Another pilot, on learning that his unit was being posted to England, sent his wife a letter telling her 'we are on our *merrie* way.'

One infantry officer remembers what it was like to have to censor the mail for the two hundred men in his unit:

> It was a long, tiresome job. I felt a kind of guilty thrill at the prospect of reading the written, personal thoughts of others and prying legally into their private lives . . . but as the days passed, censoring became a burdensome chore. Soon I could censor letters without reading them in detail. I just scanned them for place names and other restricted military matters. A censoring officer becomes quickly surfeited with reading a seemingly endless pile of letters containing most the same pattern of 'I love you', plus some hard-to-decipher handwriting and inquiries concerning the health of the family and assorted relatives and livestock. You couldn't take a personal, intrusive interest in reading fifty letters a day over a period of years even if they were the torrid love letters of Casanova.

But it didn't feel like that to the GIs, one of whom penned the following lament:

> *My honey child is far away*
> *She is a lovely frail*
> *But how can I speak of love*
> *When the censor reads my mail?*
>
> *. . . Just to think my tender words*
> *Will greet a stranger's eye*
> *Makes me so gosh awful mad*
> *I almost want to cry.*
>
> *So read my letter quickly*
> *It's not meant for you*
> *To my girl in 'Frisco*
> *I'm writing 'I love you'.*
>
> *And when you read each letter*
> *And laugh with deep delight*
> *Remember, sir, your censor too*
> *Reads everything you write.*

The troops were advised that 'letters can be written in any language and they will be censored promptly by skilled translators . . . such letters should have the language in which they are written in pencil on the flap of the envelope' – and the censors would know anyway that 'Chère mama, Liebe Mutter, Dorcha Mama, Amando Madre, Kedres Anyan, Agapite Moi Maetro, Querido Mai – they all mean the same thing – Dear Mom'.

If a soldier needed to write about something particularly personal, he could, to avoid the embarrassment of having it read by his own company officer, request a special blue envelope which would then be sent direct to the Chief Field Censor – one such privilege was allowed every two weeks.

Reading letters for purposes of military security also allowed the authorities to monitor the morale of the troops and 'if numbers of men are writing complaints about food, no furloughs, late pay, relations with the Allies or suchlike, you can bet that something will be done to remedy the situation.' It was reported, however, that the usual GI letter was pretty standard, something along the lines of 'Dear Mom, Getting along fine. I like the people and army life isn't too bad.'

But whether sent V-Mail or any other way, love letters (or 'sugar mail' as they were called) were poor recompense to men missing wives and girlfriends back home. As one disconsolate GI wrote in February 1943:

> I think about you often
> And I write you every day
> But there is so very little
> That I really want to say.
>
> It either rains or it doesn't
> It's either hot or it's cold
> The news is all uninteresting
> Because it's all been told.
>
> The only fact that matters
> Is the fact that you are there
> And I am here without you
> And it's lonesome everywhere.

It wasn't only Rainbow Corner that laid on letter-writing facilities for the GIs and tried to assuage those 'lonesome everywhere' feelings. By June 1944 there were 400 American Red Cross Clubs, catering for men on leave but also providing them with 'a home from home' near their bases. Soldiers could have a meal – and lodgings in some – at a reasonable cost, and all the clubs offered the sort of services and activities that best recreated a 'little America'. Gambling was forbidden, liquor was prohibited, and troops were only allowed to bring girls into the club at specified hours, but apart from these limitations, the clubs aimed to satisfy all the GIs' demands – and some they hadn't thought of. The clubs were the envy of the British troops who had nothing like the same range of entertainments and amusements provided for them when posted to the other end of the country or overseas, far from *their* home comforts.

The clubs in Cambridge, eventually five for enlisted men and one for officers, were typical in the range of activities they provided for GIs: they aimed to 'widen your horizons' with wrestling, weightlifting, baseball, volleyball, running, pinochle, pool, snooker, darts, dominoes, cards, clay modelling, ping-pong, bingo, portrait sketching, model-aeroplane-making, films, square-dancing, barn dances, community singing and tea dances, where some of the best talent in the ETO played – bands like the Flying Eagles, the Essex Yankees, and the Thunderbolts. There was a 'date nite' every Tuesday at the

Hobson Street Club with dancing and entertainments which included a magician and a tap-dancer. To cater for the more serious-minded, there were classical music recitals, chess and contract bridge, while contributions were solicited for an anthology of 'Yanks in England Book of Verse', and, this being Cambridge, GIs were invited to 'discuss subjects of current interest' – like politics and sport – with Cambridge University students. Or they could attend lectures given by such eminent speakers as Bertrand Russell, who gave a course of ten talks on 'American Democratic Philosophy', while another speaker lectured for several weeks on the topic of 'What to do with Germany after the war from an economic point of view'. The really intrepid could take up the invitation from the wife of a university professor who offered cakes and (British) coffee to four GIs each Sunday at eleven o'clock; from Lady Maud Darwin (of *Origin of Species* descent), who offered to play GIs at chess, followed by tea 'and a walk around her lovely garden'; from the Provost of King's who was prepared to recount the history of the college; or from G.M. Trevelyan, 'one of the great historians of England', who made himself available to meet GIs at the Bull Hotel every Saturday at 4 o'clock.

Most of the Red Cross Clubs in Britain laid on special celebrations on traditional American holidays. Some honoured Lincoln's and Washington's birthdays, most the Fourth of July, Hallowe'en, Thanksgiving, Mother's Day – and Father's Day too, though this 'was something of a poser', and not every GI was over the moon at the idea of 'an officer acting as a foster father for enlisted men' for the day.

It often took considerable ingenuity and determination by the Red Cross organizers to find the premises for their clubs, the rent of which was charged against Lend-Lease. Anona Moser found a garage and workshop in Bedford and made it into a club for the thousands of soldiers and airmen for whom Bedford was their liberty town. She begged and borrowed equipment from whomever she could – including writing to the gaming houses of Las Vegas and Reno saying that she understood that 'you guys think that it's bad luck to use a deck of cards twice' and asking for their used cards for her club: 'I got thousands of boxes of cards for the troops that way.' She was also concerned to provide accommodation for those GIs who, after a night out, were not in a fit state to make it back to their base. The Red Cross secured a building near the station once used as 'an asylum for the insane'; row after row of iron beds were installed for worse-for-wear GIs, and an army of local volunteers – including the Queen's cousin – turned out for bed-making duties.

The directors of the clubs were American, usually with experience in youth work or the leisure industry. 'Woman applying for work with service clubs had to be between twenty-five and thirty-five, had to have at least a start on college education, and had to have work experience, preferably in the recreational field,' reports 'Chi Chi' Metcalf who left her job in a dress shop in St Louis, Missouri, to work for the Red Cross in Britain and then, after D-Day, in France; 'even more important, [applicants] had to be healthy, "physically hardy", sociable and attractive . . . the standard for attractiveness in those days was not Rita Hayworth or Betty Grable, but the look of the well-scrubbed wholesome "girl next door". We were somewhere between dowdy and glamorous. We had to look friendly, not seductive.'

Local people were employed as paid workers and volunteers. 'I couldn't possibly have begun to run it without their help,' maintains Miss Moser.

The outreach programme. American Red Cross workers bringing doughnuts and coffee from their Clubmobile to US troops training for the invasion of North Africa in November 1942.

They worked round the clock cooking, peeling potatoes, scrubbing floors and trying not to worry too much about their husbands who were fighting in Crete, North Africa, Burma . . . We got our food from the States. It came over in ships. We had huge barrels of flour, great drums of lard. And what amazed me was that all these volunteers – the Englishwomen – never took even a teaspoon of flour or lard – when you think how rationing was then, that was really something.

But in her exuberance Anona Moser nearly offended the people of Bedford: 'When the club was ready, I decided to hang a Stars and Stripes from the window, and no sooner was it up than a local policeman knocked on the door and told me to take the flag down. "We haven't been taken over by America yet," he said.'

When Eleanor Roosevelt visited the US troops stationed in Britain in the autumn of 1942, she had commented that there were not enough clubs for men stationed some distance from towns and cities. The Red Cross responded by taking their hospitality to

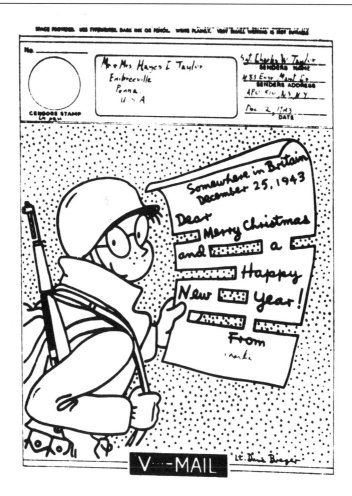

The censor came at Christmas . . . V-Mail, 1943.

those troops who couldn't get to the hospitality. Usually converted Green Line buses with space for cooking facilities and a tiny lounge, Clubmobiles were first introduced at the end of 1942 to service 149 out of the 185 detachments which were six miles or more from a club. The staff handed out doughnuts (made on special machines which turned out about seven doughnuts per minute), coffee, cigarettes, chewing-gum and newspapers without charge. Later, a public address system was added as standard equipment, and such favourites as 'Pistol-Packin' Mama' and 'Ol' Man River' were soon belting out over the English countryside.

By the end of 1943 there were 50 Clubmobiles in operation, serving a total of a million and a half doughnuts monthly. Clubmobiles welcomed troops on the quayside as they landed in Britain, visited their bases, followed them on training manoeuvres, provided food and comfort as they embarked for Normandy – and often followed them overseas to the theatre of war.

The doughnut was such an instant signal of a welcome presence to the doughboy that the small huts that began to appear all over Britain from November 1943, serving just coffee and doughnuts, were known as 'doughnut dug-outs'. These economical hospitality huts proved so popular that the build-up of troops prior to D-Day was matched by the proliferation of these 'dug-outs'.

'Flak shacks' were also an imaginative way of coping with the war provided by the American Red Cross. The USAAF had taken over large country estates to provide rest homes for airmen who had seen too much combat and needed time to get away from the war. In such places as Moulsford Manor and Furze Down, specially trained women Red Cross workers strove to create an atmosphere of tranquillity where the men, usually between twenty-five and thirty at a time, could rest, wear civilian clothes, pursue leisurely country activities – picnics, barbecues, walking, playing the church organ, helping on a local farm – and talk about anything but the horrors they had witnessed, until their battle fatigue was sufficiently soothed for them to return to their groups – or receive more specialist help if necessary.

Britain's Women's Voluntary Service – an organization first set up in 1938 as the women's auxiliary to Civil Defence – also provided hospitality to the US troops. The WVS provided the only hospitality in the early months before the American Red Cross got into its stride – WVS workers had been there to welcome the first US troops to arrive in Belfast in January 1942 – and throughout the war they continued to help out. The 'ladies in green' darned socks and sewed on 'flashes' for the Americans as they did for the British, provided local advice and information for American Red Cross personnel when they arrived in a new area, ran canteens for the GIs on railway stations and worked in US Army hospitals – running libraries, arranging flowers, talking to the patients and taking convalescent GIs for outings. They lent GI brides wedding dresses belonging to members who fervently 'hoped that they would not be needing them again' themselves, provided layettes for GI babies and, at the end of the war and after, helped organize GI brides on the first leg of their journey across the Atlantic.

There was, however, one serious limit to what they could provide: girls. 'WVS members by that time were not girls and anyway they had to keep an eye on the buns and razor blades.' So in the tireless quest to introduce the troops to 'nice girls', British 'Welcome Clubs', each with a government grant of £30, were started. The first one opened in Sunbury in Berkshire, and soon there were over 200 – some very small and open only for the few weeks that the US troops remained in the area, others much larger, like the Welcome Club housed in a cinema at Ipswich.

But there were some people to whom the name 'Welcome Club' must have had a hollow ring: black US troops. The WVS, concerned that the kind of contact that they wished to encourage in these clubs was 'not altogether applicable in the case of coloured soldiers', established separate clubs for black troops. Three 'Silver Birch' clubs were opened, two in Wales and one in Birmingham; others were proposed in the Midlands and the West Country, for the build-up for D-Day meant that the US troops now flooding into Britain and preparing to fight to free Europe were often black.

CHAPTER TEN

'BOY, ARE WE GOING TO HAVE FUN!'

THE YANKS WERE the most joyful thing that ever happened to British woman-hood . . . They had *everything* – money in particular, glamour, boldness, cigarettes, chocolate, nylons, Jeeps – and genitalia. The Yanks were sex-mad and countless British women who had virtually no experience in this line were completely bowled off their feet (and on to their backs, I suppose I should add). It was astonishing how such vast quantities of women of all ages and stations fell for them: almost every working girl aspired to 'have a Yank'. Apart from their Hollywood-style glamour which they played to great effect, they were stupendously rich by the British serviceman's standards and could treat girls to things that were beyond the Briton's ability . . . I think that never in history has there been such a conquest of women by men as was won by the American army in Britain in World War II

according to Eric Westman who adds, 'but since I was a young British serviceman and not an attractive young woman, *my* memories of GIs are pretty sour!'

The 'conquest' by the GIs of British women – 'the legitimate booty of war' – is one of the most enduring legends of the US troops' war in Britain, at least for the British. Immortalized in folk memory, in carefully hoarded letters and snapshots, novels, film, vulgar rhymes and epithets, from jokes like 'Have you heard about the new utility knickers?' 'One Yank and they're off!' to the wistful memories of women now in their sixties and seventies who still vividly recall the excitement the GIs brought to their wartime existence, to the 70,000 British girls who became GI brides and the uncounted thousands who became mothers of GI babies – in the language of the time, 'the memory lingers on'.

'You will naturally be interested in getting to know your opposite number, the British soldier, the "Tommy" you have heard and read about. You can understand that two actions on your part will slow up this friendship – swiping his girl, and not appreciating what his army has been up against. Yes, and rubbing it in that you are better paid than he is,' warned the GI's *Short Guide*. An ATS girl, stationed in Wales, remembers an evening when an American truck arrived at the camp: 'About fifteen girls had primped themselves up – as far as khaki would allow – for the occasion. As we piled into the substantial truck there were, of course, catcalls from a few of our own soldiers who happened to be nearby and shouts of "the Yanks have plenty of dough. No hope for us now!" '

Willing partners. Girls clamber aboard a 'liberty bus' or 'passion wagon' collecting them for a dance at a USAAF base.

'They had plenty of money, no doubt about that,' recalls Jean Lancaster Rennie of the GIs who frequented the American Red Cross Club where she worked in Norwich:

> They 'lived well and lay warm' was the local phrase . . . a few of them were fairly tight with their money . . . but in the main they were generous. I'm quite sure that many a girl in Norwich was taken out to dinner for the first time by a Yank . . . They brought with them colour, romance, warmth and a tremendous hospitality to our dark, shadowed island.

It was this feeling of excitement and glamour in a world where most eligible men, boyfriends and husbands were off in the forces, where rationing and the black-out added dreary inconveniences to an already uncertain life, that the GIs had such appeal.

A nineteen-year-old nurse in Exeter had the same feeling:

> Sometimes the hospital staff would put on a dance, but of course there weren't so many of our boys left in town, so we invited the American soldiers . . . they were so friendly and turned everything into fun. Some of the people in town thought at first that the GIs were a little 'wild', but either the town got used to it, or the Americans calmed down, because later on no one complained any more.

Brenda Devereux recalls:

I suppose we were as jubilant as everyone else in the country when the Americans came into the war. In Bournemouth we had seen troops of almost every colour and nationality, but when these GIs hit town, commandeering our homes, and our countryside, we were captivated at once. With their smooth, beautifully tailored uniforms, one could hardly tell a private from a colonel. They swaggered, they boasted and they threw their money about, bringing a shot in the arm to business, such as it was, and an enormous lift to the female population.

'The whole world simply changed when the Yanks arrived here in 1943,' says Averil Martin (now Logan) who had been evacuated with her London school to Selsey near Chichester in 1939: 'I thought they were sublime, they were cute, they walked differently – they loped along – and they came from all sorts of exotic places, California, Florida, New Orleans, Malibu . . .' A former nurse, who was doing war work in a factory in Leicester making engines for Spitfires, saw her first GIs at the railway station there. Her friend, Marge, 'clasped my arm excitedly and whispered "Look at all those Yanks! Boy, aren't we going to have fun!" I agreed with her fervently.'

The Yanks looked so good, too, in their smart uniforms which 'fitted in all the right places', in contrast to the thick, felt-like khaki which was the lot of the British soldier. A Shropshire man who was in the Home Guard felt it keenly: 'the presence of troops at a "do" meant competition for the village lads. The Americans were resented for their smart appearance, with uniforms of a superior cut and quality, for their money and endless supply of small luxuries.'

'Their uniforms were so nice,' enthuses a Bedford woman who lived near an American air base: 'the "fly boys" were so smart in their pinks and greens, compared to our soldiers in their thick, shapeless serge battledress. My mother used to take in their laundry, and they'd come and explain to her exactly how they wanted the pleat in their shirt ironed if they were going to a dance. It had to be just so.' 'They were so fussy about pressing their clothes,' claimed a wartime land girl stationed near Worcester. She later married a US Army medic attached to the 156th Infantry Division stationed at Broadway, and recalls that when they went to London together her GI husband-to-be complained that

> there were mostly people in uniform and all ranks kept saluting him. British officers were saying 'Good morning, sir.' He said 'Gee, English people are so friendly.' I realized that they thought he was an officer . . . Alva soon complained that his arm ached . . . so in the end he looked the other way and that solved the problem.

Not everyone was so impressed: a Liverpool girl, catching sight of the first American officer she had ever seen in the Adelphi Hotel, heard her mother, standing next to her, snort: 'Look at those ridiculous pink trousers – they'll be filthy before they know it!' And an elderly Norfolk woman was puzzled that the officers were regarded as smart in their pink trousers and olive drab jackets: 'Why their clothes don't even match!'

Even a British serviceman had to concede that the GIs were

> generally taller, bulkier and handsomer than we were. Many were blond giants, with hair cut short in 'combat crops'. Some were swarthy . . . some looked very intellectual and wore octagonal, rimless glasses. In general, I think they looked

A dance arranged by the American Red Cross
for US troops and local land girls in Suffolk.

superior to the very plebeian British serviceman. Their uniforms and their insignia were showy, beautifully fitting, of excellent material and smart. In that respect, the British soldier (in particular) looked a poor specimen beside them . . . as far as appearance went they outclassed us.

Most British girls had never encountered a real live American before the GIs arrived. Their images had been shaped by weekly visits to the cinema, where the America that was depicted – if it wasn't the Wild West of cowboy films – was a land of chromium-plated sophistication and wealth where every hour seemed to be the cocktail hour. June Barrie, who was to become a film star herself, remembers the Americans who were billeted at Knowle Greyhound Stadium in Bristol in 1942: 'It was as if the cinema had come to life.

'Almost as good as a letter from home.' Glenn Miller and his big band sound giving a concert during his tour of US bases and clubs in Britain in 1944.

They were so handsome and well groomed and *clean*.' 'And they smelled so nice,' mused another Bristol woman: 'they used deodorants and after shave – things unknown to 99 per cent of British men.' According to Eric Westman who was an under-age member of the Home Guard when the GIs first arrived in his home town of Bridgwater in Somerset, and was drafted into the Fleet Air Arm in December 1943,

> The nasal accents went down well with the girls because they gave them the glamour of film stars . . . they smoked glamorous, luxury-smelling Camels and Lucky Strikes, whereas the British had difficulty in getting hold of even the atrocious wartime cigarettes . . . and many GIs traded on their Hollywood image by claiming acquaintance with film stars and owning huge ranches or large mansions – it went down well with the British girls. Indeed many who married GIs found that their 'ranch' was a wooden shack in the mountains or similar.

Some GIs weren't merely acquainted with film stars – they were film stars. James Stewart fought a courageous war as a pilot and then a squadron leader with the 445th Bomb Group at Tibenham where he was greatly liked as a 'regular guy'. And Clark Gable, who could be seen at the cinema in the romantic epic *Gone with the Wind*, could be spotted in real life with the 351st Bomb Group at Polebrook in Northamptonshire, where he made a training film for aerial gunners – and, so it was said, exchanged the second highest salary in the whole US – $357,000 – for $600 in his new job.

'BOY, ARE WE GOING TO HAVE FUN!'

The charm of many of the GIs was as beguiling as their looks. The way that they treated women was a revelation. 'We were half starved and drably clothed, but the GIs said we looked good anyway,' recalls a woman who was a teenager in Birmingham during the GI years:

> A lot was said about them being overpaid, oversexed and over here; maybe it applied to a few but it was mainly a myth that was put about by Lord Haw-Haw in his Nazi propaganda broadcasts from Germany to upset British soldiers overseas and try to split the Allies . . . it was just that the British women and the American GIs were in the same place at the same time – it was rather pleasant really.

A Preston woman remembers a GI whistling at her in the street and calling out 'Gee you've got lovely eyes' and his friend joining in with 'She's a baby Betty Grable.' The Yanks seemed to have been 'legs men', and girls were frequently affronted to have their ankles checked out with a torch or a lighted match in the black-out before an approach was made. The more lyrical, however, praised the 'porcelain complexions' of English girls, which they put down to the damp climate.

'My first two boyfriends were Americans and I "dated" some others,' recalled a Plymouth woman who was seventeen when the GIs arrived at barracks near Devonport. 'Some of us in our mid-teens had never really known any English boys except of our own age and these soldiers seemed very glamorous to us all . . . they were so easy to talk to, speaking very naturally and casually, unlike the reticent, sometimes sniggery youths we knew.' A woman who worked in an aircraft factory agreed:

> A British soldier would take a girl for a drink, bore her to death talking about cars or sport etc. If he saw any of his 'mates', he abandoned the girl except to buy her a drink now and then until it was time to go home. With the GI it was very different. The GI would buy me a drink and entertain me as if I were the only person in the room. I know that when my back was turned he would probably make a date with another girl, but this didn't really seem to matter.

A Bedford woman, who after the war married an 8th Air Force pilot stationed at Thurleigh, remembers her first date with a local boy: 'He took me on the river in a boat – and then handed me his fishing rod and told me to put the worms on the hook for him. It was Americans for me after that.'

The generosity of the Americans was a lure, too. Many were young and single and away from home for the first time. The average weekly salary of a US private – huge compared with that of his British counterpart – was largely spending money, since accommodation, food and uniform were 'all found', and it was spent at the PX, on cigarettes, candy and presents, on drink and on girls.

As one teenager of the time recalls:

> Americans were 'cheeky' compared to our usual 'Mr Frigidaire Englishman', but what a boost to her ego when one is greeted with 'Hallo Duchess' (and you were treated like one!) or 'Hi Beautiful!' That was so GOOD! As we got to know these boys, how generous they were; we never lacked for chocolates or cigarettes or

even precious luxuries like nylons that they could get for us. Most of my friends had one particular GI Joe – and so did I.

Brenda Devereux's story was the same: 'How those gorgeous GIs could shoot a line and how we loved it. Not only that, but they were equipped up to the eyebrows with scented soap, cigarettes, food, sweets and dozens of other things we had not seen for years – it was like Christmas.'

'The difference between Americans was that they treated us English girls like duchesses . . . and they were so polite. [Jim] always said "Mam" to my mother and "Sir" to my father,' remembers a Bristol woman, who had done 'a little dance of joy' when the Americans arrived in her neighbourhood.

Grace Chawe promised a date to a GI she had met at a Land Army dance in Evesham. 'It took quite a lot of persuading from the other girls to keep that date. I guess they were thinking of the gifts the Americans were said to give. Nylons, chocs, cigarettes, gum and fruit juice that we could only dream of. I wasn't happy about their reputation but I went and had a lovely time.'

Saturday night 'hops', which had been so short of male partners when the British men joined up that the women had taken to dancing together, were transformed by the arrival of the GIs:

> And you should see them try to dance,
> They find a partner, start to prance,
> When we're half dead, they stop and smile:
> 'How'm I doin' honey chile?'

At dance halls the GIs really cut a dash because they could jitterbug. 'In Bridgwater,' reports Eric Westman,

> there was a dance hall called the Blake Hall; it was a scruffy-looking place that held a weekly hop . . . once on leave, I went inside and saw scores of girls lined up along one wall, three deep. There were some GIs who would walk up and down this line surveying the girls and then select one, who would gladly go and dance with him. I was pretty horrified at this slave-market attitude. Then a smart-looking British soldier walked along the line asking girls to dance with him, but none would. I have never forgotten it.

'American boys were the master of the jitterbug craze,' remembers Brenda Devereux: 'We English girls took to it like ducks to water. No more slow, slow, quick, quick, slow for us. This was living.' Iris Ford recalls that 'There was a lovely atmosphere' at dances at the Royal West of England Academy in Bristol, which had been turned over to the American Red Cross: 'we'd do the jitterbug, catching hold of one another's hands and gradually being twisted round, swung under their legs and then over their heads, it was quite energetic. But we were young, we could manage it.'

Averil Martin was only fourteen when the Americans arrived in Sussex. Although she was too young to go to the GI dances, she borrowed some make-up and, in the absence of nylons, painted her legs 'an ochre colour with pancake make-up', pretended that she was nineteen and went along to dance with the 'dudes'. 'Everything in England seemed so dull and corny,' she recollects:

Anglo-American relations, 1944.

the Yanks gave us cigarettes and chewing-gum – and the music was fantastic. I loved jitterbugging. I won a contest. We used to make these dresses with short, pleated skirts and when we danced they'd flare right up round our waists – so we couldn't stop the leg make-up (or the eyebrow-pencilled 'seams') at our knees . . . who wants to listen to some schmaltzy sentimental music when they're young and can dance to the 'A-Train' with the Yanks?

Connie Stanton (now Richards) did the same at Thurleigh:

I didn't want the GIs to know that I was only twelve and a half. I wanted them to think that I was sixteen. My school was so near the base that the 'snowdrops' [the Military Police] could see us in the playground . . . so I used to keep right out of sight so they wouldn't recognize me . . . and then I'd watch for the 'liberty truck' [or 'passion wagon' as it was also known] outside the American Red Cross in Bedford come to collect the local girls and take them to the base for a dance. I'd put gravy browning on my legs and borrow some 'Tangee' lipstick that some of the older girls had got from the GIs anyway, and I'd try to get in – but I only ever did once. I'd heard that Glenn Miller was coming to Milton Ernest and I didn't know who he was then, but I was *determined* to hear him play. So I stood outside the gate all dressed up and waited while the boyfriend of an older girl took her in and then came out to escort me in. Of course, my mother never knew . . . whenever I hear 'Perfidia' now, I remember that evening. It was *wonderful*.

A Plymouth woman can't forget the dances at a church hall in Devonport with

the lovely, sentimental wartime songs and the jolly jive ones, so many of which were to be ever associated with Glenn Miller. Soon after the Americans arrived . . . the dance band we had booked failed to turn up and some of the boys sent up to the barracks for a 'scratch band' to be put together and come on and play. The standard was unbelievable and from then on those boys played every week for us without charge – not always the same ones but excellent nevertheless, and the hall soon became jammed to the doors.

A Hertfordshire woman remembers going to a dance on an 8th Air Force base at Steeple Morden in Cambridgeshire:

We were transported to the base in a large GI truck escorted by two chaperones. We arrived at 8 p.m. and departed by 11 p.m. Our chaperones made sure that no one left the dance and everyone was on the truck before it took us back home . . . That first dance was unforgettable. It was as though we had entered another world. Everything was sparkling new, not like our old town hall where we usually went, and the 'Flying Eagles' band – such a collection of brass and drums unlike our town hall five-piece band. The music blared loudly and the dancers were doing the jitterbug with its collections of strange steps and athletic contortions.

Beryl McDermott (now Bann-Ashley), who worked as a 'tracer', or drawing office assistant, with the Air Ministry at Burtonwood supply depot, had an equally unforgettable evening when Bing Crosby came there

to sing to the US troops. It was a bitterly cold winter, near Christmas time. The 'tracers' were invited to see the concert. Tinker Hall, a huge hangar, was full of GIs – they were everywhere, swinging on the rafters. It was a great concert – and then the mike broke down! We all trooped out to find Bing Crosby standing on the top of an air-raid shelter, singing 'I'm Dreaming of a White Christmas'. It was snowing heavily and he stood there singing in a long white mac. It was pure silence, there were many tears. I will never forget that moment so long ago.

The music that especially evokes those GI years is swing. The big band sound of Glenn Miller playing his signature tune, 'Moonlight Serenade', or 'At Last', 'Sun Valley Serenade', 'Little Brown Jug', 'Chattanooga-Choo-Choo', 'I Know Why', 'Don't Fence Me In' or 'When the Swallows Come Back to Capistrano'; the music of Tommy Dorsey with 'I'll Never Smile Again' or 'Moonlight on the Ganges'; Jimmy Dorsey with 'I Remember You'; the music of Benny Goodman; Artie Shaw playing 'Stardust' or 'Moonglow'; melodies like 'In the Mood', 'Always in My Heart', 'One Dozen Roses', 'Sleepy Lagoon', 'All or Nothing At All', 'Someone's Rocking My Dreamboat', 'As Time Goes By', and the song that Vera Lynn made her own, although it was based on a poem by an American

Somebody's sat under the apple tree
with somebody else but him

writer living in London, Alice Duer Miller, 'The White Cliffs of Dover'. But above all, it was Glenn Miller whose tours around the US bases and clubs in Britain could pack a dance hall or fill a hangar, and whose records started tears to many a GI's eyes. 'Next to a letter from home, Captain Miller,' reported General Jimmy Doolittle who commanded the 8th Air Force from January 1944, 'your organization is the greatest morale builder in the ETO.' Miller disappeared in somewhat mysterious circumstances on a flight to Paris on 15 December 1944.

But there was other music, too. A corporal working as a film processor with an aerial photographic reconnaissance outfit stationed just outside Oxford used to spend some of his free time in the American Red Cross Club, in what had been the Clarendon Hotel.

One evening an Englishman was playing the piano, taking requests and playing from memory such pieces as 'Boop, boop ditum dadaum, watum choo' (!) and 'A Tisket a Tasket', 'Midnight Stomp' and other such pieces . . . I raised my hand and asked if he could play 'Jesu, Joy of Man's Desiring' from J. S. Bach's Cantata 147. I thought he would jump off his stool, and he turned to me with a huge smile then began to play with such tenderness and expertise as I, a small town boy from the South of the US, had never before heard. At the end of the piece he asked me, in a very halting, stammering voice, if there was anything else I wanted to hear. Yes! And so the rest of the evening he played for me classical music: Chopin, Handel, Beethoven – all from memory, and in such a professional manner I was totally astonished. Not one time did he ask for any more requests except for mine.

After the concert, the GI went up to thank the pianist for his very own concert and learned that he was the organist of St Ebbe's Church, Oxford, who had 'a very intense speech impediment . . . but could sing without missing a syllable'.

That night was the beginning of a lifelong friendship between the GI, Marshall Williams, and Donald Sprinck, which lasted until the organist and composer died in 1985.

There were GIs who liked nothing better than to stay in in the evenings and write letters home to their wives or girlfriends – like Hank Jonas from Albany, New York, 'a one-woman man who idolized his wife' and preferred to spend his evenings with the Rutter family in Warrington 'instead of going on the town with his buddies. I am sure he was one GI who went back to his wife as clean as he left her.' There were others who soon acquired a reputation as 'wolves in wolves' clothing', apt to call 'Hiya Cutie!' to anyone in skirts between fifteen and fifty. British girls were warned in a handbook issued by the NAAFI that this could lead to misunderstandings:

> The first time that an American soldier comes up to the counter and says 'Hiya Baby!', you will probably think that he is being impudent, by the time several dozen men have said it, you may have come to the conclusion that all Americans are 'fresh'. Yet to them it will be merely the normal conversational opening just as you might say 'Lovely day, isn't it?' Remember that most Americans think that English people are 'stand-offish'. If you snub them, you will merely confirm that impression.

There seemed to be ways round the problem. An engineer from New York attached to a depot group with the RAF was soon rejoicing in local British customs in a letter home to his parents:

> Strangely enough, it is considered quite proper to approach a strange woman and invite her in for a drink. An American uniform (and I expect, pocketbook [wallet]) apparently commands the scene and one might say, one has one's pick. Being no slouch, I made my selection and met a very nice young vacationer with whom I spent the evening. I had a splendid time. I might point out that the black-out is most convenient. . . . I wish you would send me the following: two boxes of cigars, one carton of Hershey Bars with almonds, hairpins and lipsticks. The last two may seem strange, but actually they are worth their weight in gold. Please, please don't worry about my safety. Believe me when I say that I'm as safe from harm as I've ever been.

If the black-out pleased those with amorous intentions, double summertime – introduced to maximize war production – had the contrary effect, for it could be midnight before it got dark. A GI stationed at Shepton Mallet in Somerset complained: 'double summertime worked against our love-making. Our GIs complained bitterly about the sunshine, which still shone at 10 p.m. It was not conducive to romance.' And *Stars and Stripes*, ever sensitive to its readers' concerns, printed a verse:

> *This British time*
> *Is an awful crime*
> *What good is a park*
> *If it ain't dark?*

CHAPTER ELEVEN

PICCADILLY COMMANDOES

'THEY WERE AS LOOSE AS A GOOSE,' wrote a US airman stationed in Suffolk. 'The only thing that was cheap in Britain were the women' was a jibe a Midlands woman still remembers. And a signalman stationed in Wales recalls:

> Although Wales was so far from London it didn't stop us having a good time. I know the GIs had a reputation for chasing girls and a lot did . . . but even in Wales it was no uncommon thing for a guy to get propositioned three times in an evening. We never got over how easy it was to make it with the girls, and not just the single ones either. One of our sergeants actually had a time with a married lady while her husband was upstairs cabinet making!

The relations between the GIs and British women were as varied and as full of prejudices and misunderstandings as were those between the GIs and the British soldiers. On the one hand, many of the American troops seemed aggressive and undiscriminating in their pursuit of British girls, while at the same time complaining about their easy availability. On the other, there often seemed to be an indulgence towards boys who will be boys, while girls were severely censored for their behaviour – an attitude hardened in wartime, when so many British men were away fighting and some British women seemed only too happy to abandon the traditional role of women in wartime of 'keeping the home fires burning' by collaborating with the occupying US forces in having a good time: 'The [GIs] may have represented "fun" whilst our boys were away, but the neighbours didn't always approve because after a dance finished at midnight, the Yanks would bring us home in their trucks, and I can remember neighbours banging on their window and saying "Get to bed!" and my father sometimes gave me a belt for being late home!'

'They used to hang around the camps for hours . . . I blame the girls' was a common reaction. A Shropshire man recalls a local square

> at 7 o'clock on a summer's night and local girls all dolled up and scrambling aboard Jeeps after first asking their escorts not to forget to give some gum or candy to their kids left behind in the street . . . some of these local girls, of course, had husbands or fiancés or sweethearts in the British armed forces and they received black looks and jeers from the older women.

The money and the luxuries that the Yanks could – and often did – splash around could quickly become a devalued currency. Although soldiers were sometimes reputed to trail

*GIs watch the world parade by from the base of the missing Eros statue
at Piccadilly Circus.*

behind girls jingling coins in their pockets as they walked, the GIs branded as 'gold diggers' some of the females they encouraged. Girls who went out with the Americans were sometimes called 'Spam-bashers', soliciting gifts of food, or 'Yankee bags'. A Yorkshire woman was 'always very suspicious of females who had lovely Jacqmar scarves and nylon stockings. We reckoned they were a bit fast and were hob-nobbing a little too freely,' and a Birmingham woman was 'very wary of Americans because I'd heard they would hold up one nylon in front of you and ask "do you want the other?" '

'I was too young at the time,' reflected a Bristol woman, 'but I don't think they took advantage more than any fellow would have taken. Maybe they were fresh, but if you are thousands of miles from home and the girls were after you, you would take what you could get, wouldn't you?'

Nevertheless, the results of this wartime laxity were disturbing. By December 1942, the number of cases of VD among US troops in Britain had risen by 70 per cent since the start of the war. Six months later, there were nearly 2,000 cases of gonorrhoea, 166 cases of syphilis and 28 other incidents of venereal infections – a rate of infection 50 per cent higher than among American troops in the US. In March 1943, a conference discussed remedial measures and moral laxity. The all-male conference diagnosed the problem:

1. The presence in the metropolis of large numbers of American soldiers far away from home restraints, fighting fit, comparatively rich and often with insufficient

to do and without the stabilizing influence of family and friends;

2. The wartime relaxation of parental control and the appearance of girls who, after their day's work in the munitions factory, etc., were anxious to have a good time and were attracted by the comparative wealth of American soldiers;

3. The black-out conditions.

Films were shown in army camps and air force bases warning of the dangers, and in May 1943 *Stars and Stripes* published a disturbing cartoon of a GI embracing a girl by a wall where 'V' for victory had been crossed out and replaced with 'VD'. Free contraceptives were issued to the troops; a US officer stationed in Chorley in Lancashire explained to a local newspaper: 'Well you know how it is. If our lads don't take 'em, the others think they're queer.' An American sergeant told his men at reveille: 'I'm told that we've got thirty thousand rubbers in the supply room. I want you people to do something about this.' US sailors tucked the small, square packets in their hat bands. A sign in the women's lavatory at Rainbow Corner, stating that prophylactics were available at the reception desk, intrigued an English girl who 'didn't know what they were, but realized that they weren't sweets'.

Discarded condoms became part of the English landscape. Used contraceptives littered a churchyard near Stockport: 'it was the only dark place in the village and near a bus stop.' 'Rubbers' were blown up to festoon the Jeeps of GIs on furlough and 'Bedford was teeming with GIs, many of whom . . . used to inflate condoms (we called them "French letters" in those days) and drop them in the river by the score, to float by the girls lying on the banks . . . Incidentally, it was alleged that the American condoms had steel tips,' recalled a British serviceman, 'but I don't know if that's true.'

A Military Policeman on patrol in London's West End was approached one night by a

> very starchy lady . . . she was at least a grandmother, and boy, was she angry. 'What are you going to do about the French letters that people keep putting through my letter box?' she asked . . . She took me by the hand and went up to her doorway. She showed me the shiny brass mail slot. 'That's for letters, young man,' she said. 'It is for letters of the Royal Mail variety . . . not these!' So saying she vanished into one of the rooms and came back with a wastepaper basket at least half full of used condoms. I don't know what i said. I can only remember being full of admiration for this very upper-crust lady who had the grit to pick up these things and then show them without batting an eyelid to a husky American MP. Actually we did keep an extra eye on her doorway but it was a hopeless situation.

A woman who subsequently married a GI remembers an American officer coming into her father's jewellery shop in Chippenham and, 'after handing in his watch for repair, he leant across the counter and 'confidentially asked my father, "Say, sir, is there a brothel in this town?" Father replied, "Oh no, we don't have brothels in this country, you'll have to wait until you get to France." ' There may not have been brothels in Chippenham, but there were certainly prostitutes in London – and many other British towns and cities, too.

In June 1943 the *New York Times* carried a despatch which described the area around Piccadilly, Leicester Square and Park Lane as

Hum!

a veritable open market . . . conditions prevail that literally startle many Americans from such cities as New York, Chicago and San Francisco, to say nothing of Middle Western towns and Southern farms . . . moreover in Shepherd Market, between Piccadilly and Mayfair, there is a courtyard where the atmosphere can be compared only to the red light districts of Genoa and Marseilles.

As Rainbow Corner was a mecca for homesick GIs on leave, so the streets around became a honey-pot for prostitutes who swarmed round offering 'Hello Yank, looking for a good time?' Robert Arbib recalls that it was a standing joke in the club that it was 'suicide' for a GI to go out in the blacked-out streets without his buddy.

The girls were everywhere. They walked along Shaftesbury Avenue and past Rainbow Corner, pausing only when there was no policeman watching. Down at Lyons Corner House on Coventry Street they came up to soldiers waiting in doorways and whispered the age-old questions. At the Underground entrance they were thickest, and as evening grew dark, they shone torches on their ankles as they walked and bumped into soldiers, murmuring, 'Hello, Yank!' 'Hello, Soldier!' . . . Around the dark estuaries of the Circus, the more elegantly clad of them would stand quietly and wait – expensive and aloof. No privates or corporals for these haughty demoiselles. They had furs and silks to pay for.

A Military Policeman – their headquarters were at 101 Piccadilly – thought of Piccadilly Circus as

the hub of GI affairs. There was never a dull moment. There was a Cockney news-seller who would yell out his wares and then *sotto voce* would also tell his customers he had 'Condoms, gents, condoms'. He had the build of Alfred Hitchcock. The prostitutes in the area were well known to us. They each had their own territory. Woe betide any girl who tried to poach – almost certainly a fight would ensue. We often pulled them apart, pointing out that while they were pulling each other's hair out they were losing customers to other girls . . . those girls worked hard for their money. London was full of foreign uniforms . . . Those girls took terrible risks. Often they were beaten up; they were robbed and several were stabbed . . . In the darkness of London in 1944 every doorway was a love nest. Amorous Yanks and all sorts were propped against willing females. We used to move them on and sometimes we arrested those unwilling to move, but it was a hopeless task.

A colonel in the US Army who visited London on leave in the spring of 1944 wrote home that though his

> whole make-up and background would make me eschew the favors of any one of these prostitutes . . . I think I should tell you that these 'ladies of the night' do not lack for customers, most of whom, I am sorry to say, wear the uniform of the United States Army. It seems that they are in every doorway. They carry small torches so that they may be seen in the black-out, and their customers do likewise. The police seem to know what goes on. I suppose because they know that however many of these girls they bring to court there are always others to take their place. They carry on their 'business' in the very shop doorway in which they stand. Once they have struck a 'bargain' with their customers, the 'service' is performed on the spot in the standing position. In this way, unless the customer demands otherwise, a girl can perform a 'service' five times more quickly than in a hotel room. Not for nothing are these girls known as 'Piccadilly commandoes'. Others of their kind who work the Hyde Park area are known as 'rangers'.

Mrs Robert Henrey, who lived in the heart of the elegant but notorious Shepherd Market, was told a story by an American woman friend who worked at Rainbow Corner:

> You know the way our boys call your ladies of easy virtue, commandoes? Lord B's son came in with an American friend . . . this afternoon. He was in uniform and, before leaving, he took off his shoulder-flash with 'Commando' embroidered on it in large letters and gave it to me as a keepsake. You can imagine the howl of delight that went up from all the GIs when he pinned it on my dress!

And an American doctor present had noticed a wartime innovation: 'most of your commandoes try to get something extra out of our boys by asking them for five dollars with which to buy new black-out curtains . . . In the old days they used to ask for a dress or a hat . . . even the oldest profession keeps abreast of the times!'

There were American servicemen who learned from prostitutes a habit that an infantryman from New Hampshire noticed: 'The English had a curious custom of fucking on foot, fully clothed.' The Piccadilly commandoes would call out, 'Hey, Yank, quick, Marble Arch style!' But soon the phrase 'wall job' entered the GIs' wartime vocabulary to denote the many girls, apart from prostitutes, who believed that they couldn't get

'Louise' painted on the wall of a hut at Knettishall in Norfolk where the 388th Bomb Group were stationed.

pregnant standing up. A Jewish chaplain from Iowa was puzzled, driving around Birmingham at about 9 p.m. in mid-June, to see some of his countrymen carrying their overcoats, until he learned they were 'wrapped around themselves and their girls as they copulated standing up'.

Prostitutes didn't only find GI clients in London and the big cities – some went out into the countryside. A Signal Corps sergeant stationed at Tidworth remembers a leave in the New Forest, when it seemed as if in every glade he was liable to stumble across 'a suitcase girl from London who had set up to await her clientele'. At Seething, an airman smuggled a 'Piccadilly commando' on to the base by putting his cap and greatcoat over her as he drove in past the sentry: 'She stayed in the Alert Room for ten days and was only discovered when the medical staff realized that all the men presenting themselves for prevention of venereal disease checks were from the same hut.'

A young GI from Oklahoma on leave in London voiced some of that restless wartime intensity: 'We would go from one pub to another, drinking just about anything on offer. From some place or other, the inevitable lady of the night would appear and I guess that many of us took advantage of their favors. It was the "live for today, tomorrow we die" mentality, I guess.'

CHAPTER TWELVE

NICE GIRLS AND THEIR LITTLE BROTHERS

'S OME OF THE AMERICAN SOLDIERS might succumb to the allure of prostitutes,' concluded the conference which looked into the spread of VD among American troops in Britain in 1943, 'but it is a mistake to say that prostitutes were the main cause of the trouble. The acquaintance between American soldiers and "good-time girls" which started with a desire for companionship on the part of the soldiers and a good time on behalf of the girls, frequently led to intercourse and the spread of venereal disease.'

As a Military Policeman stationed in Piccadilly observed:

> The 'good-time girls' were the source of the trouble and it was impossible for the police to take action against them because they were not common prostitutes and did not accost – they simply made it clear that they would welcome advances, and this was not a criminal offense . . . it was not possible to introduce legislation to make it an offense for 'good time' girls [or 'patriotutes' as such camp followers were called in America] to make the casual acquaintance of American soldiers in the street.

If the police – both military and civilian, British and American – were apt to turn a blind eye to prostitution, the British and American military and political authorities were increasingly concerned about the 'wrong sort' of liaisons between US troops and the female British population. Lieutenant-Colonel Paul Paget, chief of VD control for US troops in Britain, issued a stern warning: 'Any woman who can be "picked up" and "made" by an American soldier can be, and certainly has been, "picked up" and "made" by countless others.'

The British authorities feared for the morale of their own troops and the problems of countless illegitimate babies; their American counterparts were anxious for the stability of family life back home in the States, and concerned that undesirable girls would latch on to homesick GIs and acquire the right, through marriage, to settle in the United States. Both recognized that 'time was short and the chemistry was instant', and that the times were extraordinary: both were concerned about the rising rate of venereal disease – and of the wider implications for Anglo–American military respect and post-war co-operation of this new dimension in transatlantic relations.

The US authorities put formidable obstacles in the way of GIs marrying British girls, the British authorities and their agencies did all they could to divert GIs from 'good-time girls' and put them in touch with 'nice girls' – and both spent time and effort in trying to translate the strange rituals of the opposite sex on either side of the ocean.

Margaret Mead explained 'the American idea of a date' to the British:

> American men and boys enjoy the company of girls and women more than the British do. British boys don't go out with girls unless they have what one British boy described to me as 'an ulterior purpose, good or bad'. If they just want to spend a pleasant evening, more often they spend it with other boys. Even when boys and girls do go to the same school in Britain, they act as if they are going to separate schools.

Mead went on:

> To an American eye, the absence of flirting and backchat among secondary school boys and girls is astonishing. American boys and girls start having dates with each other in the early teens, long before they are emotionally mature enough to be interested in each other for anything really connected with sex . . . a 'date' is a quite different sort of thing from an evening spent with someone whom one hopes to marry. It exists for itself, just an evening in time, in which two people dance or go to the cinema, or have soft drinks together while they talk to each other in gay, wise-cracking style.

A date, she explained, worked to affirm each partner's popularity and attractiveness:

> The boy [proves this] by boldly demanding innumerable favors, the girl by refusing them. If a boy should fail to bid for a hundred kisses this would prove that he had a low opinion of himself, but if the girl gives in, she thereby proves that she has a low opinion of herself . . . a really successful 'date' is one in which the boy asks for everything and gets nothing but a lot of words . . . gay, witty words.

'Mothers in America,' she reassured her audience, 'approve of this dating game . . . and believe that their daughter's popularity will give her a better opportunity to make a "wise choice" when she does settle down. Dating is quite different from being in love . . . it may be called pre-courtship behavior,' categorized the anthropologist. All of this must have been very confusing for strictly brought-up British girls

> who haven't any practice in wise-cracking . . . and some of them are insulted by the speed and assurance of the American's approach to them and turn chilly, making him feel that Britain is a cold – and then he will add – little country. Some of them take his words which sound like wooing for wooing and give a kiss with real warmth, which surprises him very much. Some think that he is proposing when he isn't and want to take him home to father.

The problem, she diagnosed, lay partly in the ratio between the sexes:

up to the present there have been more men than women in America. Britain has a great surplus of women (a legacy from the First World War exacerbated by the Second) and it has been up to the women or their mothers to find husbands. The disapproval of the community falls on the man who plays fast and loose with a girl's affection. But in America there have always been more men than women, and it was felt to be difficult for a man to find himself a wife. Social disapproval falls heaviest, not on the man who deceives the girl, but on the girl who uses unfair methods to make a man marry her. Here there is a lot of room for misunderstanding.

A much-circulated poem, 'Lament of a Limey Lass', put the problem from the British girl's point of view:

> They swarm on every tram and bus,
> There isn't room for most of us,
> We walk to let them have our seats
> Then get run over by their Jeeps.
>
> Yanks say they've come to shoot and fight,
> It's true they fight . . . yes when they're tight,
> I must agree, their shooting's fine,
> They shoot a damn good Yankee line.
>
> They tell us we have teeth like pearls,
> They love our hair, the way it curls,
> Our eyes would dim the brightest stars,
> Our figures like Hedy Lamar's.
>
> And then he leaves you broken-hearted,
> The camp has moved — your love departed —
> You wait for mail that doesn't come,
> Then realize you're awfully dumb.
>
> Chorus
> It's a different town — a different place —
> To a different girl — a different face,
> 'I love you darling — please be mine'
> It's the same old Yank — the same old line.

To which a GI responded:

> The way we dance, the way we sing,
> The way we do most everything,
> The only thing we do that's right
> Is spend our money left and right.

and to the girls in particular:

> With Yankee girls you can't compare,
> The difference is, You're here, they're there.

'GOT ANY GUM, CHUM?'

which was almost exactly what a Shropshire woman reported when jealous British soldiers demanded 'What's he got that I haven't got?' of local girls who had 'wandered to American soldiers'; they replied, 'He hasn't got anything more than you've got, but he's got it here.'

A Chippenham woman remembers that by 1943 'the town girls began to be typed as officers' girls, sergeants' girls and the others. They were subdivided into those that did and those that didn't.' Those that didn't (or at least those whom the American authorities believed didn't) were to be invited to meet the troops in a carefully controlled social environment.

'The local people had formed a wholly regrettable picture of the American soldiers and had not been inviting them into their homes,' wrote an assistant at an American servicemen's club: 'I hope, with the help of the Mayoress who attended the Valentine's Day party, to change this feeling by making the boys acquainted with the better sort of girls who have been avoiding them. This should be of particular interest as the new group of soldiers move in – but it's a touchy subject and I'm keeping my fingers crossed.'

Eileen Smithers was living in Norwich 'surrounded by US Army Air Force bases', and her mother's house was on a list for providing emergency beds for officers when the Red Cross Club was full:

> I was also on a list! Most of the bases ran Saturday night dances for which transport was sent to Norwich to collect the local girls. However, there were two distinct types of Saturday night dances. Those in bases that just sent trucks to several pick-up points in the city and collected any waiting girls and those that were 'vetted' by the City Hall. The latter dances were only attended by girls with an official invitation issued from the CO of the base. To get such an invitation, a girl was interviewed at City Hall and, if approved, her name would go on the official invitation list. I went to quite a few of these dances, some were GI dances and some were officers' dances. They were very different to the mess parties I'd attended at RAF fields prior to the Americans' arrival. No hilarious games for one thing.

The American Red Cross, as official provider of rest and recreation for the growing number of American troops in Britain, also screened and selected 'nice girls' to act as hostesses for the GIs at dances and parties. To do this, they enlisted the good agencies – and local knowledge – of such bodies as the WVS and the churches to supply names of 'suitable' girls.

At Rainbow Corner, girls had to wait outside while their GI boyfriends went inside for a wash and brush-up or to collect their mail; when a dance was arranged for such an occasion as Hallowe'en or Thanksgiving, the GIs had to submit for approval the name of any partner they intended to bring forty-eight hours in advance, for approval.

'We were screened quite thoroughly,' relates a London woman who met her husband-to-be when she worked as a hostess at the Washington Club in Curzon Street, Mayfair, also run by the American Red Cross, 'and we were supposed to circulate but not fraternize or leave the club together. Of course we broke this rule . . .'

It wasn't only the US authorities who were worried about what might happen to their boys: British parents and those in wartime *loco parentis* were concerned about what might befall their girls. A land girl working near the Savernake Forest in Wiltshire had the greatest difficulty in persuading the farmer and his wife to let her go to

> Yankee dances now and again . . . so after explaining how orderly everything was, we were allowed to go on the understanding that we wouldn't be late as Tom would be waiting up for us in fatherly fashion . . . We were picked up in Swindon and transported by army truck to camp out on the downs and were always delivered safely back. We would count each other back into the truck and it was always carried out with great precision.

But the best way for the Americans and the British to get to know each other wasn't at organized social events; it was by British families inviting GIs into their homes for tea or Sunday lunch, or even to stay for their furloughs. The American Red Cross alone arranged over a quarter of a million such visits between November 1943 and the end of the war, and Anglo–American Hospitality Committees also put hosts and guests in touch with one another. People were often eager to act as hosts to the newly arrived troops. But sometimes things misfired, as when an American officer arrived with his company in Wales, where they were stationed:

> When we first arrived, these town people used to gather at the camp gate – sometimes thirty at once – all of them with invitations for soldiers to come to their house for dinner. They kept coming and there didn't seem any way to handle them. I'd go down to the gate and fill my pocket with their invitations and then – we were pretty busy getting settled – I'd forget about them. One day I heard that a local family was very offended. They'd prepared dinner for two of the soldiers and the soldiers never appeared. I found the invitation still in my pocket!

This particular unit solved the problem by forming a 'Friendship House', run by a committee of local people, who arranged sports, dances and entertainment for the troops – and a weekly hospitality schedule. 'On average 125 invitations to the soldiers from the Welsh people were received. One village, twelve miles out in the country, sent buses and forty soldiers went, dined at separate houses and had a dance in the village hall.'

There were stories of the GIs' insensitivity to the problems of rationing: 'What I don't like about the Americans,' a middle-aged woman from Gloucester said vehemently

> is that they don't seem to have the faintest understanding of war conditions over here and about how we're rationed. I asked one American to tea . . . well, I never *saw* such an appetite. He cleared us out of everything, he ate and ate and ate, he swallowed the whole week's jam ration for the family and when he'd got the table about bare, he said 'I'm only eating for politeness, you know, I had my tea before I came.'

But it wasn't usually like that. British problems with hospitality had been well drummed into most GIs. Their *Short Guide* warned them: 'One thing to be careful about – if you are invited into a British home and the host exhorts you to "eat up, there's plenty on the table", go easy. It may be the family's rations for a whole week, spread out to show their hospitality.'

Embarrassment about the paucity of the spread was undoubtedly one reason why many British families were initially less than eager to open their homes to GIs: 'After four years of war, they are ashamed of their meagre rations – a 3 ounce ration of cheese cut into tiny cubes, 2 ounces of tea, 2 ounces of butter spread thinly across a "national loaf" – and drab, threadbare homes – particularly when they think of America as a land of luxury.'

Avice Wilson invited home for tea a GI from Pennsylvania whom she had met at a dance in Chippenham:

> He had been well briefed as to our rations and refused everything except a cup of black coffee the first evening I took him home. The next time he called he brought my mother a packet of cornflakes and a wire saucepan-cleaner. Supplies were delayed and this was all he could find. Later he would bring candy and cigarettes, or a can of fruit, but either he was not a great getter of supplies or the 4th [Division] were very short.

A GI from Dade City, Florida, a truck-driver before the war, used to bring gifts to a Cardiff family, 'bread, corned beef etc from the canteen. When we stopped that, he brought us cutlery!' A woman who grew up in an Elizabethan house, which used to enchant the family's American visitors, recalls the tins of pineapple juice – 'I can still picture the labels on the tins!' – which a particular couple used to bring: 'Often they would arrive on a tandem (both men were big fellows, sixteen to seventeen stone), so it was quite a sight.'

A GI from Virginia was invited home by a girl he met at a dance:

> We had a meal which even by American standards was great – complete with ham and much more. Only afterwards did I discover that I had eaten the family's special rations for a *month*. So I soon corrected that. I went to see our mess sergeant and then the next time I turned up at this girl's home, it was as if I were Santa Claus. I brought a large can of pears and a pork loin or something like that – and a lot more stuff.

Commanding officers began to encourage their men to take official 'hospitality rations' when they went visiting – and the troops often supplemented these with food begged from the cookhouse or treats bought from the PX: this was done both in the spirit of friendship, and with the aim of minimizing the natural envy of American plenitude in the midst of British scarcity. Fathers received cigarettes, or even cigars, and a whiskey called bourbon, while mothers were presented with tinned fruit, ham, chocolate and candies.

It was often 'Mom' that the young soldiers far from home missed most. In many places the authorities – recognizing this, and seeing it as an ideal opportunity for creating the right sort of stable links with the British community – encouraged schemes whereby a local woman would 'adopt' a lonely GI for the duration, inviting him home for tea. The fourth Sunday in Lent was traditionally linked with Mothering Sunday, but 'Mother's Day' on the scale it was celebrated in America in May – trailing only Christmas and Thanksgiving as a family festival since its introduction in 1914 – was unknown in Britain. In the middle of the war, President Roosevelt called on 'the people of the United States to express the love and reverence which we feel for the mothers of our country': a number of GIs turned to British surrogates and 'adopted' a British mother for that special

Santa at war. 'Father Christmas' arrives by tank at a party given by US Army engineers for British war orphans.

day, taking her to tea and a concert laid on by various Red Cross Clubs throughout the country, while wearing a carnation in tribute to his own mother – red if she was still alive, white if not. In the same spirit, a regular visitor to a Liverpool family paid for a party for the couple's twenty-fifth wedding anniversary and 'even bought my mother a corsage of orchids. She'd never had anything so lovely. After her death in 1971, thirty years later, we found the flowers pressed in her Bible.'

If it was hard to be away from home and at war in a foreign land on Mother's Day, it was even harder at Christmas. As many troops as possible were given the day off, Jewish soldiers would volunteer for duty, and for those men who could not be spared, the army cooks prepared a traditional Christmas dinner.

But if possible the troops were to be entertained in British homes – 'filling the chairs left empty by British fighting men'. The soldiers who accepted invitations to family meals were provided with special rations for each day's stay: 'a typical package will contain fruit or tomato juice, evaporated milk, peas, bacon, sugar, coffee, lard or shortening, butter, rice or available substitutes.' In view of this cornucopia, perhaps it is not surprising that so many invitations were extended to the US troops that first Christmas in 1942 that 'the ratio is estimated at fifty invitations for every one soldier available' and a plea went out for more GIs to come forward 'and accept some more of those invitations'.

GIs entertain Brownies from London's blitzed East End at a party they threw for Thanksgiving Day in 1943 at the Hans Crescent American Red Cross Club.

One GI was invited to spend Christmas at a Land Army girl's home which was 'a two-storey stone cottage. No plumbing, but gorgeous fireplaces.' He turned up on a bicycle laden down with

> legal rations of Spam and powdered coffee, chocolate and soap, and other items from the camp stores . . . we all sat down that day to a Christmas dinner – and scene – that might have made Charles Dickens the only true recorder . . . I don't recall what we had for dinner, but at long last the plum pudding – and all the renewed laughter at the clumsy struggle I had . . . till with a victorious 'whoop', I gained the threepenny bit.

It wasn't only extra rations that the GIs brought into British homes at Christmas: 'they taught us about Advent calendars and burning Advent candles and hanging gingerbread biscuits on the Christmas tree – but we showed them Christmas crackers which they'd never seen before and were greatly taken with!'

If the US troops brought new delights to many young British women, it was the same with the children. Many GIs were not long out of childhood themselves and the uninhibited curiosity and open admiration which British children usually displayed for the Yanks made it easier to get to know them than their elders. And for family men, time spent with the children was perhaps some compensation for missing their own children who were growing up while they were away at war.

The currency of the relationship was chewing-gum. A Hertfordshire man, seven years of age when the Americans came to his home town, recollects: 'my friends and I constantly chased them with cries of "Got any gum, chum?" It must have been very irritating to say the least and I don't recall actually getting any gum, whatever that was, but my uncle told me that this was the correct way to greet Americans.'

Chewing-gum reached parts that had never been exercised with such ferocity before, and to whose who deplored the Americanization of Britain, vistas of endlessly chomping young jaws was final proof of a world gone to the vulgar. The 'gum-chummers', as a Seething airman labelled them, seemed to materialize like magic whenever a GI appeared. Chewing-gum was a prized possession, to be asked for, cajoled for – and bartered for. Connie Stanton used to swap hard-boiled eggs from her mother's hens for sticks of gum with the base guards at Milton Ernest; chewing-gum was used as a bribe to get local kids to go for fish and chips, or exchanged for jam jars, coat-hangers (which the sartorially minded GIs seemed always to be short of) or even, optimistically, for sisters. Once secured, the gum was treasured, chewed long after all taste had been extracted, carefully stuck on the bedpost at night to be masticated afresh in the morning, or traded in elaborate exchanges. Some children showed particular initiative in securing this booty. A master at Dulwich College preparatory school, which had been evacuated to Wales, noticed that when the US tank convoys rumbled through the village, one tank frequently stopped for a time outside the front door before starting off again. Upon investigation, he found that 'one of the more ingenious boys, whose bedroom window was on a level with the tank turrets as they passed, had found it very convenient to hang out a pole with the notice, "Any gum, chum?" and a kind of fishing net attached, and, until I had discovered it, was reaping a very rich reward from our gallant allies.'

At a time when sweets and chocolate were almost non-existent, and sugar was strictly rationed, chocolate Hershey Bars, 'Babe Ruths', and hard candy (boiled sweets) like 'Life-Savers' were much coveted. A Liverpudlian, aged five in 1942, was walking along the street with his older sister 'one bleak winter afternoon, and winters in Liverpool at that time were very bleak', when they met a GI who

> asked us did we like chocolates. I wasn't sure because I couldn't quite place what it was, but my sister wasn't stupid and said she loved them and he gave us a huge box. That today would be the equivalent of a small win on the pools. We were both astounded by such unbelievable kindness that we still remember it today. Now I am older and more cynical I would put it down to what is known here as the 'knock back' from his girlfriend and not wishing to advertise the fact by taking the box of chocolates back to camp, he gave them to the first kids he saw.

A thirteen-year-old living in Bude in Cornwall 'on meagre British wartime rations . . . couldn't believe the food available to the 29th Ranger Battalion stationed there . . . I well remember coming home daily from school and making straight for the mess hall.' He and his friends 'would stand around the exit (probably looking like refugees) until invariably being invited in to clear up some of the surplus meatballs, tinned fruit, etc. that always seemed to be available. I'm ashamed to say that after all that we would happily go home to our own tea.'

The GIs gave British children their first glimpse of another great American subculture, one which would stay with many of them well into adulthood – the 'funnies', comic strips featuring such characters as Superman, Captain Marvel, L'il Abner, Loony Toons, Red

Ryder, the Katzenjammer Kids, and Bugs Bunny. One fourteen-year-old acquired a lifelong addiction to American crime stories as an Air Training Corps cadet at Biggin Hill in Kent. A B-24 Liberator, damaged on a mission to France, had crashed nearby: 'All the crew, with the exception of the pilot, had baled out. I clambered aboard and found my way to the Plexiglas bombardier's position at the front of the aircraft on the "scrounge". Among the items "won" was a paperback novel by Ellery Queen. Thereafter I became an *aficionado* of the private eye.'

'Hank', who was billeted with a Bristol family in the months before D-Day, maintained that in civilian life he was a cowboy. The son of the house was sceptical: a cowboy with rimless glasses? But one day

> I was roping the trellis fence on next door's wall with a lasso made from an old sash cord when Hank came along. 'Bet you can't lasso me,' I shouted, thrusting the rope in his hand. Hank looked at the rope, made a couple of practice casts, then the rope snaked out, the noose settling over my shoulders at extreme range. Hank hauled me in and removed my lariat. 'You haven't got the right knot,' he said, 'let me show you' . . . under his instruction I soon mastered the right knot: the terror of the South Street pecos galloped away to show his pals his lariat with a real cowboy knot.

Other children learned from the GIs how to play baseball, and some villages could even muster a scratch team. Others acquired less desirable skills. MPs guarding a crashed aircraft at Leiston in Suffolk bribed some local boys with tobacco to fetch them fish and chips: 'We chewed it and spat it out like cowboys did in the movies . . . we were as sick as dogs, but by the time the war was over, we were experts at chewing and smoking.' A boy living near an American army camp in Pembrokeshire recalls cadging single cigarettes from the GIs. 'They'd give us brands such as Camel, Philip Morris, A1 . . . I remember having twenty-one cigarettes in one night . . . it's no wonder most of us kids smoked at nine or ten.' One night he met a GI 'who had no gum and no cigs, but took out of his pocket a cigar that was about twelve inches long and an inch in diameter, tapering at the ends. We lit it up on the local playing field and because this was our first cigar we were away from school for two days – our mothers unaware of the cause of our sickness and headaches.' The same adventurous boy learnt to drive by taking a Jeep parked outside a local woman's house by a courting US captain, and traversing thirty miles over rough country roads with his friends. When the time came for the American to drive back to camp, 'he must have wondered why his Jeep did so few miles to the gallon.'

'Christmas, New Year, birthdays – any old birthday – Hallowe'en, Fourth of July, Thanksgiving, whatever celebration the GIs cooked up, there was *always* – bombs or no bombs – a party for the kids,' relates Jean Lancaster Rennie. A Hertfordshire man who was evacuated to Middlesbrough as a child recalls how

> at Christmas the Americans threw a superb party for the schoolchildren in the town hall. It was one of those grim public buildings of the time, with sandbags all around the lower ground floor. The [GIs] had decorated the interior with lots of flags – Stars and Stripes and Union Jacks – together with tinsel and paper chains . . . they served an immense amount of food, not only the cakes, jellies and

'Sweet Pea', the little girl 'adopted' by the 306th Bomb Group at Thurleigh through the Stars and Stripes *war orphan scheme, christens an airplane.*

blancmange but many sweet dishes that we hadn't seen for ages due to rationing. We were all given a present from 'Santa', who had an American accent . . . I had a box of cardboard infantrymen. They had 'Stars and Stripes' stickers and my hosts had to reassure me that they were on 'our side'.

For those invited to 'Operation Reindeer' at Shipdham air base in Norfolk, 'coming into the huge hangar was like coming into Aladdin's cave . . . with coloured lights, streamers, silver bells and a Christmas tree reaching up to the skies.' Such trees would often be festooned with 'chaff' – the thin strips of metallic foil thrown out of the aircraft to confuse German radar during a raid.

'There were sweets, sacks of sweets, stacks of sweets everywhere and every now and then a great shower of sweets would be thrown into the air and the children scrambling and screaming in sheer delight tumbled into an exuberant mass for a fistful of this treasure.' The GIs would have saved up their sweet rations for weeks to provide this feast, and spent many evenings making toys, collecting money so they could buy whatever they could find in the shops, and writing home for small toys to be sent for the high point of the party – the arrival of Santa Claus. Usually he came by Jeep, but at Shipdham 'a droning was heard in the sky . . . nearer and nearer it came. It was silver and "snow" covered . . . a Piper Cub plane straight from Santa Claus Land. The propeller slowed and stopped – and sure enough there he was. Father Christmas, with a red robe and white beard and a big bulging sack, stepped out of the plane.' On one occasion, the venerable old man 'arrived' in a Flying Fortress and the children were allowed to scramble in and out of this huge 'sledge'.

The parties were thrown to foster good relations with the local community, and to bring some pleasure to wartime children for whom fun was pretty thin on the ground and who were growing up deprived of toys and treats – and often of at least one parent as well. Many of the children who came to GI parties were evacuees: at Colchester in 1943 the Military Police stationed there threw a Christmas party for ninety children whose fathers were prisoners-of-war and many GIs held parties for local orphanages and entertained children in hospital or in homes for the handicapped.

The American Red Cross and *Stars and Stripes* joined forces to start an orphans fund; each unit which collected £100 could 'adopt' an orphan, or a child who had lost one parent, for a year. They could specify their requirements – 'a blue-eyed, blonde girl', 'a red-haired boy, no older than five'. These children, and there were nearly 600 of them, would be sent sweets, toys and new clothes by their benefactors, as well as being taken on trips and entertained; they would often visit the units, where miniature uniforms might have been made for these 'mascots'. The 306th Bomb Group at Thurleigh had wanted to adopt a boy and had even settled on a name, 'Butch'; when the day came, there weren't any boys available, so instead they took a three-year-old girl, Maureen, nicknamed her 'Sweet Pea', and got her to christen a bomber after herself by dipping her hand in red paint and holding her up to plant her palm print on its fuselage.

Local papers would report the GIs' generosity: 'US Host to Northants Children', 'Yanks Play Santa Claus at Wellingborough', 'US Santa Claus at Kettering'. But a staff sergeant with the 820th Engineers thought a headline that appeared in the *Rushden Echo and Argus* was particularly apt: 'Americans Revel in Children's Visit,' it read.

CHAPTER THIRTEEN

'COME HOME AND MEET FATHER'

THE QUEUE AT THE FISH AND CHIP SHOP was considered a good place to meet Yanks – or maybe at a dance or at the Red Cross Club. It was often the daughter of the house who would first invite a soldier or an airman she'd met home for tea. And it was not all that unusual for the visitor, like all invaders, to end up by carrying off the woman. Some 70,000 British women were destined to become GI brides – though the course of wartime true love did not always run smooth.

Eileen Smithers, whose mother's house in Norwich was an emergency billet for US officers, 'only ever dated one of them, a Texan called "Red" because of the colour of his hair'. He was a 'very serious formal young man' who would insist on walking her to wherever she was going and made sure that if she had a date she had her 'mad money' – enough for a taxi home if necessary. They went for long walks and cycle rides, sailing on the Norfolk Broads – and 'of course to the cinema!' But it wasn't an entirely compatible friendship. 'He was the only Yank I ever knew who didn't dance and I was mad about dancing, especially jive and jitterbug,' so it was something of a surprise when, after about a year,

> my mother informed me that he had asked her permission to get engaged and to marry me, having previously written and obtained his father's permission to marry a Limey! I was considerably shocked and not a little annoyed by this. When I asked him why he hadn't discussed the matter with me first, he replied that was how it was done where he came from. As we hadn't even held hands, let alone kissed each other, I just wouldn't take him seriously. I think I hurt his feelings.

One woman remembers that the GIs she dated as an eighteen-year-old civil servant in 1942 would often 'want to get engaged' after a few evenings out, but she concluded that 'this was only the war talking', while her family and friends 'were surprised to see me dating a GI' – a not uncommon reaction. Sometimes this was simple snobbery. A Liverpool woman recalls neighbours saying to her mother: 'I saw *your* Pamela out with a Yank last night' – with the use of *your* as opposed to *our* denoting North Country disapproval. Fathers were often suspicious of the man's intentions: the girlfriend of a ferry pilot was instructed by her father to 'question me on (1) Did I have a wife? (2) Did I have a girl back home? I remember it was at the Swan Hotel and [Jean's] face was as red as the port wine we were drinking.' A woman from Aberdare, who had frequently sworn she would never 'be seen dead with a Yank', decided that she wanted to marry the one she'd met on the eve of D-Day. Her father sent her out of the room when her suitor arrived for tea in order to grill him about his marital status. 'My Louis got the "third degree" . . . and when we finally left the house he said "Boy, that was tough – but I respect your father for what he did."'

Parents often opposed such wartime romances because they were likely to mean that their daughters would emigrate to the United States at the end of the war. In the days before frequent air travel, a single flight across the Atlantic cost around £175, a sea passage between £40 and £65, while the average weekly wage in Britain in 1940 was £4.10s. Many feared they would never see their daughters again – and to the daughters 'going to America seemed like going to the moon.'

'Mum kept asking me what was wrong with British boys,' one woman recalls, and many dads weren't too keen on their daughters dating 'those bloody Yanks' – let alone marrying them. The father of a Cornish land girl expressed 'heartfelt feelings of relief' when the 291st Infantry moved out of Newlyn in June 1944 'without capturing any of us'.

A woman who became a GI bride recalls that for several months her father refused to sign the necessary papers for her to marry:

> I guess he was anxious for the future of his daughter, but of course I was very young and headstrong. The months crept by and I never gave up. I would put them on the table every evening where he would sit. He always picked them up and put them on one side without a word . . . it was so frustrating. Many nights I sobbed into my pillow. Finally one night my father sat at the table and looked down at the papers. He looked at me and I could see that there were tears in his eyes. 'You both mean business, I can see there is nothing to be gained by going on like this' . . . and he signed the papers.

Another girl, faced with an intransigent father, defiantly insisted: 'If you won't sign the papers, there may not be a wedding – but there'll be a honeymoon anyway.' He signed. The father of a Newcastle woman never forgave her for marrying a GI – 'he tried to prevent my marriage by appealing to the British and American embassies.'

But while the parents of a woman who was working as a telephonist in Wales during the war were 'naturally not very happy' when they learned she and her GI boyfriend had decided to marry, once they realized that their daughter had really made up her mind, 'Mother did everything possible to make it a happy time' – including 'giving up eight clothes coupons so that Jack would have pyjamas to take on honeymoon'.

Indeed some parents were full of encouragement. A woman who met her future husband while working as a hostess at Rainbow Corner found that her parents gave her 'a lot of support . . . they felt there was no future for young people in England – and I would have a much better life in the States.'

On the whole, the US authorities discouraged their servicemen from marrying – and particularly from marrying abroad. A single man undistracted by family responsibilities was considered more likely to be single-minded in his war effort, and more likely to make the strong ties with his 'buddies' which could generate the selfless courage that war might demand. It was common currency, too, that wartime marriages were doomed to failure. (In fact, the evidence rather contradicted this: it was estimated that some 80 per cent of the 8,000 marriages contracted overseas during the First World War were successful – or at least lasted.) And then there was public opinion back home, which was hardly enthusiastic about having the flower of American manhood return from foreign wars accompanied by foreign wives, at the expense of American women seeking husbands.

In June 1942, the US War Department issued a regulation requiring troops stationed overseas to seek the approval of their commanding officers two months in advance of a proposed wedding. Furthermore, a potential bridegroom was warned that 'he will not be allowed any special privileges or special living arrangements different from those provided for single men and women', and the wife of a US serviceman married in the ETO 'will not necessarily be allowed to accompany her husband to a change of station or on his return to the US'. Failure to comply with the regulations could lead to a court martial and sometimes immediate despatch to a combat zone. But if the woman was pregnant the waiting period was sometimes waived.

The GI's commanding officer also interviewed the potential bride – though this could be delayed by bureaucratic red tape for more than a year after the initial application had been filed. A GI who applied to marry a Worcestershire woman in the autumn of 1942 was granted permission only in December 1943: 'They tried to discourage us at first because so many servicemen were marrying British girls. They thought they would later regret it.' Her GI fiancé was transferred to Northern Ireland for three months. On his return, he asked if his application had been sent on. It had not, but the CO conceded: 'So you still want to marry this girl? Well, I guess we'll just have to go ahead and send it in!' And a woman then living in Leicester relates that 'one of my husband's officers remarked that he should wait until he was back in the US and marry an American girl. My husband replied that it was a matter of opinion. He was demoted in rank.'

Enquiries were made about the girl's background – the American Red Cross was supposed to be enlisted for this task, until they refused to do so. The men had to get letters from home confirming that they had jobs to return to, savings in the bank and parents prepared to support the young couple if need be. The girls dreaded the form-filling and the interviews with their fiancés' CO or chaplain, during the course of which they were interrogated as to their fitness to be the wives of Americans – and as to whether they were pregnant. Before marrying a GI sergeant 'I had to sign fifteen documents in all,' remembers a civilian employee of the 68th General Hospital. 'The Commanding Officer had to sign them, my father had to sign them, my mother had to sign them and Arnold had to sign them . . . and then they talk of Americans and lightning romance . . . nonsense!'

There was one category of request to marry that was almost always refused: a proposed marriage between a white woman and a black GI. It was suggested that 'further publicity should be given in the press to the regulations of the American Army concerning marriage. These are still far too little understood by young women and girls both in town and country. To these rules should be added the statement that in nineteen out of forty-eight states, mixed marriages of colour are illegal' – these being mainly the segregationist states of the South.

It was not only the COs who proved obstructive on occasions: letters appeared in newspapers all over the US protesting against the outbreak of overseas weddings. One GI – a former correspondent for *Stars and Stripes*, who had himself married an Englishwoman

– roused a storm of protest on both sides of the Atlantic by an article he wrote in the *New York Times* at the end of the war, explaining why, in his view, such marriages so often happened. Women overseas

> seemed to be there for the sole purpose of being pleasant to the men . . . while American women insist on a big share in the running of things, few European women want to be engineers, architects or bank presidents. They are mainly interested in the fundamental business of getting married, having children and making the best homes that their means or conditions will allow. They feel they can attain their goals by being easy on the nerves of their men folk.

But many thought there was something more fundamental at stake than the desirability of a British bride. A Californian woman, writing to the Press in June 1942, questioned

> the right of the War Department to deny any sound-bodied American his right to mate. Is not self-determination in marriage one of the basic American liberties we uphold? Surely if our young men are prepared to offer their lives as shields for the protection of the rest of us, we should equally be prepared to care for the offspring when the need arises. America is made up of 'foreigners' isn't it?

But, of course, relations between the sexes were further complicated by the troops' distance from home and the nature of war. A newly promoted US sergeant took his overcoat and jacket to an ATS barracks to ask if someone could sew his stripes on – upside down in British eyes (a custom defiantly adopted after the American Revolution). When he collected the coat, he found a scrap of paper in the pocket which read:

> *If you are single*
> *Drop me a line,*
> *But if you're married*
> *Never mind.*

The next day the soldier sent back two shirts, two chevrons and the following reply:

> *Have you ever seen any Yanks*
> *(Men in their very best mind)*
> *Who would say to a girl*
> *(I bet you're a pearl)*
> *That they had left a family behind?*

Stories were told of girls being shown photographs of 'sisters' who were really wives, and the personal effects of one airman shot down on a mission were said to have revealed that not only was he married back home in Michigan, but in London and King's Lynn too. As a Norfolk girl said goodbye to her boyfriend in the 8th Air Force, she recalls, 'Marriage was on our minds, but there were obstacles. He said that he was enduring an incompatible marriage. At that piece of news, I said "Oh no, not another one of those." We girls were always listening to tales of "My wife doesn't understand me." '

It was clear that there were cases where absence made the heart more accommodating, and for some GIs it was a case of 'If you can't be near the one you love, then love the one you're near.' When GIs asked a woman who was working in the administrative offices of

" Just like it said in the invite, Tex—'Widow and five single daughters would like to entertain party of American soldiers for Christmas'."

the US forces in Burton, Staffordshire, for a date, she would decline, explaining that her fiancé was serving with the RAF in Rhodesia: 'That doesn't matter' was the usual reply.

Particularly distressing is the story of a Cheshire woman who, 'after a whirlwind courtship', was asked by a US staff sergeant, then working as a quartermaster at Southern Base Headquarters at Salisbury, 'to become engaged and on my nineteenth birthday he presented me with a beautiful sapphire and diamond engagement ring.' They celebrated with a huge party at which she and 'Bob led the dancing to my favourite tune, "Star Eyes",' high in the hit parade at the time. Wedding plans went ahead for the ceremony set for Boxing Day 1943 at St George's, Hanover Square, with the bride, 'determined not to get married in my khaki uniform', busying herself getting a trousseau. Her fiancé seemed strangely slow in completing the necessary application to his CO, so eventually the bride-to-be took matters in hand herself 'to speed things up'. When she was summoned to the CO's office she noticed that he was fingering the pages of a file lying open on the desk in front of him. As she talked on about her father's delight at the wedding, 'he suddenly banged his hand down on the desk and with a look of anger on his face said, "Goddamn all liars! There is only one way to tell you what I have to," and reading from the file in front of him, he quoted "Name: Robert Maxwell. Dependants: wife, Maria Dorita; child, Judith Mary, born 1938".'

A Newbury woman noticed that there were GIs who 'plastered their Jeeps with the names of their girlfriends "back home" – perhaps as a warning, or to preclude involvement with an English girl'. The girlfriend of Britain's first 'official' GI, Private Henke, was a founder member of the 'Always in My Heart' club; its members in twenty-three cities pledged 'to keep faith with their fighting sweethearts: everything will be kept *status quo* until the boys come home.' But life was not always like that – either in Britain or the US. US wartime legislation meant that if a GI stationed overseas refused to consent to a divorce, it was often impossible to end the marriage while he was still in uniform, for the US judiciary were very reluctant to imperil the sanctity of family life in wartime. After

VJ-Day, when the restraints were removed, petitions for divorce doubled. In pre-war Britain, most applications for divorce alleging adultery were filed by women; by the end of the war two out of every three petitions were filed by husbands.

'A passing fad with post-war complications' was the cynical view of these wartime romances. The consequences in terms of illegitimate babies will never be accurately known – though the pre-war average of 5.5 per 1,000 births shot up to 16.1 per 1,000 in 1945. A man born in the Midlands in 1943 relates the midwife's remark to his mother as she held up the new infant: 'Well, Mrs Thorne, that's the first born the right side this month.' Babies born to married women were registered as legitimate unless notified as otherwise, so children born to married women but fathered by a man other than their husband may well not have shown up in the statistics. In the case of single girls, the baby's parentage was often concealed, and it was brought up within the mother's family, with the mother becoming her own child's 'sister' or 'aunt'. Alternatively, the baby might be offered for immediate adoption. Abortions were illegal, and, if possible to secure, either very expensive, or dangerous, or both. Almost everyone could recall cases of such wartime pregnancies among their acquaintances; an eighteen-year-old factory worker living in a hostel near High Wycombe calculated that out 'of the fifty girls I started with, only eighteen of us were still there at the end of the war. All the others got pregnant.' And there was the cause célèbre of Sergeant Thomson, who fathered quadruplets on a certain Miss Nora Carpenter, but whose unyielding wife refused him his freedom to marry her.

The US military authorities could be as unhelpful in these situations as they were slow moving when it came to processing applications to marry. A padre tells of a woman who came to claim that her daughter was pregnant by a GI, and when asked his name, volunteered 'Joe'. 'They're all called GI Joe,' responded the CO unhelpfully. A man who did not want to take responsibility for his fecundity often only had to tell his CO that he was 'drunk at the time' to secure a new posting, never to be heard of again by the unfortunate girl.

There were crude boasts about this particular baby boom: 'We were making up for drinking the pubs dry, by filling up the nurseries,' or 'Next time round, just send the uniforms, the bastards will be there already'; while on a road leading to Burtonwood supply depot, it was said that a sign had been erected which warned 'Watch out for that child. It might be yours.'

But despite the obstacles, and the clampdown forbidding all weddings prior to D-Day, thousands of British girls overcame their families' reservations, their neighbours' disapproval and the rigidity of the US authorities to marry their GI in wartime Britain, wearing a corsage on their uniform, or a borrowed wedding dress, or a pre-war suit set off with a new hat (hats were never rationed), or perhaps even an entirely new outfit obtained with saved and borrowed coupons. Their bridesmaids might wear dresses made from 'damaged parachute silk provided by my fiancé', or maybe butter muslin. A woman working as a volunteer at the Red Cross Club in Newbury decided that neither she nor her husband-to-be was greatly in favour of wartime marriages, but the padre warned that unless they were married it might be years before she would get transport over to America. With the wedding arranged, transport difficulties meant that her fiancé only arrived the lunchtime before the big day. There was no time to assemble the choir, but the organist played and the family rallied round to provide 'jellies and blancmange and

*'Getting his feet under the table.' Sergeant Carleton Fournier,
who married an English woman from a Norfolk village, receives
advice and instruction from his new in-laws.*

other goodies for the reception'; and Nora Lambert became Mrs Schneider in a dress borrowed from a friend who had just got married, her mother's veil and orange blossom, with the bridesmaids in dresses which she had bought through an advert in the local paper ('so, no coupons!'). The wedding ring was often sent from the States in a set with an engagement ring – 'as if our jewellery wasn't good enough,' bristled a woman, reviving memories of her war years in Norwich. The wedding cake might be a wartime rations sponge with an iced cardboard confection borrowed from the baker plopped on top; there was no icing sugar in wartime ('Roses are Red, Violets are Blue, Sugar is Sweet, Remember?' was inscribed in one bride's card). A corner-shopkeeper's wife, invited to a wedding, was so envious of the marzipan on the young couple's cake that she did a deal with them for a piece in exchange for 'several glasses of wine'. The food at a wedding reception was likely to be a masterpiece of improvisation. Guests ate whatever was available – in one case, reported by Norman Longmate, peas on toast fingers in place of the traditional canapés. If the groom was on good terms with his cookhouse, there could be joints of ham, tubs of ice cream and tins of fruit. When a Bristol girl married a GI, her brother remembers that she was

> bashful in her borrowed wedding dress and her bridesmaids' dresses, none of which fitted properly, but no one seemed to notice . . . They had a nice reception thanks to the generosity of the Yanks who brought enormous tins of Spam and

145

WARTIME WEDDINGS
ABOVE *WAC Mary Elizabeth Elliot married Sergeant Wallace R. Best, flanked by an armed guard of honour, at an English village church and* LEFT *Edward P. Yeater from Cedar Rapids, Iowa, married an English girl, Barbara Broome, at St Deny's Church, Evington, on 17 July 1945. The couple first met at the Palais de Danse Hall in Leicester.*

peaches, and Doreen's customers [on her milk round] clubbed together with their meagre rations and made her a lovely wedding cake.

An American ferry pilot who proposed to his wife in Barbara's Bun Shop in Bedford – and was accepted – managed to secure a precious bottle of vodka and watched in bemusement as his best man thoughtfully poured it into a large jug of orange juice reserved for the elderly ladies at the reception. 'When I last saw them they were crying and laughing . . . and one of them told [my mother-in-law] what a lovely wedding it was, and what was that exquisite drink?' There was also an excellent trifle at the reception and a wedding cake which his co-pilot enjoyed so much that 'he took big chunks . . . with him when he left for a mission. I never saw him again. He was lost over the Channel on a foggy day.'

Honeymoons, if possible at all, were often brief. One GI had fifty minutes in which to get married and return to his unit. He sought the help of the Red Cross:

> He burst into the office at 1.10 p.m. and said he had to be married and back with his unit by 2.00 p.m. as the unit was pulling out that afternoon . . . the registrar at the local registry office was out rent collecting, and anyway forty-eight hours' notice was necessary prior to the ceremony. A telephone call to the soldier's CO explaining the situation was sufficient to give the man another hour, but 3 o'clock was the deadline. Another phone call was made, this time to the Catholic minister, who, after conversation with the bishop, carried out the ceremony just in time to return the soldier to his unit without being AWOL.

A woman who grew up during the war in the small hotel her parents ran in Cornwall remembers that 'on provision of a marriage certificate, my parents allowed many happy young couples to snatch whatever brief time they could together at the hotel. I can't remember their names, but I know at least two of those couples whose liaison was brought to a tragic end in the Normandy landings.'

The ferry pilot, John Doktor, had had a particular hotel recommended to him for his honeymoon.

> They served thick steaks and great food and drink. We travelled from the prettiest part of England to rain-drenched Manchester and the bedroom had one antler hat stand and a creaking iron bedstead. Jean said, 'I will not stay: get something else quick,' which I did. To our horror we looked behind the curtains and viewed a dance floor. We couldn't go to bed until the dance closed at midnight. And the chambermaid came in at 5.30 a.m. with a steaming teapot, and I asked her gently to remove herself – and her pot.

So began married life for one Anglo–American couple – 'a life perforated with hellos and goodbyes'. It was the same story for thousands. Men were posted, trained, or flew on missions, and finally joined the invasion of Europe. For the GI brides there were classes run by the Red Cross and booklets telling them what to expect in their new lives. Then they settled down to what was likely to prove a long, frustrating and somewhat worrisome wait for the time when it was peace again and they would be able to set sail for their husbands' native land – and check out these glowing descriptions of the 'new country' for themselves.

CHAPTER FOURTEEN

FIGHTING A WAR ON TWO FRONTS

'THEY FOUGHT SEPARATELY and died equally,' was the epitaph written for his fellow black GIs by Ralph Ellison, a writer and musician who served in the merchant marine and spent time in Wales with the US Army in 1943. During the Second World War, as in all wars since the American Revolution, US troops were segregated. With the arrival of US forces in the United Kingdom in 1942, many British people were forced to confront – usually for the first time – questions of racial attitudes.

The desire of the British government to minimize any non-white presence in Britain had been explicit in the First World War. And at the time when the first US troops were arriving in the UK during the Second World War, the 'accepted view' in Whitehall of the coloured troops from the British Empire was made equally explicit in a Foreign Office report: 'The recruitment to the United Kingdom of coloured British subjects, whose remaining in the United Kingdom after the war might create a social problem, is not considered desirable.' Or, as the lady prayed in Westminster Abbey in John Betjeman's 1940 poem:

> Keep our Empire undismembered,
> Guide our Forces by Thy Hand,
> Gallant blacks from far Jamaica,
> Honduras and Togoland;
> Protect them Lord in all their fights,
> And, even more, protect the whites.

The same attitude was adopted towards black American troops. But the objections of British government, voiced through the Chiefs of Staff to Washington, and seconded by the US Army authorities in Britain, were overridden by the US War Department, which decided that 'in planning for the shipment of troops to the British Isles, including Northern Ireland, colored troops may be included in reasonable proportions for any type of service unit.' 'Reasonable proportions' meant in practice that the number of blacks in the Army was to be roughly in proportion to the number of blacks in the US population, namely, about one in ten – and that some of these were to be sent to serve abroad. The first black American troops landed in Britain in May 1942; by late that summer about 12,000 had arrived.

The US Army was an almost entirely segregated army; it was not until 1947 that a presidential order ended military apartheid. When blacks, severely hit by the Depression, began to enlist in the Army in 1940, which they did at a rate much greater than their proportion of the population, they were assigned almost exclusively to segregated units and trained almost entirely for non-combatant tasks as labourers, transport operators, stevedores, kitchen and domestic staff and stewards. Blacks could not enlist in the Army Air Corps or in the Marine Corps – élite services by definition – though many were employed on air force bases doing a variety of ancillary tasks, some of them hazardous, such as transporting and loading bombs. Drafted men fared no better. *Yank* magazine carried a wry comment in 1942 about blacks being denied a role in combat: 'What do you call a Negro with three Purple Hearts?' (awarded for death or injury in action) 'A fiction.'

In the First World War, Army-designed tests in the US examined levels of education rather than 'intelligence', and blacks, then largely from the South and denied formal educational opportunities, generally fell below the national average. This confirmed the Army in its assumption that blacks were inferior to whites, and to a large extent the same premise shaped military policy throughout the Second World War. In the words of Henry Stimson, Secretary of War, 'In tactical organization, in physical location, in human contacts, the Negro soldier is separated from the white soldier as completely as possible.' In the months preceding the re-election of President Roosevelt in November 1940, a few token moves were made towards 'the development . . . of policies looking to the fair and effective utilization of Negroes'. The Army agreed to organize some black combat units and to train some black aviators, and a black officer, Colonel Benjamin O. Davis, was promoted to the rank of brigadier-general. But there were no moves to 'intermingle colored and white enlisted personnel in the same regimental organizations'. The GI army that came to Britain in 1942 was, in all essentials, segregated – a 'Jim Crow army'.

The policy was implemented in guidelines issued by General Eisenhower, Commander of the European Theater of Operations. On arrival in Britain, US troops had to be cautioned against making racial slurs and to be instructed about the lack of a colour bar in Britain and the need to respect this custom; but, as far as possible, black and white troops were to be kept apart, at work and off duty. Thus Eisenhower hoped to restrict black troops to the western ports of Britain – places like Liverpool, Cardiff and Bristol – where the small black British population was concentrated for the most part.

To keep black and white soldiers apart when off base a system of 'rotating passes' was introduced whereby blacks were allowed to go into the local town on one night and whites on another – black Wednesdays and white Thursdays. Where this was clearly impractical, some pubs and dance halls would be allocated for whites only, others for blacks only. (Passes were ostensibly allocated by unit, but since the units were racially homogeneous, the result was the same.) Thus in Launceston, a small town on the edge of Bodmin Moor in Cornwall – where a gun battle was fought between black and white troops in September 1943 – there was a 'black' fish and chip shop, and a 'white' one, and the white GIs didn't look kindly on a black soldier entering 'theirs'. There were 'black' and 'white' dances at the town hall (alternating between the two races on Saturday nights); a local man recalls that 'the white Military Police . . . were kept busy with many incidents – and they didn't hesitate to use their clubs like baseball bats on the heads of the recalcitrants.'

Officially, the British government distanced itself from the US Army's policy. On 4 September 1942, the Home Office issued a circular to all chief constables:

> It is not the policy of His Majesty's Government that any discrimination as regards the treatment of coloured troops should be made by the British authorities. The Secretary of State, therefore, would be glad if you would be good enough to take steps to ensure that the police do not make any approach to the proprietors of public houses, restaurants, cinemas, or other places of entertainment with a view to discriminating against coloured troops.

Furthermore, the British police 'should not make themselves responsible in any way for the enforcement of such orders'.

But if there was no official support for the US measures of segregation, there were many in government and local administration who were anxious to place strict limits on contacts between the black US troops and the British population, particularly the female population.

In August 1942, a conference at the War Office in London agreed that British officers should explain American racial attitudes so that their own troops, especially those women who were members of the ATS, might avoid contact with black GIs. A few days later, the senior administrative officer of Southern Command, in which a high proportion of the black troops were stationed, went still further in issuing advice to his local subordinates. The blacks, he explained, 'had a simple mental outlook and lacked the white man's ability to think and plan'. In the US Army, he continued, they lived their own lives but 'they are sympathetically treated by the white man' who 'feels his moral duty to them as if to a child'. British men and women in the armed forces should 'adjust their attitude so that it conforms to that of the white American citizen', and, in particular, he added, soldiers 'should not make intimate friends with them, taking them to cinemas and bars', nor should white women 'associate with coloured men . . . they should not walk out, dance, or drink with them.'

The British government was balancing on a knife edge – covertly supporting US Army segregation while overtly declining to assist in implementing it. This stance was the result of several considerations. One was the importance of maintaining good relations with the US; a second was a desire to foster harmony between British and American troops – or at least white US troops – who were going to have to fight together across Europe; a third was concern about the shape of the post-war order and, in particular, anxiety that the US should not revert to its traditional isolationism. Convinced by Roosevelt's cautious conduct up to Pearl Harbor that 'public opinion' largely determined US foreign policy, the British government spent huge amounts of time, effort and money in welcoming and entertaining the GIs; far more attention was paid to them than to those despatched by less important political allies, including the very numerous Canadian troops. It was fervently hoped that this hospitality would pay dividends in the post-war world: as David Reynolds points out, it was thought vital to conciliate the power-brokers in Congress, notably the Southern Democrats, who would help to decide whether the Anglo–American alliance would persist and whether Britain would receive essential foreign aid after the fighting was over. Churchill was also anxious that Britain and America should stand together after the war to resist the 'menace of Bolshevism' posed by an increasingly powerful Soviet Union. For all these reasons, the British government was intent on not offending US racial sensibilities.

GIs outside Horace Gurney's pub at Bovingdon in Hertfordshire in 1942. One of a series of photographs released by the Ministry of Information in 1942 to show the arrival of black US troops in Britain.

At the same time, many in British government and administration were influenced by a set of deeply ingrained racial stereotypes, reinforced by a sense of Empire. These led to an attitude of natural white superiority and a belief that there were definable 'races' with fixed, inherited differences of moral and intellectual capacity.

Nor were such attitudes confined to official circles. They found expression in the popular song published in 1944 and written by the authors of 'In the Quartermaster's Store' – 'Choc'late Soldier from the USA':

> *Choc'late drop, always fast asleep*
> *Dozin' in his cozy bed . . .*
> *They used to call him Lazybones in Harlem,*
> *Lazy good for nothin' all the day;*
> *But now they're mighty proud of him in Harlem*
> *CHOC'LATE SOLDIER FROM THE USA.*

And they affected even the more 'enlightened': for example, while insisting that 'any American Negro who comes to Britain must be treated on a basis of absolute equality, and remember *never* to call a Negro a nigger', the poet Louis MacNeice, in his pamphlet *Meet the Army*, thought it advisable to explain that it must be remembered . . . that while the Negroes form a very large section (one in twelve) of the American nation, they are in the unique position of being descended from slaves: this memory of slavery, being still fresh, retains a psychological hold on both the Negroes themselves and on many of their white fellow citizens (especially those in the old slave states, i.e. the 'South'); from this they will only gradually break free.

The BOLERO plan for the build-up of US troops had a target of one million GIs in Britain by April 1943. If 10 per cent of these were to be black, that would mean a total of 100,000 US blacks in Britain – and the authorities feared for public order.

In the early 1940s, the permanent black community in Britain was small – probably no more than 7,000 or 8,000 in 1939 – and unless they lived in a big city or a port, most British people had never met a black person. The first black GIs – especially in rural areas – were something of a novelty, hitherto seen only on the cinema screen, often in a banjo-strumming musical or as a faithful and subservient family retainer. Moreover, the black GI was a temporary visitor and so wasn't perceived to pose a threat to white jobs in the way in which post-war black immigrants would be. So, although Britain was not devoid of racial prejudice at the time, the attitude among most ordinary people seems to have been: 'They're all soldiers. They've all come to fight the same war'. As both blacks and whites had come 3,000 miles or more to help win the war, many Britons saw no reason to distinguish between one American and another. Others went further: 'I don't mind the Yanks, but I can't say that I care much for the white chaps they've brought with them.' In similar vein, a British publican was quoted in *Stars and Stripes* as saying: 'My pub is open to anyone who behaves himself. The Negroes could teach some of our boys some manners'; again, a canteen worker in Hull reported in February 1943 that 'We find the coloured troops much nicer to deal with . . . in canteen life and such, we like serving them, they are always so courteous and have a very natural charm that most whites miss. Candidly I'd far rather serve a regiment of the dusky lads than a couple of whites . . .' A Marlborough woman agreed: 'Everyone here adores the Negro troops. All the girls go to their dances, but nobody likes the white Americans. They swagger about as if they were the only people fighting this war, they all get so drunk and look so untidy, whilst the Negroes are very polite, and smarter.'

Black troops were often considered by the British to be less loud and pushy than their white colleagues; and indeed one of the US authorities' motives for perpetuating effective segregation was a fear that their wartime experiences in Britain might encourage the blacks to get 'uppity' and demand greater civil rights on their return home. In fact, more than three-quarters of the black troops who came to the UK were from the still largely rural South where the Depression had perpetuated a low standard of living: they were not beneficiaries of the American dream, nor were highly mechanized homes and large cars part of their lot back home. The result was that they found British living conditions less 'backward' and were far less prone than their white counterparts to make derogatory remarks about the British way of life.

Many British people were genuinely disturbed by the treatment they saw meted out to the blacks by their white compatriots. They responded at a human level to their humiliation, and some also felt that such prejudice sat ill in a war being fought to destroy

FIGHTING A WAR ON TWO FRONTS

An open-air service conducted in the fields around a US Army camp 'somewhere in England' in the summer of 1942. 'A harmonium gives them a lead — and from all round the voices join in: "Glory, Glory, Hallelujah",' said Picture Post.

Nazism and its racial attitudes: 'a Jim Crow army cannot fight for a free world.' 'I think the treatment of the coloured races of the US Army etc by the white fellows is disgusting,' said a Cambridge man, 'the coloured are prohibited from going to certain pubs, dancing halls, cinemas, just because the white fellows are snobbish. After all, both races are doing the same job of work.' 'I have personally seen the American troops kick, and I mean, kick, coloured soldiers off the pavements, and when asked why, reply "stinking black pigs" or "black trash" or "uppity niggers",' reported a Birmingham man. A woman working in a NAAFI at Tidworth was shocked at the way the black soldiers were treated: 'They had every dirty job there was, latrine-cleaning, road-sweeping.' And a Chippenham woman who was to marry an American officer recalls 'a Southern boy' from the 11th Armored Division 'who was appalled at my grandmother's "black Mammy" knitting bag. "Ma'am," he commented politely, "we shoot niggers where I come from." '

Young people, in particular, were often mystified by racial incidents. A Northern Irish woman who was fifteen in 1942 remembers such an occasion:

> when the Belfast bus stopped at the bus queue in Lisburn, several GIs boarded, some were coloured. When the bus was full, the conductor barred the door with his outstretched arm saying 'Sorry, full up.' A white American who couldn't get on stretched into the bus and drew out an unsuspecting coloured soldier. Nelson [the bus conductor] stepped out to block the white man's access and told the coloured man to get back into the bus and said to the white man 'No colour bar here, mate.' It was many years before I understood about a colour bar.

A girl living in Devon, where thousands of troops descended in readiness for the D-Day landings, recalled 'the famous Gettysburg address, "All men are created equal", when [she saw] the hypocrisy of the officers in the big house, other ranks billeted in our houses and yet the blacks were in tents in the park. Even as a child I thought it disgraceful that they were second-class citizens.' A wartime teenager who used to run errands for the American troops stationed at Huyton, near Liverpool, was amazed to hear the GIs shouting and screaming from behind the wire fence which surrounded the camp:

> the shouting spread to every GI behind the fence and as the words became clearer I realized that they were yelling abuse at the lone soldier walking along on our side of the wire. He was, of course, a black man, and all the men in the camp were white. I was about fourteen at the time and I could not understand why the sight of a black man walking along the road could arouse so much hatred and abuse. I still can't.

Frequently publicans refused to be dictated to by the US authorities about whom they could serve and whom they couldn't, and welcomed 'any soldier of any colour who behaved himself and could pay for his drink'. A Bristol woman recalls two black soldiers coming into the Colston Arms where her father was the landlord.

> They called for two beers . . . their voices carried into the back bar, and one of the white Americans [who were regulars] came through to check. When he saw the two coloureds he told my father not to serve them – rather late, because he already had. Here's the odd thing: prejudiced as my father was, he was more

infuriated at being told whom he should serve, and told the coloureds that they were welcome to stay. However they drank up immediately and left. I went outside to tell them they need not have done so. They told me that the reason they left was that my father had treated them so well, it would have been the scene of considerable damage had they remained . . . Their parting words as they left were 'It's like this in the States, but things'll be different after the war.'

Yet there were also prejudices and tensions between black GIs and some of the British. In September 1942, the wife of a vicar in Worle, Somerset, took it upon herself to advise the local population about their behaviour towards the black troops. She told shopkeepers that they should serve the black troops, but tell them not to come again; women who found themselves sitting next to a black GI in the cinema should move; people should cross the road to avoid meeting blacks, and, of course, 'they must have no social relationship with coloured troops' and 'on no account must coloured troops be invited into the homes of white women.' Such advice, though quickly repudiated in the Press – 'We must have no colour bar here,' responded journalist-politicians like Brendan Bracken and Tom Driberg – may have come nearer to coinciding with the private views of some in government and certain members of the British aristocracy. Thus the Duke of Marlborough thought that in areas where black troops 'are quartered it is unwise and dangerous to go out into the roads and country lanes after dark and there is a growing resentment that these conditions should be allowed to exist.' And a story, perhaps apocryphal, was nevertheless reported with glee in the *New Statesman*: a grand English lady, wishing to do her bit for the war effort, wrote to the commander of a US unit stationed locally to invite half a dozen men for Sunday lunch, and scribbled on the invitation 'No Jews please'. When she opened the door on the appointed Sunday, there stood six large black GIs. Horrified, she exclaimed that there must be some mistake. 'Oh no, ma'am,' one of them replied, 'Colonel Cohen no make any mistake.'

Much more immediately threatening to the peace, however, were black–white tensions among the American troops. Eisenhower described one important cause:

> The British population, except in large cities and among wealthy classes, lacks the racial consciousness which is so strong in the United States. The small-town British girl would go to a movie or a dance with a Negro quite as readily as she would go with anyone else, a practice that our white soldiers could not understand. Brawls often resulted and our white soldiers were further bewildered when they found that the British press took a firm stand on the side of the Negro.

A quartermaster corporal in Northern Ireland forecast problems: 'It seems that several outfits of colored troops preceded us over here and have succeeded pretty well in salting away the local feminine pulchritude . . . the girls really go for them in preference to the white boys, a fact that irks the boys no end.'

There were violent incidents: in Manchester the sight of a black sailor kissing a white girl at the railway station set off a series of incidents which led to all GIs being banned from places of entertainment in the city for a fortnight, and there were rumours of black soldiers being castrated or stabbed for dancing with white girls.

In 1943, tensions between American blacks and whites over women and segregated places of entertainment erupted in mutinies and shoot-outs, with simmering resentment among the blacks about over-zealous actions by the Military Police: at Bamber Bridge near Preston in Lancashire a black GI was killed; there were shooting incidents in Bristol as well as in Launceston; and in December 1944, when some blacks were driven out of a pub in Newbury, Berkshire, a gun fight developed in which two black GIs and the publican's wife were killed.

But it was the fear of miscegenation that united American whites and many of the British in their attempts to keep black soldiers apart from British women. Myths of the sexual rapacity of the blacks led predictably to condemnation of the behaviour of 'easy girls'. A civilian in Leamington Spa found it 'horrible to see the white girls running around with the blacks – but they do say once a black, never a white, don't they?' A Somerset man, seeing a number of local girls peering through the hedge at a black GI camp, diagnosed that they were 'prick-mazed they be, prick-mazed'.

Girls realized sadly that to dance with a black man was to run the risk of becoming a permanent wallflower at white dances. At a local dance hall near Glasgow, a factory worker recognized that 'If you danced with coloured Americans, you were blacklisted by the white ones. They kept a list at the camp of these girls and passed it to the new troops coming in.' And at a dance near Warrington, when

> two black Americans came in, the band stopped, the dance stopped, and two white Americans walked across the floor and took hold of the blacks by their collar and threw them out of the front door: then the dance went on. I asked one American why, it was an awful thing to do. He said they were not going to breathe the same air as a black.

A first lieutenant stationed near Wellingborough was vehement on the subject: 'I've seen nice-looking English girls out with American Negro soldiers as black as spades. I have not only seen the Negro boys dancing with white girls, but we have actually seen them standing in doorways *kissing them goodnight*.'

But Mary Ruau (then Kemp) recalls a dance at her home town in Bridgwater when a contingent of black GIs arrived, and sat out the dancing.

> Nobody talked to them. We thought it was very rude so we decided to ask the band to play a Palais Glide and make it a 'ladies' choice' and my sister and I and some friends went over to ask them to dance, which they did. And that broke the ice. But afterwards someone came up to my father and asked him what he thought his daughters were doing dancing with coloured troops. My father replied that he was proud of us, 'they're our allies, too,' he said, 'they'll bleed and suffer and die just like white men.'

However, official opinion in Britain was firm in its opposition to black–white romances and marriages, pointing out that such unions were illegal in the segregated Southern states from where many of the black troops came. The December 1942 issue of *Army Bureau of Current Affairs Bulletin* warned that 'in our present society such unions are not desirable, since the children resulting from them are neither one thing nor another and are thus badly handicapped in the struggle for life.' A Conservative Member of Parliament, Maurice

GI dancing in Frisco's Club off Piccadilly, July 1943. Picture Post *described the soldier's partner as 'the white girl who likes Frisco's. She's smart, apparently well-to-do and is said to come from Mayfair . . . This is London's Harlem,' declared the magazine.*

Petherick, went so far as to demand that the Foreign Secretary should 'arrange with the American government to send [the black troops] to North Africa, or to go and fertilize the Italians who are used to it anyway'.

In fact, despite sensational Press reports of tens of thousands of 'brown babies' or 'tan Yanks', as they were sometimes offensively referred to, the number of illegitimate babies fathered by black GIs has been estimated at no more than 1,200–1,700 – as compared with the estimate of 22,000 children fathered out of wedlock by white GIs in Britain – and this when a total of three million servicemen passed through Britain between 1942 and 1945.

It is hard to see what the black troops were supposed to do for any sort of female company in Britain. There were some 130,000 black GIs in Britain during the Second World War: it was not until a few months before the end of the war that 800 black WACs arrived in Birmingham, to add to the 130 black women nurses and Red Cross workers already in Britain. 'I am tired of this place,' a black GI wrote home. 'If I could see some colored girls I would feel better. I am sick of these fay broads, they are no good, but [due] to nature I have to put up with them.' Another black soldier stationed at the Scout Dyke army base in Yorkshire wrote to the *Huddersfield Examiner* in September 1943 in response to criticism of the behaviour of black troops:

> We do not criticize your local pub for we happen to realize that it is your life. Would it be asking too much of the population to realize that we are actually bored because it has nothing to offer? . . . We are a very small contingent of soldiers thousands of miles from home, who have made . . . the best of our position and get what pleasure may be had in the locality . . . Please do not for a moment harbour the hallucination that we have no race pride, that we wouldn't glory in the possibility of spending our 'hard-earned' finance on young ladies of our own race. It hasn't occurred to you that no one will be able to fill the void that the absence of Negro girls has created.

CHAPTER FIFTEEN

THE MIGHTY EIGHTH

In our new planes, with our new crews. we bombed,
The ranges by the desert or the shore,
Fired at towed targets, waited for our scores –
And turned into replacements and woke up
One morning, over England, operational.

From *Losses* by Randall Jarrell.

'THE SKY WAS ALWAYS FULL,' remembers a Norfolk man who was fourteen in 1942. A woman working at the American Red Cross Club in Norwich was struck by the fact that 'in a district that had for centuries heard few other sounds than the monotonous mooing of contented cattle or the frantic bellow of a cow in calf . . . a new sound now dominated the air . . . dawn brought the drone of bombers.'

Throughout the thousand days that the 8th Air Force was operating from Britain, its bombers flew a total of 330,523 sorties – including bombing raids (or missions), training flights, and transport flights to drop supplies over occupied Europe. By 1944 a mission – flown on one of the 459 days between 17 August 1942 and 8 May 1945 on which heavy bombers set off from the United States bases in eastern Britain to attack enemy targets – would take off with an average of 1,400 heavy bombers supported by up to 800 fighter planes to drop an estimated 3,300 tons of bombs.

The most significant building in the life of the bombardment group stationed on one of these 8th Air Force bases might seem to have been the operations briefing room, but preparations for a mission started long before that tense moment when the crews were let in on the secret of the target for that day.

The decision to fly would have been taken at the 8th's HQ at High Wycombe (code-named 'Pinewood'), where General Ira Eaker and his staff, working from a list of priority targets supplied by the Supreme Allied HQ, had sifted through intelligence and operational information to determine both how many bombers should be sent to the target and how many planes the various bomb groups would be able to muster (depending on how heavy their recent losses had been, and whether replacements had arrived), which fighter groups should be used, what was known about enemy anti-aircraft batteries, and which was the best route to avoid their flak. But the one imponderable which kept everyone on alert was the weather. The bombers had to be able to assemble in formation, and they couldn't do that in fog, or low, heavy cloud; they had to be able to fly across occupied Europe at higher than 18,000 feet or, on daylight missions, German flak would pick off the planes at a suicidal rate; and a formation was very hard to hold flying blind through cloud. And over the target there had to be enough breaks in the cloud for the bombardiers to aim their bomb loads – until the introduction of PFF or Pathfinder planes, in which the ball turret had been removed and radar equipment installed, made targeting a different matter.

The crews who were 'on alert' were those who would be flying the next combat mission – and in 1942–3, the shortage of replacement staff meant that pilots and crew were on alert for most missions. Crews on alert were restricted to base.

On the base at Grafton Underwood there was an amber light in the bar: if it was switched to green during the evening, the forecast was unpropitious and the mission was off. A red light meant that the mission was on. The bar would then close around eight o'clock and everyone who was scheduled to fly would try to get some sleep.

While the aircrew slept, the operations crew planned and checked the details of the raid, and the ground crew set to work to get the planes ready to fly, delivering and loading fuel and bombs – high explosive for buildings, fragmentation bombs for moving targets, trains and troops. Loading would take from around 11 o'clock at night until 3 or 4 next morning. It could be dangerous work. At Alconbury in May 1943, the ground crew was loading bombs into a B-17 when one of the bombs detonated and set off several others. Nineteen men were killed and twenty-one injured, and four B-17s standing on the runway were destroyed. At Ridgewell in the early hours of 13 June 1943, bombs being loaded into a B-17 exploded, destroying the Fortress and another plane, damaging another eleven and killing twenty-three men. The work was usually freezing cold – as it was for the armament section, loading the .50-calibre links for the waist gunners, checking gun turrets and bomb sights, and for the crew chiefs taking off the canvas covers and testing the four engines and running an instrument check, turning the engines off as soon as possible to conserve the expensive high-octane fuel. There were reckoned to be about ten ground staff for every man in the air; and they worked through the night before each mission, servicing, checking and loading – as responsible in their way as the flight crew would be in theirs for the success of the mission.

It was still pitch black when the mechanics – or 'grease monkeys', as they were known – tapped the final rivet back and firmly secured the last bomb door. The flying crews were woken at about 4 a.m. for a 6.30 take-off: the orderlies would flash a torch in the faces of the sleeping crews to wake them. The men who were scheduled to fly would have tied a towel round the end of their bunk, but it was firmly believed that anyone seen to be sleeping with a smile on his face would be woken up for the hell of it. Lateness for a briefing wasn't tolerated, so, as a pilot stationed at Grafton Underwood recalled, 'You had to get your clothes on real quick . . . You had to take time to shave though, because you wore an oxygen mask real tight against your face, and the mixture of breath condensation and gunsmoke would irritate your face badly even if you *had* shaved.'

Then it was off by Jeep or bike or on foot, carrying a torch (which the Yanks called a flashlight) covered in 'not less than two thicknesses of tissue paper', to the mess hall for breakfast. Most days that meant that the men were served up what the GIs dubbed

The target for today. Briefing for the 8th Air Force's first independent mission to Rouen from Polebrook and Grafton Underwood, Northamptonshire, in August 1942.

'square eggs' (powdered eggs cut into cubes), but on mission mornings the aircrews tucked into 'combat eggs' (precious fresh eggs), toast and mugs of coffee. As the war correspondent Ernie Pyle observed: 'a young airman died clean-shaven and well fed.'

After chow, it was off in the Jeep for a briefing session. The men filed into the base briefing room – often a Nissen hut – and sat on benches or wooden chairs. Many would be smoking – 'we put up a haze that rivalled a Pittsburgh smog' – and talking and joking nervously. There was none of the usual reluctance to sit in the front row; everyone wanted to get a good look at the target map, though this was covered with a curtain or sheet until the base commanding officer strode into the room and gestured to the S-2 (the intelligence officer), who then dramatically pulled it aside. There were catcalls and jeers from the men, and someone usually called out the wartime slogan, 'Is your journey really necessary?' It was at this moment that the men learned whether their mission was likely to be a 'milk run' – over targets in occupied countries, from which the crews were reasonably likely to get home without being hit by flak or enemy planes, not that there was ever any guarantee that a mission would be a 'milk run' for attacks could appear from nowhere – or the stomach-churning prospect of a long and dangerous flight into Germany, which by 1944 could even include a daylight mission to the 'Big B' (Berlin).

Elmer Bendiner, who flew with the 379th Bomb Group stationed at Kimbolton, remembers when the curtain was swept across the map of Western Europe on 17 August

1943. The red yarn indicating their flight route began at the assembly point over the Wash, stretched over the Channel across Holland to the German border, and across the Mosel and the Rhine before ending in a pin 'puncturing Germany at a place called Schweinfurt'. It was, in fact, the 8th Air Force's first raid into Germany and it was to prove perilous – yet it was the prime purpose for which the 8th had been sent to Britain in May 1942. They had come to prepare for – and then support – a combined Allied land, sea and air operation across the Channel to continental Europe, and this meant first smashing the heart of the German war machine from the air.

Although by 1942 the RAF were raining bombs on industrial centres in Germany at night with the aim of crippling industry and destroying civilian morale, the USAAF's approach was one of daylight precision bombing, delivered by heavy bombers flying at high altitudes in tight formation. The targets were specific, worked out after a careful, if ultimately volatile and somewhat flawed, analysis of the strengths and weaknesses of Germany's war production industries. It was a policy which owed something to the traditional US reverence for the marksmanship of the squirrel rifle of frontier days, when the scarcity of powder and shot put accuracy at a premium – underlined by the fact that the B-17s, the great Flying Fortresses, were, as their name implied, heavy planes, developed for the defence of the US with a good record of safety under attack, but a bomb load of only 4,000 pounds.

The 8th Air Force's first independent raid flew on 17 August 1942 when twelve B-17s took off from Grafton Underwood and six from Polebrook. General Eaker, Commander of the 8th Air Force Bomber Command, was flying the lead plane, 'Yankee Doodle', on a mission to bomb the railway marshalling yards of Rouen in north-east France. (Also flying the mission was Paul W. Tibbets, who, three years later, on 6 August 1945, would pilot the 'Enola Gay', the plane that dropped the Atom Bomb on Hiroshima.) As the only casualty on the Rouen raid was caused by a pigeon smashing into the Plexiglas nose of a returning bomber, and as the target was fairly decisively hit by planes flying a good deal higher than when training in the American desert, where crews were trained to pick off the proverbial pickle barrel, the raid was seen as confirmation of the practicality and effectiveness of daylight precision bombing.

But although daylight precision bombing might be perfectly feasible in the clear skies above the deserts of Texas and Arizona, it was less so in the cloud-filled skies of Europe. The weather in Britain in the autumn and winter of 1942 was so bad that there were only eight days on which it was possible to fly missions.

In 1943 only 14 per cent of USAAF bombs fell within 1,000 feet of the target and only 32 per cent within 2,000 feet and although the figures did improve in 1944, it remained a difficult and imprecise task to bomb a target accurately from 25,000 feet under heavy fire: it was 'like dropping a lump of sugar in a teacup' from a great height. As a US economist remarked after the war: 'nothing was subject to such assault as open agricultural land.'

Strategic targets were set – and then revised – in the light of an analysis of Germany's war industries and their capacity to recover from bomb damage. The top priority was to make the skies as safe as possible for the invasion planned for the spring of 1944. Aircraft factories became number one targets, followed by factories manufacturing ball-bearings (vital in aircraft production), oil refineries, factories producing synthetic rubber and tyres, and military transport vehicles. Submarine construction yards and bases had headed an

*A ball turrett gunner curls himself into his post where he might remain
for the entire mission of five or six hours.*

earlier list, but by the summer of 1943 the submarine menace was beginning to subside,
and in any case, the fifteen-foot concrete submarine pens had proved almost impervious
to aerial bombardment.

The crews were given details of the mission by the various experts involved. Allan
Healey recounts, in his history of the 467th Bomb Group stationed at Rackheath, that

> by map, picture and diagram the whole operation was explained. S-2 (Intelli-
> gence) put on the route, target and expected reaction from flak and fighters, S-3
> (Operation and Planning) gave the operational data; Weather told of the
> conditions to and from the target . . . All [was] cut and dried; an operation of
> death told like a commuter's timetable.

Next came the synchronization of watches or 'time tick': 'The CO would say something
like "Gentlemen, it is now three forty-five minus twenty seconds . . . ten seconds . . .
nine seconds . . . two . . . one . . . hack." ' Finally, navigators were given a special
additional briefing, as bombardiers and radio operators queued up to receive 'flimsy'
sheets of information about their own particular duties.

The crews piled into the equipment room to pull on their flight gear: electrically
heated flying suits – essential for high flying altitudes, given that the temperature could
drop to minus 50 degrees, the planes were unheated and the air rushed in through the
waist gunner's windows (which weren't windows at all but openings cut out of the

No life for a dog. 'Lucky' is sent back to base as his master climbs into his Mustang fighter plane.

fuselage behind the wings). Some airmen refused to wear the suits, because 'when I sweated, I'd short the damned thing out.' On top of the suits came flak jackets, aprons lined with metal panels, and flying jackets, and over the lot, bulky 'Mae Wests', inflatable life jackets named after the film star 'for obvious reasons'. Sheepskin-lined boots, helmets with earpieces and an oxygen mask, a throat microphone on an elastic band round the neck, and a parachute completed the outfit. At least one airman always checked his pack as he strapped it on, after hearing rumours of GI-issue blankets being stuffed into the pack after the parachute itself had been given away to a girlfriend – for silk was much in demand to make dresses during wartime rationing. An aircrew would routinely check their oxygen supply, including the portable bottles they used if they needed to move around the plane; at the altitude the crews would be flying, oxygen was as essential to the men as petrol was to the planes. An escape pack, containing a phrase card in English, German and French and four photographs in civilian clothes, would be slipped into a special zip pocket at the knee of their trousers so that there would be no danger of losing it if they had to bale out, and sometimes a small knife between their shoes and flying boots. Like all US servicemen, each airman wore two dog tags round his neck giving his name and army number. In case of death, if the body was recovered, one would be hung on a rifle or a branch above a temporary grave so that the body could be located later and interred in a permanent cemetery, for no GIs were buried on Axis soil; the other would be sent back to the US as proof of identification. For Jews flying on missions over Germany the dog tags were often 'edited' for fear that their owners would suffer from Nazi anti-Semitic persecution if they were captured; an armaments officer from Grafton Underwood, who volunteered to fly on several missions, Nathan Mazer, had his dog tag read 'Nathan Mac Mazer'.

Then it was out on to the runways to 'hurry up and wait'; sometimes for a tense hour or more – with checks run and ready to go, but dependent on the weatherman. If, at the last moment, it was decided to scrub the mission, red flares would be fired from the operations buildings; green flares going up meant start the engines and be ready to taxi out. No one was pleased by a scrubbed mission at this stage: 'we didn't feel relieved. We felt cheated.'

On the flight deck were the pilot and the co-pilot, who flew forward on the deck, elevated above the bomb bay and shielded by a bulkhead of armour plating from bursts of flak coming from the rear. The radio operator had his equipment lined along the wall behind the co-pilot, the flight engineer was up on the flight deck too, though in combat he would take up a position as a top turret gunner. The turrets were the most hazardous positions to fly, not only because they were the most exposed but also because if it became necessary to bale out, it took time to squeeze through the narrow opening. The worst of the four turret positions was the ball gunner's. He was usually about eighteen or nineteen and agile; once the plane had taken off he had to curl up inside the ball turret, then the doors were shut and he was cranked down below the belly of the plane. Apart from a tiny escape hatch, he could not get out until he was cranked back up. If the hydraulic mechanism was shot up, he had to be cranked up manually before the plane could land. 'A threat of being court-martialled and a stick of dynamite' could not have forced John McClane, a navigator with the 44th Bomb Group, into what his 'mind's eye perceived as a death trap'. The navigator and the bombardier sat in the nose of the plane

'And all who fly in her.' The padre blesses the crew of a B-17 Flying Fortress at the start of a bombing raid.

with the map of Hitler's Europe spread out below them – if they cared to look. One navigator remembers that he kept his helmet jammed down over his eyes so that he could see his instruments, but not the flak and fighter planes the crew seemed to fly straight into. Others worked at a small table facing the tail of the plane – usually with a view of the pilot's legs. Two gunners stood at the waist of the plane, each manning a .50-calibre gun. The aircraft would get bitterly cold at 20–30,000 feet so that even when they had to take off their sheepskin gloves to do some task, the men never removed the silk gloves they wore underneath; at that temperature, their skin would stick to the metal.

The USAAF flew two types of heavy bomber to war in Europe. The 8th Air Force regarded the B-17s with particular pride; they symbolized US air power in the minds of the Press and public alike and they were perceived to be almost as safe as their soubriquet of 'Flying Fortress' suggested. They were, indeed, capable of withstanding a considerable amount of enemy damage. Fortresses limped home from raids with huge holes in their fuselages, wingtips missing, propellers distorted and tail spans hanging. But whereas the British Lancaster could carry 17,000 pounds of bombs, the B-17s could take only 4,000.

The four-engined B-24s, the 'Liberators', which could carry up to 8,000 pounds of bombs, began to arrive in England in September 1942, and there was much rivalry between their crews and those of the B-17s. The planes were stationed at different bases to accommodate their different servicing needs and operational requirements. The 1st Division of the 8th Air Force, which spread over Cambridgeshire, Huntingdonshire, Northamptonshire and Bedfordshire, flew B-17s; the 2nd Division, stationed mainly in Norfolk, flew B-24s; the 3rd Division, with bases in Norfolk, Suffolk and Essex, was a mixture of both up to August 1944, but thereafter only B-17s stood on its fields.

The B-17 crews mocked the B-24s' squat appearance and insisted that they were actually the crates in which their own planes had been shipped to England. 'On the ground it looked like a flying-boat out of water,' admitted a navigator who flew B-24s from Seething, 'it wasn't very photogenic.' The men who flew the Liberators deprecated the Flying Fortresses as 'medium bombers' because of their smaller bomb capacity, while the B-17 crews responded that the Liberators were 'pregnant cows'. The Liberator had fewer guns than the Fortress, but carried a much heavier bomb load and also flew faster at medium altitudes. However, at the higher altitudes at which the USAAF operated – incurring the scorn of the RAF, who sneered that the only injuries they were likely to sustain would be frostbite – the B-24s were slower and found it harder to keep stable in formation.

The same crews usually flew the same planes, until they were damaged beyond repair, and they 'customized' their craft. Most had names: the choice was the pilot's. As in Randall Jarrell's poem:

> In bombers named for girls, we burned
> The cities we had learned about in schools
> Till our lives wore out . . .

There was 'Beau Jac' (for beautiful Jacqueline), 'Suzy Q' (a pilot's daughter), 'Ginger' (a red-headed girlfriend), the famous 'Memphis Belle' (named for a good friend of the Tennessee pilot), 'Sweet Pea' (the nickname of the little girl whom the 306th Bomb Group had 'adopted' under the auspices of the *Stars and Stripes* Orphan Fund), 'Miss Mickey Finn' (a compliment to the knockout punch someone's woman packed), 'Piccadilly Lilly', 'Lili Marlene', 'Ice-Cold Katie' (after the popular song 'Ice-Cold Katie with a Floy Floy'; though none of the crew of this plane from the 448th Bomb Group was really sure what a 'floy floy' was). Sometimes the names were macho: 'Dog Breath', 'Hellzadroppin', 'The Avenger', 'Dry Martini', 'The Playboy', 'Wahoo', 'Holy Joe', 'Flaming Marines', 'Wolves Inc', 'Eight Ball' (though after a devastating attack when it limped home on two engines with a wing half torn off, this plane was rechristened 'No Balls At All'). Sometimes they were jokes: 'Purty Baby', 'Mountin' Time', 'Virgin on the Verge', 'Iza Available'; a tail gunner had stencilled between the guns of a B-17, 'It's more blessed to give than to receive.' Sometimes they were more than a little obscure: 'Tondelayo', a plane named by a pilot in the 379th Bomb Group, was called after a character Hedy Lamar played in *White Cargo*. Sometimes they had a touch of nobility; the 388th Bomb Group stationed at Knettishall flew a plane inscribed with the name 'Tom Paine' in honour of the author of *The Rights of Man* who had been born in Thetford, Norfolk, and went to Pennsylvania in 1774. It bore his statement that 'Tyranny, like Hell, is not easily conquered.' And sometimes they were simply accurate – like the plane christened 'Flak Magnet'.

Many of the planes were decorated with fine examples of 'nose art'. There were pin-ups of luscious, if sometimes improbable, ladies in the airbrush style of Petty and Vargas; cartoon characters – an illustrator who had worked at Walt Disney's studio in Hollywood emblazoned his plane with Mickey Mouse, Pluto and Donald Duck – and fierce figures of menace comparable to the ancient bowsprits of Japanese warships. Originally, the planes had been painted olive drab, with the division's symbol and the bomb group's identifying letter stencilled on the tail, and the squadron codes in large letters on the fuselage, but from April 1944 new planes came in a natural silver metal, with the tails painted in the group's colours.

Despite the bravado, the airmen were well aware of the dangers. 'You weren't a bit scared. You were a helluva lot scared – every mission – and fear took a quantum leap the nearer the end of your tour you got.' A group commander in the 8th Air Force saw an advertisement in a magazine which asked: 'Who's afraid of the new Focke-Wulf?' referring to the Luftwaffe fighter plane. He cut out the advertisement, signed it and pinned it to the bulletin board. The entire group signed as well, and then it was posted back to the advertiser in the United States. 'They have a saying that nobody's afraid on his first five raids, and he's only moderately afraid on his next ten raids, but that he really sweats out all the rest of them,' was how it was for a bombardier from Oregon who won a Purple Heart for injuries he received on a raid over Augsburg.

John McClane, a navigator who was stationed at Shipdham, thought that anyone who believed that

> a mission was like they show it in the movies with a gunner shooting down one of the attacking fighter planes and saying something to the effect of, 'That's for my buddy, Joe, come on you SOBs and I'll give you the same medicine,' must believe in the tooth fairy also. The truth is that bomber crews were in an extreme state of fear and the only thing on their minds was the hope that the Nazis would break off the action before they were shot down.

There may not be any atheists in a foxhole, there certainly weren't many atheists on a bombing mission. Few were the airmen who didn't pray at one time or other, 'Please God, you gotta get me through this one.' As all fliers insist, 'there was no hierarchy on a mission'; each member of the crew was only too well aware of how much he depended on the others.

Elmer Bendiner expressed the philosophy that kept crews flying:

> You know it's going to happen to somebody, but it's not going to happen to you. It's going to happen to the other guy . . . I was certain that I would survive . . . but only if I followed my private ritual. Only if I went out and found a poppy to put in my buttonhole. I had worn poppies before and survived. I am a reasonable man, but in matters of life and death I do not exclude talismans.

The crews were often highly superstitious, even ritualistic: they would dress for a mission taking extreme care to put on their clothes and equipment in exactly the same order as they had on every previous raid; some insisted on using exactly the same latrine at the same hour; more than one would always wear odd socks. A navigator had a doll he'd take on every raid – 'and the one time he forgot, he didn't come back!' Another 'flyboy' wore the same scarf around his neck on each flight – a silk strip torn from a parachute that had saved his life on an earlier mission.

Other rituals developed. At Thurleigh, in Bedfordshire, wartime home of the 306th Bomb Group, airmen often bought eggs from a farmer's wife, Mrs Payne, and the legend grew that everyone who bought eggs from her before a raid would return home safely. In the bars and mess halls there were other customs to be observed, such as a Toby jug turned to face the wall when the crews left and only turned round again on their safe return. One day when a stray cat that patrolled the base at Seething didn't turn up to 'see the crew off', as it had seemed to do on every previous raid, the crew were very apprehensive; in the event the mission was aborted before it reached France because of bad weather.

Once these rituals had been observed, the briefing absorbed and the mechanical checks completed, the crew was ready. At the green flare, the planes would taxi down the runways ready for take-off. Bitter experience had taught the necessity of the 'big birds' flying in tight formation as protection against Luftwaffe fighter planes, so very precise instructions had to be given and followed to ensure that planes taking off from different airfields dotted over East Anglia converged in pattern ready for the flight across the Channel. An assembly plane would fly ahead as their marker. This was usually a 'tired old plane' that was no longer in combat use, brightly painted in yellow and black chequerboard squares or in stripes or dots to make it easy to follow. At each base, the planes took off at thirty-second intervals when the weather was clear – and waited a further thirty seconds if it wasn't. They would then fly straight ahead for a given time, climbing in altitude as they did so, turn above the assembly point – the Wash, for example – and form the squadron into a box formation, and then the squadron would form a group, and this group would link with other groups to fill the air with the drone of aircraft. The complete formation would set off: 'with contrails forming at the wingtips of hundreds of planes, the beauty of the sight would have to be seen to be comprehended.' Forming up was an exacting and demanding task for both pilots and navigators. Collisions at this stage were not infrequent – perhaps 5 per cent of the 8th Air Force, some 300 planes, were lost in accidents during assembly.

The formations were plotted round the clock so that they could be identified over the radio: 'enemy fighters at twelve o'clock high; two o'clock low, pull back into formation.' The most experienced pilot, co-pilot and crew usually flew the lead plane and the newest replacements on base took the last position. The wingmen flew at 'coffin corner' or the 'Purple Heart' position – the low rear left – which had the least protection from the other planes in the formation from attack by enemy fighters.

Once the planes had been organized in the familiar V-shaped formation, they set out across the Channel, noticing to their relief that at this point they were surrounded by their 'little friends' – fighter escort planes, which were stationed further forward, nearer the coast.

As the formation flew across the sea, climbing to about 20,000 feet, each plane tested its weapons – tail guns, turret guns, bombardier guns – until the North Sea 'must have had a solid lead bottom'.

The planes did not fly straight to the target, but took a 'Cook's tour' to keep the Luftwaffe guessing where to concentrate their defences. John McClane recalls that

Nose art. 'Buffalo Gal', one of the planes belonging to the 448th Bomb Group stationed at Seething in Norfolk.

we would fly towards a particular potential target, only to turn in another direction about the time the Germans had alerted their AA [anti-aircraft] batteries and fighters . . . Sometimes the city we pointed towards would already be throwing up a flak barrage even though we had no intention of making this our target. Somehow this seemed to amuse us.

Once the planes had crossed the coast of the continent, they would often run into flak from German anti-aircraft guns. A navigator, Frank Nelson, recalled his first mission in *One Last Look*:

Sitting up there, looking around and really sort of enjoying myself, I leaned forward to get a better look at Europe. Just as I did, it sounded like someone had fired a forty-five pistol beside my ear. I looked round and saw a big hole in one side of my compartment and another big hole in the other. The piece of flak that had made them had gone exactly where my head had been a moment ago. That, by golly, impressed me.

The crews hated flak even more than enemy fighters. They could fight back at planes, but all they could do with flak was to fly through it and hope. The flak charts handed out at the briefings were supposed to help the crews to avoid the heaviest concentrations, but flak would often come up when the men were least expecting it in ominous black spurts

The ground crew watch as an 8th Air Force plane leaves on a mission, knowing that their job is done and that it's over to the air crew now.

which sounded like pebbles on the metal of the aircraft. Its effect could be devastating, ripping holes in the fuselage, tearing off tails and wingtips, and penetrating the fuselage in a rain of steel splinters.

The airmen were confounded by the flak. 'They always seemed to know where you were going – I don't know how the hell they knew, but they always did.' In an attempt to confuse the radar the waist gunners would toss 'chaff' or 'window' – bundles of metalized strips – out of their planes, falling like confetti on to the ground below. It was said that the streets of some German cities were covered in chaff, like a glittering sea of ticker tape. An Iowan airman recalls:

> Presumably this distorted the German aim, and perhaps it did, but we still almost always came back with flak holes in our plane . . . Berlin, Munich, Bremen, Hamburg, Schweinfurt . . . were [places] which put up an apparently impenetrable carpet of flak over their cities as we approached and we somehow flew right into and out of that carpet after dropping our bombs, and many of us survived the experience.

As the formation of bombers approached their assigned target, they were 'sitting ducks for enemy ground fire, sometimes as many as 300 guns were trained on the ships and many didn't make it through the carpet.' John McClane explains:

We could take evasive action after we had dropped our bombs but on the bomb run from the IP (Initial Point) to the drop point, the bombardier took control of the plane with his bomb sight. His concentration was 100 per cent through the sight tracking the target. The flak would be exploding all around us, planes could be burning, wings coming off, men parachuting through the sky but the bombardier could not care less. His job was to make the effort all the ground personnel and the flight crews [had made] worth the cost. What would be the use of going through all this if the bomb load was not on target? The rest of us were helpless, the pilots were not flying the plane, the gunners were not defending us. I had no navigation to consider until after bombs away. We were sitting ducks . . . The Germans had some psychological tricks . . . on one mission over northern France, the flak exploded with red smoke instead of black. It did not make the flak more deadly, but [it] sure as heck scared the fire out of us not knowing what it was . . . When the action got hot and heavy, even though it was 40 degrees below zero or more, I would always perspire so heavily that sweat would come out from under my flight helmet and freeze along my forehead. I would pick the ice off with my fingers when the action was over.

Flak accounted for a third of bombers lost and two-thirds of those damaged in 1943. Between June and August 1944, two-thirds of the 700 bombers lost were due to flak, and 98 per cent of the damage was flak damage. The Luftwaffe was the other hazard. On outward missions, the fighter escort P-47s, Thunderbolts, and P-38s, Lightnings, would have to fall away before the German border. This left the Forts and the Liberators to fly on alone, trying to keep in tight formation – their only defence against the attacks of Messerschmitts and Focke-Wulfs. The German fighters would attack by flying straight at the nose of the first plane in the convoy, shells volleying from their wings, in an attempt to break up the formation and stop it reaching its target. The only response the B-17s and B-24s could muster was to return fire from the front guns and the top and ball-turret gunners – not very effectively.

The crux of the problem was that the targets the Allies most needed to hit lay deep in the heart of Germany – areas that were beyond the range of fighter escorts until 1944. Throughout the summer and autumn of 1943, US 8th Air Force losses were devastatingly heavy: sixteen of the 107 B-17s sent to attack an aircraft factory at Bremen in April 1943 were brought down, and that meant the loss of 160 highly trained flyers. On 17 August 1943 (the anniversary of the first 8th Air Force raid) the raids on the plant at Schweinfurt which produced over half the ball-bearings made in Germany, and on the Messerschmitt aircraft complex at nearby Regensburg, were the deepest penetration into enemy territory to date – and they were very costly. Although 315 US bombers dropped 724 tons of bombs, 36 planes were lost in air combat over Regensburg and 24 over Schweinfurt, a further 17 were classed as 'E' Category – damaged beyond economical repair – and 121 needed major repairs before they were fit to fly again. On 6 September 1943, 45 out of the 386 Flying Fortresses that set off never returned. On 'Black Thursday', 14 October 1943, 291 Flying Fortresses flew on deep penetration raids into Germany: only 30 returned undamaged and 62 were lost. Overall the 8th Air Force lost 148 planes that week. The strategy of daylight bombing seemed to be incurring unacceptably heavy losses.

Debriefing. Crews stationed at Grafton Underwood, Northamptonshire, relive the mission they have just completed.

Meanwhile, the Luftwaffe was still expanding in strength and growing in combat sophistication. For the 8th Air Force, partial cover was not much of an improvement on no cover at all as an attack on Rennes in April 1943 demonstrated when German fighters waited until the P-47 escort planes had turned homewards before attacking, with the loss of six US planes. The addition of drop fuel tanks made of paper or light metal increased the fighters' range by about 100 miles, but it was not until early 1944 that a plane was developed that was capable both of accompanying the bombers as far as Berlin and back, and engaging in high-altitude, fuel-consuming dog-fights. The P-51 Mustang, yoking a new, highly powered British engine to an American craft, had the necessary range and could also reach speeds of 440 miles an hour; it was reported that when Goering first saw the Mustangs escorting a USAAF formation he declared flatly: 'We have lost the war.'

There was reputed to be a bombardier with the 448th Bomb Group who would sleep peacefully throughout the flak assaults and the fighter attacks, only to jerk awake as the B-24 neared its target and it was time for him to play his vital part in the mission. In the early days of bomber raids, individual bombardiers released their bombs over the target whenever they considered this would be most effective, but bombing was soon systematized: highly qualified crew flew the lead squadron and set the bombing pattern by

One of theirs. An 8th Air Force captain tabling another Luftwaffe plane shot down by his fighter.

dropping smoke-streamers at the bomb-away point; then the rest of the group opened their doors simultaneously at the scheduled altitude on receiving the order 'Bombs away'. Towards the end of the war, loads of around 4,000 tons of bombs rained down on ball-bearing factories, marshalling yards, aircraft factories, oil refineries, or whatever that particular day's target was.

The planes would remain over the target for several minutes until all their bombs had been released; then they would turn and head for a prearranged location, where they would try to pull themselves back into formation for the long flight back to base, through a renewed barrage of flak and fighter plane attacks.

While the planes were in the skies over Europe, the ground crews were 'sweating out' the mission, calculating when the planes might be expected back. The crews and the base staff would strain their ears for the low drone of the returning bombers and scan the skies for the first plane to appear over the horizon, with the once-neat formation now straggling, battered and damaged 'like geese who had flown over too many hunters' guns'. Some planes made it on only three of their four engines, with lacerated tail wings or gaping holes in the fuselages. Ambulances and rescue trucks would be lined up on the runway perimeter in readiness; planes carrying dead or injured crew would fire off a double red flare so that the other planes would hold back, allowing them to land first while the rescue services raced across the tarmac with their fire-fighting equipment, stretchers and plasma.

The navigator (left) and pilot (wearing a flak jacket) inspect the flak damage to 'Miss Emily', a B-26 Marauder medium bomber.

Landing was always dangerous – particularly with a damaged plane. Sometimes the brakes would fail and the plane would go screaming off the runway and end up safely in a field of turnips if the crew were lucky, or combust and turn into a lethal inferno in seconds; sometimes the wheels would jam, or only one would descend, and the plane could veer over or be forced to make a belly landing.

Some planes just managed to limp across the Channel and put down at another airfield – RAF or USAAF, and there would be an anxious time until the base phone rang.

Some planes had been hit, but their crews managed to bale out. It was easier to get out of a Fort or a Liberator than an RAF Lancaster bomber, which was notoriously difficult for a pilot to escape from. If the crew managed to get their parachutes open in time – airmen were instructed to hold off pulling the rip cord until the last possible moment, so that German fighters wouldn't be able to follow the ballooning parachutes down – and if they weren't sucked back by the engine stream, they might well land on the ground to face death or capture in Germany or occupied Europe.

If they were unfortunate enough to land in the sea, the airmen would inflate their Mae Wests, which contained a phial of dye to colour the water in the area around them, to make it easier for searching rescue craft to locate them. Four and a half thousand 8th Air Force crewmen came down in the North Sea or the Channel – they had precisely thirty seconds to get out of their ditched plane if it came down with them – of whom 35 per cent were rescued. Ernie Pyle relates how whenever a flier was pulled out of the

'IT *COULD* BE DONE . . .'

The 'Memphis Belle', the first 8th Air Force plane to complete twenty-five operational missions, leaves Bassingbourn, Cambridgeshire, on 9 June 1943 to return to the US for a fund- and morale-raising tour.

North Sea or the Channel, his RAF rescuers would give him a little felt insignia of a fish skipping over water – the membership badge of the 'Goldfish Club' – to be sewn *under* one's lapel.

The local population, too, would 'count them out and count them back'. Aircraft recognition ousted birdwatching as a country pursuit; local people often felt very proprietary about 'their boys', who had often become part of the community, and saddened when planes did not return.

Invariably, there were some planes that did not. The Reverend James Good Brown, the chaplain at Ridgewell, remembered the CO standing on the upper walk of the control tower scanning the horizon:

> It was the ETA [estimated time of arrival]. We saw in the distance tiny objects which we thought were 'our' planes. When they got close enough, we began to count. We had sent out twenty-one planes: only nineteen returned. The men's faces at my side turned a grayish colour – but they kept back the tears. They were not prepared for that shock on our very first mission.

On the day that the 95th Bomb Group lost 10 planes and 103 men, the CO at Framlingham paced up and down in despair with tears in his eyes, repeating, 'What's happened to my boys? What's happened to my boys?'

'BUT THE ODDS WERE AGAINST . . .'

In June 1943, the sad task of packing up the kit of a pilot who did not return from a mission fell to his fellow officer. It was returned to his grieving family in the US, and by next morning he would have been 'replaced' on the base.

Sometimes, the losses seemed almost insupportable. James Good Brown recorded that:

> We arrived on June 5th 1943. We flew our first mission on June 22nd 1943. We had lost half our group by August 17th . . . we had lost the other half by October . . . from here on we were an entirely new outfit. The name 381st remains the same. The flying personnel is different. No longer can it be looked on as a family . . . replacements now come in almost every day and before we learn to know them, they have gone in combat.

A navigator at Grafton Underwood eventually refused to eat in the flying officers' mess: there had been so many losses that 'I didn't know any of them anymore. I ate with the ground crew instead. They were still the same men as when I'd arrived.' After the raid from which a hundred men of the 381st Bomb Group at Ridgewell never came back, 'morning brought a severe letdown in morale. Very few men showed up . . . the usual chatter and banter was absent. We ate in silence. I found myself looking round for faces that I knew I would never see again,' wrote the group's chaplain.

One group had sent out ten planes as part of the 8th Air Force's first major mission to Berlin on 4 March 1944 to have only two return. As a result, a seventeen-year-old gunner found himself the oldest gunner in the squadron. In general the crews were very young: gunners eighteen or nineteen, pilots of twenty-one or -two, and anyone over thirty was liable to be known as 'Pop' or 'Pappy'. And many of them were never going to get much older; in 1943 and 1944, the average life of an 8th Air Force bomber crew was fifteen missions. To begin with, the assigned tour of duty was twenty-five missions. Death provided the shortfall. As a navigator who had been an actuary pointed out: 'Mathematically there just ain't any way we're going to live through this thing.'

In late 1943 the tour of duty was extended to thirty missions. For Joseph Hallock, a bombardier who had been counting off his missions, this was almost unbearable:

> at about the halfway mark, the number of missions we'd have to fly was raised from twenty-five to thirty. That was one hell of a heartbreaker. Supposedly they'd changed the rules because flying had got safer, but you couldn't make us think in terms of being safer. Those extra five raids might as well have been fifty.

Too many missions had the same consequences: there would be a space left on the hard-standing; someone would have the unenviable task of going through an airman's locker and sending all that it was deemed suitable to send home to his wife or family; and the base commander would have to sit down and write the letters he could never get used to writing – 'I very much regret to inform you . . .' Half of all the US Army Air Force casualties in all the theatres of the Second World War were incurred by the 8th Air Force. During the 1,008 days that the 'mighty Eighth' was in action, it lost nearly 5,000 planes and sustained over 45,000 dead, wounded and missing in the battle of the air.

> . . . our bodies lay among
> The people we had killed and never seen.
> When we lasted long enough they gave us medals
> When we died they said, 'Our casualties were low.'

wrote Randall Jarrell.

For those who survived to clamber out of their planes after a mission which could have lasted some eight to ten hours – giving a premium to those who 'could hold water like a camel' – the first welcome sight to greet them was often the Clubmobile with coffee and doughnuts. Then the crews would be picked up by truck and taken back to the base to be debriefed. They were given a shot of whisky, or more if there was call for it: a gunner recalls that once

> we were forty-five minutes overdue at the base and everyone had almost stopped looking for us. We had only one engine and a big hole in the fuselage. Part of a wing was gone . . . The thing I remember most was when I got out of the plane they had a whole bottle of scotch waiting for us.

Then each crew would be interrogated by the intelligence officer. They were quizzed about the mission: what had they seen of the raid? had they hit the target? how many times? had they seen any of the 8th's planes go down? had any crew managed to bale out? where? were the Luftwaffe doing anything differently these days? had they hit any Focke-Wulfs? how many? Everyone had a different story. After hours in the air, the crews were stiff, frozen, exhausted, stunned and shaken by their experiences and relieved to be alive. They gave their estimates of the success of the raid, how many parachutes they'd seen and the number of German planes they'd destroyed or disabled – in the confusion of the battle, these were often optimistic, with several crews sometimes claiming the same plane. The film from the automatic cameras sited on the bomb bay was developed and analysed, and this gave a clearer picture of the damage. 'The results of the interrogation were never made known to us,' recalls William Ruck, a radio operator with the 448th Bomb Group who flew thirty missions from Seething:

> After interrogation we would go back to our barracks and a few other crews might join us to talk it over, but we never had a complete picture. If a plane was shot down, a new plane was in its place the next morning. If a crew didn't return from a mission their personal effects were packed up immediately and a new crew installed in their barracks, so there was always the same number of planes on the field and the same number of people in the squadron. Unless you personally knew the men who didn't return from a mission, you never really knew they had gone. The German news broadcasts would quote a ridiculously high figure for 8th losses after a raid, and the BBC news would quote a ridiculously low number of losses for the same raid. Only the commanders knew and they weren't letting anyone know except *their* commanders.

Then it was back to their hut to rest, with an awareness of the empty beds and the knowledge that there would probably be another alert in twenty-four hours. If the weather was bad, with endless cloud and heavy rain, it could take crews many months to clock up the twenty-five or thirty missions that would enable them to go home, but for some, when the weather held, it could be a matter of four or five stressful months.

Yet as Crew Number 21 of 713 Bomb Squadron, 448th Bomb Group, flew to bomb the Normandy beaches on D-Day, their radio operator looked down as they crossed the Channel and 'couldn't help but think that we had only two missions to go and our combat war would be over, while the troops down there were just beginning theirs . . .'

CHAPTER SIXTEEN

OPERATION OVERLOAD

I CAN RECALL SO VIVIDLY waking very early one morning to the rumble of heavy vehicles and racing to the front windows to see what appeared to be a never-ending convoy of young men in full battle order on vehicles of every description. Gone were the devil-may-care young men we had known so well who only two nights ago had come to say their fond farewells,' recalls a woman whose parents kept an hotel in Bude in Cornwall during the war: 'We had no idea that this was to be more than just another exercise, but within four days they were in France.'

'Every day over the past year we'd heard the bombers go out, and every evening we had heard them return home. But that day there was something different about the familiar sound,' remembers Jean Lancaster Rennie, who watched from her wartime home in Norfolk:

> It was different enough to send us, at dawn, from our beds to windows that looked out on chimney pots and slates and beyond to the clear blue sky with tiny white clouds, playing among the glitter of new bombers – and the dull glare of old ones as sunbeams glanced across the nose cones . . . They seemed to come from nowhere . . . In perfect, geometric formation, they roared overhead . . . they kept coming and coming . . . as if the whole sky belonged to them as they roared away to deal death and destruction.

It was D-Day, 6 June 1944. The major operation of the war had started: the Allied troops were crossing the Channel in a desperate assault on Hitler's 'Fortress Europe'. The US troops in Britain, who by now totalled 1,526,965, had always known that their only way home lay across the beaches of France and that they were going to have to fight all the way. Now the fight was starting – and many of them would never make it.

It was the climax of Operation BOLERO, for in addition to the million and a half troops stationed in the United Kingdom, equipment and supplies had been pouring into the country in preparation for the invasion. The south of England had become an arsenal. Tanks, trucks, amphibious craft and Jeeps were lined up in serried ranks on parking lots and in fields. Planes and gliders stood, wingtips touching, on the airfields. Troops near Greenham Common in Berkshire took advantage of the imports to move out of their mud-lapped tents and into a snug, dry packing-case city, converted from the crates in which the gliders had been delivered for assembly. Bombs, weapons, ammunition and other supplies were crammed into every available storage space, and spilt out to be

OPERATION OVERLOAD

TRAINING FOR D-DAY

BELOW *GIs in full kit and equipment navigate the Serpentine in London's Hyde Park.*

BOTTOM *Scaling rope ladders as practice for shinning down ships to landing craft and up the cliffs of the Normandy beaches.*

stacked in endless rows along the roadsides and byways of the country. The invasion was officially code-named Operation OVERLORD, but it soon became Operation OVER-LOAD. GIs joked that it was only the barrage balloons that were keeping the British Isles afloat: cut the strings and the country would sink into the sea under the weight of American men and matériel. It was to be the realization of Anglo–American co-operation – and its most acute test.

This co-operation had not been achieved without disagreement, misunderstanding and compromise. Ever since Pearl Harbor, the Americans had been determined to confront Hitler's army on the continent as soon as possible, as part of the logic of their 'Europe First' policy. Roosevelt and his Chiefs of Staff had become increasingly impatient with what they regarded as British vacillations and military sideshows in the Mediterranean which deflected men and equipment from what the US believed to be the essential strategy of an all-out attack on the coast of France, deliberately planned for a fixed future date. In contrast, right up to the eve of D-Day, the British, who had had experience of the German Wehrmacht in 1940, were more inclined to proceed cautiously in a series of attacks rather than to launch an all-or-nothing assault. In the autumn of 1943, the US Chiefs of Staff claimed that the British had come to believe that

> OVERLORD is no longer necessary . . . in their view continued Mediterranean operations coupled with POINTBLANK [the combined Allied Bombing Offensive] and the crushing of the Russian offensive, will be sufficient to cause the internal collapse of Germany and thus bring about her military defeat without undergoing what they consider an almost certain 'bloodbath'.

Indeed, in February 1944, Winston Churchill, his worst fears confirmed by the disastrous Dieppe Raid of August 1942 in which over 1,000 Allied troops – mainly Canadian – had been killed, and a further 2,000 taken prisoner and all vehicles and equipment lost, had demanded of his military advisers: 'Why are we trying to do this?' And Sir Alan Brooke, Chief of the Imperial General Staff, wrote on the very eve of D-Day: 'At the best, it will come very short of the expectations of the bulk of the people, namely those who know nothing about its difficulties. At its worst, it may well be the most ghastly disaster of the whole war.' In fact, Churchill had never doubted the necessity of a cross-Channel invasion of Europe: his fears were over the question of timing, and the readiness of men and equipment. Wherever Allied soldiers had confronted the formidable Wehrmacht on terms of comparable strength, the Germans had prevailed. The historically powerful German army had reached its apogee under Hitler, and by May 1944, German war production still made Germany a formidable foe.

At the Teheran Conference in November 1943, under pressure from Stalin who was deeply mistrustful of Allied intentions over a 'second front' which would take the war to Hitler on the Western Front, a date of 1 May 1944 had finally been agreed for D-Day. On 7 December 1943, on his way home from Teheran, Roosevelt stopped off at Tunis to meet Eisenhower. After a great deal of deliberation, Roosevelt had made his decision: 'Well, Ike,' he said, 'you are going to command OVERLORD.'

In planning OVERLORD, Eisenhower shared the conviction of his countrymen that the Germans would only be vanquished on the ground, but nevertheless he was equally aware of the imbalance of trained forces and equipment. Convinced that LCTs (Landing Craft

ON THE MOVE
BELOW *Often there was no time to say goodbye.*
BOTTOM *East End women rush to offer sandwiches and cakes as the
US Army moves off.*

Tanks) – essential equipment for this ambitious amphibious operation – were in short supply since they were still being deployed in the Mediterranean, Eisenhower postponed the date until 5 June 1944.

The final plan was for a seaborne Allied assault by five divisions on a fifty-mile stretch of coast from near Cabourg on the Normandy coast to Quineville on the Cotentin Peninsula. It was neither the closest nor the easiest point of attack, but the natural choice, the Pas de Calais, had been rejected as being too strongly fortified with German troops and defences. The invasion from the sea would be preceded by the drop of three airborne divisions whose mission was to seize and protect the inland exits from the beaches and hold back German reinforcements, and by the bombers from the RAF and the 8th and recently formed 9th US Air Force, which were to bomb beach fortifications just in advance of the landings and give air support to the flotillas.

The US forces would attack on the right flank and would aim to capture the deep-water port of Cherbourg, Brest, and the Loire ports; then, once in Allied hands, it would be possible to reinforce the troops directly by sea from America. The initial US landing force would comprise 130,000 men, with another 1,200,000 to follow within the next three months (D + 90). Convoys of supplies flooded into the British ports – artillery shells from Illinois, Jeeps from Detroit, blood plasma from Tennessee, and cheese and K-rations from Wisconsin. As Max Hastings points out, the GIs were not going to be short of rations, they would be issued with 6¼ pounds a day in contrast to the German soldier's 3½ pounds; on the other hand, a US rifle company would carry 21,000 rounds of ammunition, a German, 56,000.

The fact that the US troops were to form the right flank of the assault meant a massive movement of men and supplies within the United Kingdom. While the 8th Air Force largely continued to operate from its bases in East Anglia, the seaside towns and coves from Dorset along the coast of Devon to the tip of Cornwall became host to hundreds and thousands of combat units and their services, including those moved from elsewhere in Britain and those which now came flooding through British ports every day from Italy and North Africa as well as from the US itself.

Omar Bradley, Commander of the US 1st Army, set up his headquarters at Clifton College, a boys' public school in Bristol. There, with many of his staff forced to cram into beds intended for junior boys, plans were laid under a statute of Earl Haig. This was hardly auspicious; Haig, Commander-in-Chief of the British Armies on the Western Front in the First World War, had won a harsh reputation for profligacy with men's lives.

The twenty US divisions, hundreds and thousands of special forces, corps troops, headquarter troops, lines of communication personnel, and service and supply forces were packed into Nissen and Quonset huts, tents and requisitioned country houses, while officers were often billeted in private houses, to await – and to train for – the invasion of 'the far shore', as the Americans called it.

The relentless influx of troops into areas which normally saw few outsiders other than summer holiday visitors was often an eye-opener for the locals. In Lyme Regis, the Americans took a tin bath to the pub to have it filled with local cider; the inhabitants of Launceston were entertained with a revue called *Dixieland*, staged in the town hall; and in the village of Newlyn, the girls – like young women elsewhere in England before them – were 'delighted at the sudden influx of partners and greatly impressed by the compliments which the GIs gave so naturally . . . We were greatly flattered and it was a new experience in that far end of England.'

John Keegan, who was to grow up to be a distinguished military historian, remembers how the part of the West Country to which he and his family had been evacuated

> overflowed almost overnight with GIs. How different they looked from our own jumble-sale-quality champions, beautifully clothed in smooth khaki as fine in cut and quality as a British officer's . . . and armed with glistening, modern, automatic weapons. Thompson sub-machine guns, Winchester carbines, Garand self-loading rifles. More striking still were the number, size and elegance of the vehicles in which they paraded about the countryside in stately convoy. The British Army's transport was a sad collection of underpowered makeshifts, whose dun paint flaked from their tin-pot bodywork. The Americans travelled in magnificent olive-green, pressed-steel, four-wheel-drive juggernauts, decked with what car salesmen would call optional extras of a sort never seen on their domestic equivalents – deep-treaded spare tyres, winches, towing cables, fire extinguishers. There were towering GMC six-by-sixes, compact and powerful Dodge four-by-fours, and, pilot fishing the rest or buzzing nimbly about the lanes on independent errands like the beach buggies of an era still thirty years ahead, tiny and entrancing Jeeps, caparisoned with whiplash aerials and sketchy canvas hoods which drummed with the rhythm of a cowboy's saddlebags rising and falling to the canter of his horse across the prairie.

Standing by the roadside one day to watch this cavalcade, the young Keegan was thrown 'perhaps a month's rations of sweet things' – Hershey Bars, hard candy, sugar cubes 'casually disbursed in a few seconds' – and concluded that clearly 'something [was] going on in the west of England about which Hitler should be very worried indeed.'

There was an urgent need for more training areas. Although 165,000 acres of farmland had already been requisitioned, the Secretary of State for War had to demand a further 140,000 acres of good agricultural land in Oxfordshire, Hampshire and Wiltshire which, it was considered, would provide the necessary firm sub-soil and natural features essential for realistic training – and that despite the warnings of the Minister of Agriculture that 'it will mean that my efforts to maintain and even increase . . . the 1943 level of home food production will be severely affected.'

A woman who farmed 400 acres at Inkpen in Berkshire had had some of her land requisitioned for the US troops to train – and was not best pleased:

> The troops would arrive in luxury coaches in the morning, leaving them to block the lane all day, walk down the hill to the battle area (apparently American soldiers don't march) and begin the battle. Unfortunately they seldom warned me that they were coming, so sometimes we were at work, ploughing, drilling, threshing and so on in their area, and had to abandon work and beat a hasty retreat to avoid the bullets and shells, all of which was very annoying and disorganizing . . . I don't know how many of their people got shot, it was a miracle they never shot any of us . . . I once saw them using a flame-thrower, a ghastly weapon, and they completely burned up a little spinney with it . . . the

place became strewn with unexploded ammunition . . . they dug slit trenches all over the fields which was a great hazard for the tractors, especially at harvest time when the corn was thick and hid these deep holes.

Charles Cawthon was relocated with his 2nd Battalion of the 116th Infantry Regiment to 'a small wartime British Army camp outside the picture postcard village of Bridestowe on the edge of Dartmoor'. Training

> started off in a fumbling way, for there was only a vague idea as to what we were supposed to do. At first, it was all conducted on land, using homemade mock-ups of landing craft. Dartmoor was probably as good a land area for this as any, for it seemed afloat in rain. Its vast, rolling, pitching stretches of spongy turf were usually clouded in mist – a desolate, eerie, sometimes bleakly beautiful place. We came to know, but never to love, Dartmoor as we tramped across it, shivered in its cold winds and slept on its liquid surface.

The company practised beach assault training – on land: fortified areas, surrounded by barbed wire and riddled with bunkers, were staked out for assault practices, though Cawthon felt 'our efforts seemed unreal then, and even more so looking back on them now.' They marched past the eighteen-foot granite walls of Dartmoor prison, 'where over a century before some five thousand Americans, captured in the War of 1812, had been held in disease and hunger'. After some time spent with wooden mock-ups serving as assault landing craft, while a cargo net hung from the eaves of a building stood for the side of a ship which the troops would need to clamber down to reach the landing craft as they neared Normandy, a beach assault training centre was established at Woolacombe on the north Devon coast, and mechanics were able to practise waterproofing vehicles and fitting the snorkel devices which would enable them to drive through surf. The troops practised as thirty-man boat teams made up of rifle and machine-gun sections – the capacity of a personnel landing craft organized to fight independently against the complexes of bunkers and field fortifications they expected to encounter in the landing areas. The military knew that the Normandy beachheads would be barricaded with barbed wire, defended with bunkers and gun emplacements, made treacherous with mines, and studded with devices known as Rommelsspargel (Rommel's asparagus) – poles sticking out of the sand to prevent gliders landing. But no one knew how many troops or how much heavy artillery lay in wait on the far shore.

The US troops spent most of the winter of 1943–4 training – a training that became more demanding and rigorous as winter turned into the beautiful spring of 1944. Top brass paid frequent unannounced visits to the troops to raise morale, monitor performance and infuse a warlike spirit by making sure that the men remembered exactly where to buckle their helmet straps and never to leave more than a cupful of food in the company garbage can after meals and that they knew off by heart the alignment of gun sights and the procedure for squeezing the trigger, while 'the division's battle cry of "29 Let's *Go*" was a required shout in everything we did,' remembers Cawthon.

John Downing was sent to the west coast of Scotland with his infantry unit to train in amphibious warfare. British veterans of the disastrous Dieppe Raid taught what they had learned the hard way and drummed into US infantrymen that ubiquitous call of the amphibious landing: 'Get off the beach! Get off the beach!' Downing offered up a silent prayer that 'the actual landings would work out better than this maneuver. Our confused stumbling around blindly in the dark of early morning did nothing to increase my confidence in my ability as a combat leader.'

This intensive training was designed to be as like the real thing as possible, so real weapons and live ammunition were used. Inevitably, such authenticity involved tragic accidents. Cawthon visited in hospital a 'particularly handsome H Company lad, sightless for life from a premature explosion of a demolitions charge'. A month or so later, he watched as a beach was being cleared of British anti-invasion mines so that it could be used for practice landings. A soldier from the Ammunition and Pioneer Patrol approached an uncovered mine and touched it with the tip of his boot. 'There was a blinding flash and a clap of sound, and he disappeared as by a magician's sleight of hand. The illusion terminated in pieces of anatomy plopping into the sand around us.'

Invasion exercises designed to simulate landing conditions in France took place on a stretch of shingle beach in Devon known as South Hams. With low-lying ground and a steep cliff, the area provided as similar conditions as possible to those the troops would encounter in Normandy. The villages and hamlets of the area became ghost towns; the population of 3,000 was evacuated so that the troops could practise manoeuvres using live ammunition. The Bishop of Exeter pinned a notice on the boarded-up doors of the village churches exhorting GIs to respect the fact that 'These fields are as dear to those who have left them as are the homes and graves and fields which you, the Allies, have left behind you. They hope to return one day to find them waiting to welcome them home.' The villagers were not permitted to return to their homes until more than two months after D-Day; they found that every window had been broken, Slapton church had received a direct hit, and, despite being well sandbagged, a stained-glass window had been totally shattered.

Six weeks before D-Day came a terrible precursor. Over 700 US soldiers were killed and three tank landing craft were sunk on 28 April 1944, when American troops were training off Slapton Sands in Devon. Nine German E-boats intercepted the convoys on exercise TIGER and roared through firing torpedoes. The LCTs were maimed and powerless, and two sank at once. Apart from the human tragedy, Eisenhower reported that the incident had reduced the reserve of LCTs to nil; there was also a short-lived anxiety that one of the six officers involved, who had information about the D-Day landings, had been taken prisoner and might, under interrogation, reveal vital evidence that could jeopardize the invasion. In fact, all had perished. However, the Germans, realizing that they had devastated a training exercise, were reinforced in their belief that an invasion was imminent.

The element of surprise in the D-Day landings was crucial. Not only was it essential that the Germans should not know when the invasion would take place: above all, they must not know where. An American major-general had blurted out over cocktails that the invasion would take place before 15 June. He was promptly demoted and sent home. Another scare was started when a package of top-secret OVERLORD papers was discovered in a Chicago post office. An inquiry revealed that a sergeant had put the wrong thing in an envelope he had sent home to his sister. On successive days, the *Daily Telegraph* crossword clues included 'OVERLORD', 'OMAHA', 'NEPTUNE' and 'UTAH', the code names of the Allied beaches, but this was soon dismissed as 'coincidence'. On 4 June a teletype operator at Associated Press had practice-typed what was on everyone's mind on what she thought was a disconnected machine. Instead it told New York, and within seconds the 'urgent flash' had gone round the world: EISENHOWER'S HQ AN-NOUNCES ALLIED LANDINGS IN FRANCE. An immediate disclaimer was issued. But nobody knew what German intelligence had picked up.

Operation FORTITUDE was a fantasy invasion force supposedly destined for the Pas de Calais – the most logical place to launch a cross-Channel attack, where many of the German military leaders, though not Hitler himself, expected the Allied landing. To give substance to this deception, General Patton commanded a wholly fictitious 'First Army Group' (FUSAG), which massed in south-east England with a huge array of dummy landing craft, military vehicles, camps and wireless communications, and on D-Day would carry out simultaneous dummy drops of what would appear to be paratroopers armed with firecrackers for simulated gunpower to divert and confuse the Wehrmacht.

On the last days of May, vast columns of men and vehicles blocked the roads of south-west England as they streamed towards the concentration areas. There they were issued with special equipment and their vehicles were waterproofed before taking off for marshalling areas close to the points of embarkation.

Buildings had to be knocked down, roads widened or newly built, bridges strengthened, and hard-standing and lay-bys constructed to accommodate the huge amphibious trucks and gigantic transporters which poured into British ports, laden with tanks and bulldozers. Some unintended demolition occurred when transporters got stuck under road bridges, knocked down parapets and took the corners off innumerable buildings. A Cornish woman recalls a tank which took a wrong turning in Bude

> and got stuck across the bottom of our little road, I suppose they did not have experience of such small roads . . . They called up two more tanks to try to pull clear the one that was stuck. Imagine how those three huge tanks shook our little cottage! My mum flew into the sergeant in charge . . . She won the day and the three tanks were left until they were able to bring special removal trucks the next morning. Two days later there was a knock on the door and there stood the sergeant with a box of 'goodies' for the kids to say how sorry he was for frightening the children.

A teacher in Dorset was particularly alarmed at the sight of a truck carrying two Sherman tanks. 'It must have required tremendous skill, and a heavy engine, to drive this heavy load through our narrow streets. Our narrow country roads were unsuitable for Sherman tanks.' She found the noise of the tanks pulling up the steep hill deafening: 'it was impossible to speak . . . I arranged with the pupils that I would dictate until these tanks drew near, and then they should study their notes while we endured the deafening sound outside.' She recalls that employers gave their staff an extra quarter of an hour for lunch because the town had become so congested with the convoys blocking the narrow streets that it took twice as long to get around.

The troops had never been sure when they were in training whether it was 'the real thing' or just another exercise; now it became increasingly clear that D-Day was fast approaching. Often there wasn't time to say goodbye. A young woman working on a farm

HURRY UP AND WAIT

BELOW *Life goes on in a Southampton household as US vehicles and armour stand ready for departure on 5 June 1944.*

BOTTOM *'Good luck, soldier.' General Dwight D. Eisenhower, Commander in Chief Supreme Allied Forces in Europe, gives a last-minute pep talk to the paratroopers of the 101st Airborne Division stationed at Greenham Common as they prepare to take off for Normandy on 5 June 1944.*

near Chippenham recalls that the GIs from a nearby camp moved off at seven o'clock on a Sunday morning. 'I was on my way to work and . . . got off my bike and stood and waved for a while. Now I'm older I should probably cry with the realization, but then I just accepted that they had not come to sit the whole war out. I had never failed to see an American in the town each time I went to school or work. Now it seemed peculiarly empty.' Robert Arbib met 'his' engineers as he drove up the A1:

> Everywhere along that road, and all the others in England, there were endless convoys of army vehicles – miles and miles of them . . . moving along bumper to bumper – division after division. [The 820th Engineers] had pulled out of their aerodrome in Suffolk, and were headed south, to take part in the invasion. As bulldozers rumbled past, and the motorgraders and the shovels and the trucks, I stood up in the back of the Jeep and shouted and waved. 'So long, Pete! Good luck, Tommy! . . . Take it easy now, John . . . Good luck, good luck!'

As the convoys stopped along the roads, women came out with cups of tea, scones and whatever they could spare for the departing GIs, and in thanks the GIs would fling their small change to the local children, who clamoured for gum to the end.

A GI serving with the chemical division of the supply services at Shepton Mallet found on his return from leave that some of his company, sensing that the invasion was imminent, hadn't waited for the off:

> in the small hours of one morning, they loaded up a Jeep with guns, ammunition and several cases of whiskey. Thus equipped they sallied forth. Quite how they would join the invasion didn't seem to occur to them, for they had neither boats nor water-wings. They were returned to us next morning by the MPs with multiple hangovers – and minus stripes, Jeeps and whiskey.

Finally it *was* time to go and the convoy set off:

> we would drive for five minutes at a time and then stop for what would seem like endless hours . . . It was a miracle that it all worked, as tens and thousands of men and their vehicles slowly funnelled down to the south shore to pick up the places assigned to them. To do it on time and then do it over and over again throughout the hours of daylight and darkness marked a major triumph in the bureaucratic mind.

Elsewhere during that hot and wearing day, the convoy had stopped outside a row of houses where a group of

> men, women and children all stood watching the never-ending column of tanks and trucks manned by their sweating crews. They waved now and then, but to tell the truth, they were waved out. Overcome by the awesome sight of this enormous cavalcade, they just stood still. We somehow became aware of their anxiety and feeling for us. It was as if we had assumed the object of all their hopes and fears for the coming struggle.

However cheerful the troops may have seemed as they drove off in convoys, waving and shouting and showering the children with their last taste of GI candy and gum, many were realistic about the hazards they faced, often leaving addresses – 'you will write to my mom, won't you?' – and prized personal possessions with British families they had got to know. A Sussex woman awoke one morning in early June to find packages on her windowsill left by members of the 4th Cavalry Regiment which had been stationed nearby: these turned out to be 'wallets with mothers' and girls' pictures and suchlike treasures, asking me to take care of them until they could call again'. A Bristol man was charged with the safekeeping of a near-complete set of Shakespeare's plays which a GI billeted with him had been collecting. John Keegan remembers an American soldier his parents befriended asking them to keep safe a small pile of personal possessions which he had collected. When Keegan heard that 'Sontag won't be coming back', the boy inspected the treasure trove to find that it consisted of a GI torch, a webbing belt and a Pocket Book edition on wartime paper of *A Tree Grows in Brooklyn*.

Others faced the possibilities in other ways. Henry Giles ceremoniously burned the letters from the woman he would marry after the war, 'having no way to keep them'. But he had been writing to his fiancée twice a day – 'and I have an almost uncontrollable desire to write more' – though it didn't seem as if much mail was getting through to her in recent weeks, and that which was had clearly been opened, read by the censor and resealed: 'that has never happened before, so she has had her "Alert" too . . . women aren't fools. Stop their mail and they begin to add two and two and come up with four . . . Looks to me as if the top brass might as well have taken full page ads in all the big newspapers and announced the news.'

By the beginning of June, the seaborne assault troops who were going to be the first wave of soldiers across the Channel were confined to marshalling areas close to the embarkation points where they were kept incommunicado behind barbed-wire fences and patrolling sentries. 'If we were prisoners-of-war we couldn't be more closely guarded. There's not only a barbed-wire fence all around the camp, but there are guards posted everywhere . . . It really hits you that the only way out is through France and Germany. It's strictly a one-way road.'

Troops bound for Normandy were issued with life jackets, seasickness pills, gas masks and protective clothing. 'Our invasion uniforms turned out to be impregnated chemically as protection against gas,' recalls an infantryman: 'they felt stiff and uncomfortable and odiferous – and would go slimy when they got wet. The old canvas lace-up leggings still worn at the time got the same treatment. I reckon the Krauts would have smelt us coming if it had been a night landing.'

Each soldier was handed a leaflet about getting on with the French civilians – which included a warning not to mention the defeat of 1940. It wasn't at all well received: 'This is a real lulu. For instance "Some French are good and some are bad" . . . What do they do? Put armbands on 'em so we can tell 'em apart?' *Stars and Stripes*, as usual a lexicon of international understanding, reassured the troops: 'Don't be surprised if a Frenchman steps up to you and kisses you. That doesn't mean he's a queer. It means he's emotional, French and darn glad to see you.'

A recording of a speech by Eisenhower was relayed as the men sat around waiting – and talking: 'What do you think we've had all this training for? They've got us pinpointed,' 'Sure, we'll be the suckers who hit the beaches,' 'They say the Engineers will take 90 per cent casualties,' 'God! do you *have* to talk about it?'

Sergeant Giles reflected that: 'It's a strange feeling . . . to know you're heading for war – really on your way – a very queer, helpless, frightening feeling. But the rent's due and we have to move on.'

Brigadier-General Norman Cota, who had seen action in North Africa, spoke soberly to the advanced HQ group of 29th Division, of which he was deputy commander:

> This is different from any other exercise that you've had so far. The little discrepancies that we tried to correct on Slapton Sands are going to be magnified and are going to give way to incidents that you at first may view as chaotic. The air and naval bombardments are reassuring. But you're going to find confusion. The landing craft aren't going in on schedule, and people are going to be landed in the wrong place. Some won't be landed at all. The enemy will try, and will have some success, in preventing our gaining lodgement. But we will improvise, carry on, not lose our heads.

Cota was right. That's how it would be.

CHAPTER SEVENTEEN

THE FAR SHORE

BY 4 JUNE 1944 EVERYTHING WAS READY for D-Day, planned for the next day. The men who were to be the first wave of invaders on the Normandy beaches were packed tight in their transports with too much to carry, too much to wear and much too much time to think.

But the weather wasn't ready. The sea was rough, there was a strong wind and driving rain, and the sky was too overcast to allow the use of the air forces. This was the decisive factor – the vulnerability of the ground troops required heavy air cover to storm the Normandy beaches. In the early hours of Sunday, 4 June, Eisenhower took the decision to postpone the invasion for twenty-four hours. The US and British fleets were pulled back to port to refuel and to wait. For the men already cramped in their transport ships it meant another night of discomfort, boredom and apprehension.

During the day, the weather did not improve much: the sea was still rough and the sky overcast, and the wind whipped the craft waiting in harbour. The forecast was uncertain, but it did look as if there would be sufficient break in the cloud to permit bombing on Monday night – 5 June – though the cloud would close in again on the Tuesday. It certainly wasn't the weather anybody would have chosen for an invasion, but if it were tolerable Eisenhower knew they would have to go. If he didn't go the next day, tidal conditions would mean that the invasion couldn't be launched until 19 June, a wait of nearly two more weeks. That would mean that the troops would have to disembark and hang around a confined, sealed area, eroding their morale further and endangering security. There would be no moon for the parachute drop, and two weeks of good fighting weather would be lost. Moreover, though the Allies could not be sure of this, the German forces were as yet only in that state of 'defensive readiness' that they had been all spring. It couldn't last: the German commanders knew an invasion was near but they considered the weather was too bad for the Allies to attempt a Channel crossing. Indeed, the weather had inhibited the Luftwaffe from flying air reconnaissance flights during the first five days of June, and had caused German naval patrols and mine-laying operations for the night of 5–6 June to be cancelled. Moreover German intelligence had effectively ignored the signal they had been told was to alert the Resistance forces to prepare for an invasion – the broadcast of a verse from Paul Verlaine's poem 'Chanson d'Automne'. The first line, *Les sanglots longs des violons*, had been broadcast by the BBC on 1 June; on 4 June it transmitted the second, *Blessent mon coeur d'une langueur monotone*, which signalled that the invasion was less than forty-eight hours away. Intelligence informed the German High

Command: Rommel had set off in the opposite direction, home to celebrate his wife's birthday and to get in touch with Hitler about stepping up the mobile response troops.

The Allied High Command met again that evening to consider the situation. As Eisenhower put it: 'the question is, how long can you hang this operation on the end of a limb and let it hang there?' At quarter to ten on the night of Sunday, 4 June 1944, he announced his decision: 'I'm quite positive that we must give the order . . . I don't like it, but there it is . . . I don't see how we can possibly do anything else.' The invasion was on for 6 June.

Then he sat at his portable table and scrawled a press release on a piece of paper: 'Our landings . . . have failed . . . and I have withdrawn the troops . . . my decision to attack was based upon the best information available. The troops, the air forces and the navy did all that bravery and devotion to duty could do. If any blame or fault attaches to the attempt, it is mine alone.' He folded the note, put it carefully in his pocket and carried it around with him for the next few days.

Then on D-1, the Supreme Allied Commander drove to Newbury, where the 101st Airborne Division was loading for the flight to Normandy. Privately, it had been predicted that these troops, who would parachute on to the beaches in advance of the seaborne infantry in order to blow up bridges and mine the approach roads to the beaches to block German reinforcements coming from inland, would suffer 70 per cent casualties. Their faces blackened, the men talked to Eisenhower who reassured them that they had the best possible equipment and leaders. A sergeant piped up, 'Hell, we ain't worried, General, it's the Krauts who ought to be worrying now.'

The parachutists of the 101st and of the 82nd had been segregated in readiness since 30 May. They were all volunteers who had joined for adventure – and, in John Keegan's words, 'had survived the strenuous training, the nine-mile runs, the "Gimme 25" [push-ups] and the endless "Hubba-hubbas" [hurry, hurry in what drill instructors inexplicably believed to be Hebrew], had jumped in practices by day and by night and were now ready to try the real thing'. Cooped up and waiting for the off, they were fed on a high-protein diet and played endless high-stake card games, watched films and scrapped among themselves. Jim Kurz of the 82nd Airborne was confident:

> We were going to be the key that unlocked the door to Hitler's fortress . . . Our mission was to take and defend the crossing of the Merderet River that led to Chef du Pont and the road that continued to Utah Beach. The main mission of the 82nd was to keep the Germans in the west from mounting a counter-attack on the incoming forces on Utah Beach . . . that was the set-up, and after that we ceased to worry. All we had to do now was to wait for D-Day to come. Meanwhile we ate well, saw a different movie every night, played volleyball and softball, and attended briefing meetings that updated us with the latest information.

Films proved the most popular choice of amusement for the 377th Parachute Artillery, the gunner regiment of the 101st: they were watching the Ted Lewis comedy *Is Everybody Happy?* when the order came over the public address system that D-Day was on.

Each of the 822 aircraft to be used for the drop carried a 'stick' of eighteen fully laden parachutists, along with the pilot, co-pilot, navigator and chief crew. Parachuting was a

Grim-faced US infantrymen pack into a landing ship on 5 June 1944.

precise and dangerous form of warfare. Pilots had to fly in close formation at heights of about 600–700 feet and at low speeds of 120 mph to allow their cargo to jump: this made them easy targets for anti-aircraft fire, yet the instruction had gone out, 'Do *not* take avoiding action.' The pilots of the C-47s (or Dakotas as the British called the planes) who were to deliver the parachutists were, in the main, transport and carrier fliers who had had no experience of combat flying. They were totally unprepared for the barrage of flak that hit them, disorientated by the cloud cover and unused to flying at the slow and steady speeds required for a safe parachute exit. The main danger was not that the parachutes wouldn't open – that only rarely happened – but that parachutists would drop too close to the ground to be able to open their 'chutes in time.

The men were so heavily equipped that they were only able to clamber aboard the planes with the utmost difficulty. Private Donald Burgett of the 506th Parachute Infantry, 101st Airborne Division, was wearing

> one suit of olive drab, worn underneath my jump suit . . . helmet, boots, gloves, main parachute, reserve parachute, Mae West, rifle, '45 automatic pistol, trench knife, jump knife, hunting knife, machete, one cartridge belt, two bandoliers, two cans of machine-gun ammo totalling 676 rounds of .30 ammo, 66 rounds of .45 ammo, one Hawkins mine capable of blowing off the tracks of a tank, four blocks

of TNT, one entrenching tool with two blasting caps taped on the outside of the steel part, three first aid kits, two morphine needles, one gas mask, a canteen of water, three days' supply of K-rations, two days' supply of D-rations (hard tropical chocolate bars), six fragmentation grenades, one Gammon grenade, one orange smoke and one red smoke grenade, one orange panel, one blanket, one raincoat, one change of socks and underwear, two cartons of cigarettes and a few other odds and ends . . . Other things would be dropped in equipment bundles that we would pick up later on the ground. Torpedoes, extra bazooka rockets, machine-gun ammo, medical supplies, food and heavy explosives. When all the troops were aboard, a loudspeaker came on and the pilot read us a mimeographed message from General Ike wishing us Godspeed. A canteen cup of whiskey would have been more appreciated . . .

And Burgett had a .45 pistol. Troops weren't issued pistols, but his father had sent one over from Detroit in a package containing a cake. Burgett was so weighted down that he had to be 'lifted bodily [by two Air Corps men who offered to help and who] with much boosting and grunting shoved me into the plane where I pulled myself along with the aid of the crew chief' – and rode to France kneeling on the floor, which led a journalist who was flying with the 506th to think that the men spent the crossing in prayer.

The K-rations, which were going to be the men's staple fare for many days, came in a small waxed box which just fitted into the pockets of their fatigue jackets. It contained the usual provisions, including the synthetic lemon powder which one infantryman was to find useful later: he thought that the Calvados he was given in France 'tasted like liquid paint neat', yet was quite drinkable once the lemon powder had been mixed in.

At 10.15 p.m., as night fell on 5 June, the propellers of the C-47s began to turn ready for take-off on airfields strung out from Devon to East Anglia. The planes flew off into a cloudless night until they reached the French coast, where the perpetual bad weather began to close in again.

D-Day was fifteen minutes old when the first airborne troops were dropped from planes and gliders at either end of the fifty-mile assault front to pave the way for the seaborne landings on the beaches. The British 6th Airborne division landed on the eastern end, charged with seizing bridges over the Orne River near Caen and destroying others in an attempt to seal the left flank of the Allied bridgehead, while 13,000 parachutists of the US 82nd and 101st divisions were dropped over a wide area around the town of St Mère Eglise to the west to secure the causeways leading from what had been designated by the planners as UTAH Beach. The men floated down like pollen, many dropped or blown miles off course. Some landed in the sea and drowned; some never left their planes, which were hit by flak and plummeted to earth in flames; others were picked off by the enemy as they floated towards the ground; others jumped too late and too low with insufficient time for their parachutes to unfurl, and were killed when they hit the ground. Donald Burgett was dropped at less than 300 feet rather than the specified 600–700; the hedgehopping of the pilot 'to save his own ass', in Burgett's view, meant that seventeen men 'hit the ground before their 'chute had time to open. They made a sound like large ripe pumpkins being thrown to burst against the ground . . . I hope that [dirty SOB pilot] gets shot down in the Channel and drowns real slow,' he fumed.

Others dropped into ditches or marshy beaches, which the Germans had flooded in order to strengthen their defences, and, unable to get free from their harnesses, drowned; others were impaled on 'Rommel's asparagus' or dangled from the high branches of trees – or, in one case, from the steeple of the church at St Mère Eglise – and, if they could not be cut down in time by their companions, would be taken prisoner or shot by the Germans; others were accidentally dropped behind enemy lines and were never heard of again or spent the rest of the war as POWs. Only two battalions made a 'good drop' – that is, they dropped and were concentrated in the planned zone. Altogether 4,000 airborne troops failed to join their units after the drop, and in some cases it was many days – seventeen for one group – before they were able to link up. Meanwhile those men who were able to slash themselves out of their harnesses wandered around clicking the metallic Christmas cracker 'crickets' they had been issued with as a means of making contact with each other. Most had lost their radio sets and also found it difficult at night to follow the usual daylight procedure for linking up by watching the direction of the aircraft stream. But despite the heavy losses of men and equipment, what appeared to be a disaster, with the men scattered so widely, proved to be a strength for it confused the enemy and engaged him in skirmishes rather than a co-ordinated counter-attack which could have massed towards the beaches.

The 29th Infantry Division had been practising for D-Day for what seemed like months on Slapton Sands:

> Again and again we loaded on to landing craft that pitched and rolled out into the Channel and then roared landward to drop ramps over which we lumbered to flounder through surf to the beach and go through the assault drills. So often repeated, these drills became a ritual dance performed by fire, flame-thrower and demolition teams displaying then advancing, in stylized movement, to blast paths through barbed wire, throw flames through the apertures of bunkers and blast them with explosives. Battalion and regimental staffs entered on cue to direct further movements.

It was clear from this and from the frequent visits of the military top brass, including Eisenhower and Montgomery, that the 29th had been chosen for a key role in the landings. All told, only five infantry divisions, along with the three airborne divisions and the supporting engineers and armour, were to take part in the initial assault on the Normandy beaches on 6 June.

From training in Devon, the company moved to Blandford in Dorset and then, at the end of May, to the marshalling area to join up with the other divisions of 'O' force, the US naval force that was to make the assault on the stretch of the Normandy coast designated as OMAHA Beach. Supported by tank companies, their DD (dual-drive Sherman) tanks fitted with canvas 'skirts' to enable them to float ashore, the 116th Regiment was charged with the task of opening the two roads inland from OMAHA up the cliffs for the wave upon wave of US troops which would first have to fight through the concrete bunkers, barbed wire, mines and fire trenches standing between the Allies and occupied Europe.

The infantrymen's task was to be helped as far as possible by Allied air power which would strafe targets identified from aerial reconnaissance photographs; in the final thirty minutes before the troops were scheduled to come ashore, beach defences were to be saturated by aerial and naval bombardment which would also crater the beach with ready-made foxholes for the assault troops.

The bombers had clear instructions as they left their bases in the early hours of 6 June: there must be no possibility of a SNAFU (Situation Normal: All Fouled Up) on this critical day. Timing was vital. The planes would be dropping their bombs on the same beaches as the ground troops would be landing on. The crews were issued instructions: 'You may bomb early, but not late.' Overnight the planes had been painted with wide black and white stripes that encircled the fuselage and wings: it was feared that the Germans might try to infiltrate the formations with planes they had rebuilt from RAF and USAAF planes shot down on missions, so this element of surprise was crucial. All Allied craft were routed in a gigantic circle of one-way traffic. There could be no change of course or turning back for any reason whatsoever. Fighter planes were ordered to shoot down any plane flying in the wrong direction, invasion stripes or not.

As the planes took off in groups of six rather than the usual formation, it seemed to those flying – and those watching – that the entire 8th Air Force was in the sky that day; every plane that was available had been mustered, and many flew at least two, if not more, sorties to France. And as they flew they caught the first glimpse, through the heavy cloud, of the invasion fleet – of the sea filled with 'the largest number of ships ever assembled in the history of mankind', as one navigator marvelled – 6,483 vessels in all.

The bombers leaving their bases gave most people their first intimation of the arrival of the long-awaited D-Day. An 8th Air Force flight engineer spent a restless night listening to the RAF bombers flying over Suffolk to the coast and 'as dawn approached our planes began their droning. Actually thousands of them . . . The sky looked like we were being invaded by locusts . . . the Luftwaffe had had its day and now we were having ours.'

Following the saturation bombing, banks of rockets were to be launched from offshore naval craft, and tanks were to fire from the landing crafts – and only then were the infantrymen to pour ashore. The infantrymen were as fully laden as the parachutists. Each soldier was carrying a total of 168 pounds. The pockets of their special assault jackets were stuffed with grenades, K-rations, mess tins, a raincoat, a morphine syringe, seasickness pills, water purification tablets, DDT dusting powder, paste to put on their boots to counteract any chemically contaminated areas, TNT for blasting foxholes and 200 francs to trade with the French; their waists were belted with ammunition and equipment, and each infantryman carried his own weapon.

Twelve miles out from the shore, the US troops swung over the side of their carriers and scrambled down the nets into the rectangular metal boxes that were their landing craft. The landing craft were then winched down into the rough sea, where the troops rode 'like sardines in an open can, feet awash in bilge water and altogether uncomfortable' for anything up to three hours until the craft bumped the shore and the ramp was let down. Those who had survived thus far were tossed out in their life-belts, and often had to scramble to shore up to their necks in water.

The GIs who landed on OMAHA and UTAH beaches found that their careful training was thrown into chaos by what confronted them in France: the aerial bombardment had not 'softened up' the defence; low cloud had prevented the planned air attack, those bombs that were dropped had not smashed into the beach defences but had landed many

The far shore. US medics administer first aid to US casualties of D-Day, while other troops dig themselves into fox holes in the sand.

miles inland; the strong seas had swamped most of the tanks and artillery, and had swept many of the troops far down the coast from their planned points of attack.

The current swept the American landing craft of Force 'U' 2,000 yards south of the area where they were supposed to land on UTAH Beach according to the OVERLORD plan. It was a fortuitous accident since the 4th Infantry Division happened on one of the least heavily defended stretches of the Normandy coastline. Twenty-eight of its thirty-three amphibious DD tanks were washed ashore at H Hour, 06.30, and the combat troops landed and were able to storm the 500 yards across the beaches to the first entrenchments under only sporadic fire. The first infantry wave was followed by engineers, who started to clear the beach and blast gaps in the sea wall. Within H + 3 hours, the beaches were cleared and troops were coming ashore in the nearest thing to textbook precision that would be seen that day: Force U had 'arrived transport area without incident'. 21,000 troops and 1,700 vehicles pressed forward towards the small town of St Mère Eglise, which was already in the hands of elements of the 82nd Airborne. All told, 23,000 men of Force U landed on D-Day, with only 197 casualties. The force suffered much heavier losses in the training disaster at Slapton Sands than it did on UTAH beach.

It was a very different story for Force 'O' on OMAHA Beach. The 1st and 29th Infantry Divisions were buffeted and soaked by waves up to six feet high: in the rough seas, one battalion of tanks did not even attempt to launch; another lost twenty-seven out of twenty-nine, which either sank or were destroyed by fire from the beach. The five-mile stretch of beach was soon an inferno of burning tanks, vehicles and equipment. There was noise so deafening that it was impossible to think; troops were pinned down by enemy fire, the dead and wounded lying in the water and scattered all over the beach. At noon, General Omar Bradley, Commander of the US 1st Army, aboard the USS *Augusta* moored offshore, faced a terrible dilemma. A force of 25,000 men and 4,400 additional vehicles was due to arrive on the second tide. OMAHA was a vital link in the Allied forces. UTAH was twenty miles from the British zone with its only links by sea. To send the troops there would break the front, yet to divert them east to the British forces on GOLD, which was an option Bradley considered, would in his opinion confuse and overload the British landings. If OMAHA was abandoned, Cherbourg would be forfeited and the western flank, an integral part of the full frontal assault of D-Day, would be lost, making the Allied invasion much easier to contain and defeat. Despite the fact that hundreds of US troops had died in those first hours on OMAHA, that over 40 per cent of the engineers had been killed, that only a handful of obstacles had been exploded and that it appeared that no soldiers had been able to cross the 200-yard beach and start to scale the steep 150-foot scrub-covered bluffs which cut the beach off from the surrounding countryside, Bradley finally decided: the fight for OMAHA had to continue.

In fact, the breakthrough had already begun about an hour earlier. Through individual acts of outstanding bravery and exhortation – 'We can't stay here,' 'Get off the beach,' 'Two kinds of people are staying on this beach. The dead and those who are going to die. Now get the hell out of here,' 'Come on up, the SOBs are cleaned out' – those troops who could, crawled through pill boxes and round obstacles towards the cliffs. As Bradley recognized, 'the battle belonged that morning to the thin, wet line of khaki that dragged itself ashore on the Channel coast of France.' By nightfall the beachhead had been secured. US forces controlled a perimeter a mile deep beyond OMAHA and the 4th Infantry Division which had landed at UTAH was able to link up with the 82nd Airborne Division west of the causeways from the beach.

As night fell on D-Day the Allies had tenuously breached the Atlantic Wall along a fifty-mile front: the US troops at UTAH and OMAHA, the British on GOLD and SWORD, the Canadians on JUNO – all linking for the fight inland across Normandy. More than 23,000 airborne troops, 15,500 of them American, had dropped into occupied France on the night 5–6 June, and 55,000 American and 75,215 British and Canadian troops came ashore during D-Day. If the advance of the US forces fell short of the planned objectives, the main object had been achieved: that of landing GIs on the 'far shore'. At nightfall Lieutenant Cawthon surveyed the debris and the dead on OMAHA Beach and felt 'the void of friends gone' on that day:

> Together we had been through months and years of wartime confusions and strains; marched countless tedious miles; lived in mud and dust, heat and cold. I knew their problems, both duty and personal, and they knew mine; the battalion and its business occupied very nearly all our time and thoughts, and it did not matter what else we might have or not have in common. Then it all came down to this brief first day of battle on the coast of Normandy, and for so many of them, it all ended. For the rest of us, what has been since has not been the same.

CHAPTER EIGHTEEN

OVER THERE

NSOMNIACS IN NEW YORK heard it at 3.32 a.m. on Tuesday, 6 June: 'Under the command of General Eisenhower, Allied naval forces, supported by strong air forces, began landing Allied armies this morning on the coast of France.' Then Eisenhower's message to the Allied Expeditionary Force was broadcast:

> You are about to embark on a great crusade . . . in the company with our brave Allies and brothers in arms on other fronts, you will bring about the destruction of the German war machine, elimination of the Nazi tyranny over the oppressed people of Europe, and security for ourselves in a free world . . . and we will accept nothing less than full victory . . . Good luck and let us all beseech the blessing of almighty God upon this great and noble undertaking.

Taxi drivers, who'd heard it on their car intercoms, pulled into the kerb and shouted to passers-by, factory workers on night shift paused to listen, and some to pray, and the neon flashes in Times Square told anyone who was around – 'It's On'.

Most Americans only heard the news of the Normandy landings when they woke the next morning. At ten o'clock that morning, President Roosevelt broadcast a prayer he had specially written for the occasion: 'Almighty God – our sons, pride of our nation, this day have set out upon a mighty endeavor, a struggle to preserve our Republic, our religion and our civilization and to set free a struggling humanity.'

By the end of D-Day, nearly 155,000 Allied troops were established across nearly 80 square miles of France: 55,000 Americans had come ashore, plus the 15,500 who had parachuted or glided across the Channel. Anglo–American co-operation had secured a bridgehead in Normandy. American troop carriers and gliders had transported British paratroopers, while US infantrymen were carried to the beaches in British troop ships in a frontal assault against the German defences of occupied Europe.

One out of every eleven Americans who had taken part in the cross-Channel invasion was dead, missing or wounded. There were some 6,000 American casualties (of whom 700 were airborne troops): more than half the total Allied casualties of that day.

By the end of July 1944, the Americans were the majority Allied force in France, with 980,000 troops compared with 660,000 British, and by VE-Day some 3,000,000 US troops were fighting on the continent. Although some US troops came directly from America, or had been redeployed from the Mediterranean theatre, in the weeks after D-Day troops continued to pour out of Britain as reinforcements flooded in.

After that first day, the troops knew what awaited them on the 'far shore'. They could no longer share the optimism of Private Linley Higgins who, on D-Day, was

> dumb enough not to feel the slightest trepidation. We really thought that at any moment the whole Reich was going to collapse. We saw what we had. Heard what they didn't have. We really thought that we only had to step off that beach and all the Krauts would put up their hands.

As the forces embarked from Weymouth, Portland, Portsmouth, Southampton and Falmouth, the dead and injured from Normandy were being brought ashore, and fleets of ambulances were awaiting the stretcher parties. The injured GIs were transported to hospitals which had been on alert for invasion casualties for months, and would receive medical treatment to enable them to return to the States for discharge or further treatment, or to go back to the battlefields of Europe and fight some more.

The battle for France was slow as the troops fought out the 'battle of the hedgerows' across Normandy. It was, in Bradley's phrase, 'tough and costly, a slugger's match, too slow a process'. By 26 June, the Americans were in Cherbourg; on 10 July, D+33, the British entered Caen. Allied troops fought through the cold, and wet summer to push the German armies back and on 18 July US troops took St Lô with the loss of 5,000 men. On 25 July 1944, the Americans launched Operation COBRA in Normandy and had succeeded in breaking out of the Cherbourg Peninsula by the end of the month, while the US 1st Army 'kept moving' to help seize Rennes and close the Falaise Pocket. The battle for Normandy ended on 19 August with 209,672 casualties, of whom 36,976 were dead. Combined British and Canadian casualties were two-thirds those of the Americans. The failure of the Arnhem airborne attack in September ended any hope of winning the war in '44, and American casualties were very high during the 'Battle of the Bulge' of Christmas 1944 when von Rundstedt's troops mounted a massive – and final – counter-attack across the Ardennes. In a nightmare of cold, fog and chaos, the US Army had more troops involved, and suffered more casualties, than in any previous battle in its history.

By February 1945, Allied troops were advancing across Germany and by mid-March divisions of the 1st and 3rd Army had crossed the Rhine upstream from Mainz – and were pressing on towards the Elbe. Less than two months later, on the afternoon of 6 May 1945, a German delegation headed by General Jodl, Chief of Staff of the disintegrating German Army, arrived at Eisenhower's headquarters, housed in a school building in Rheims in northern France. At 1.41 a.m. on 7 May, the unconditional surrender of all German forces was signed. On 8 May *Stars and Stripes* carried its largest headline ever – 'GERMANY QUITS'.

By VE-Day there were less than a quarter of a million GIs left in Britain. The vast majority had been fighting on the continent and would now be on their way home or heading for the other theatre of war in the Pacific where the conflict continued for another three months – VJ-Day was not until 15 August 1945.

· · ·

For the GIs coming to Britain, as long ago as the early spring of 1942 in some cases, it had been a journey to war, but they may have come to like what they found, as Robert Arbib certainly did:

" I don't care if the war is nearly over—I'm not selling my cab for a fiver for a souvenir."

Every Englishman you meet apologizes. They all say, 'Too bad you are seeing England in wartime. Too bad you cannot see England at her best.' And dammit this *is* England at her best. Right here and now. Perhaps the streets were dirty and the shopfronts needed paint. Perhaps England is prettier when the iron railings are back round the parks and the lights are on in London. Perhaps life will be more comfortable when there is plenty of good food once more and hot water and soap are no longer rationed. Perhaps, too, the girls will be prettier when they can buy new clothes and wear stockings again and the grime disappears from under their fingernails and hard muscles from their arms and legs ... But to some of you, who remember other things – who knew a country wholly united behind one danger which made all men friends, where sacrifice came not only to the soldier ... where everyone shared in the work, where terror and trouble could not subjugate humor ... this was a nation at its best.

Or they may not, as an anonymous versifier felt:

> This isle's not worth saving I don't think,
> Cut those balloons loose – let the damn thing sink.
> I'm not complaining, but I bet you know
> Life's rougher than hell in the ETO.

But whatever they felt, as the journalist Ernie Pyle knew, there was one goal that obsessed every American, and 'That goal was home.' (Not that Pyle made it home; he was killed by a Japanese machine-gun sniper on Ie Shima, a small island west of Okinawa, on 18 April 1945.)

As a Lancashire man observed wryly, 'If ever the people of Chorley thought of saying "Yanks go home", that was exactly what the Yanks wanted to do.'

With the coming of peace, priority home was given to the wounded – of whom there were at their peak 150,000 in British hospitals. Other troops were subject to a complicated points system based on length of service since September 1940 and on family circumstances, with bonus points for each medal awarded. The ships that had brought the GIs 'over here' – including the *Queens*, and the *Aquitania* – were among the 370 taking 50,000 troops a month back 'over there'.

There were soon to be further calls on the 'demob' ships: GI brides wanting transport to the States to rejoin their husbands. Although some brides left for the US before the end of the war, the flood of 70,000 eventual British brides into the US began in earnest when the *Argentina* docked in New York on 4 February 1946 carrying 452 brides, 30 of them pregnant, 173 children and one GI husband whose wife was a WAC. The youngest bride, bound for North Carolina, was sixteen, the oldest forty-four. They had been welcomed aboard by the captain who reminded them that 'even now, on the decks of an American ship, you are on American soil . . . may you find warm hearts and kindness.' And as if to emphasize their new life, each woman was known by her first name plus the name of her destination; so there would be a Pamela Idaho, several Joan Minnesotas, a Pat Oregon, a Betty Texas and an Edith Wyoming. Newspapers called the brides 'Pilgrim Mothers' and dubbed the whole venture 'Operation DIAPER'.

But it hadn't been easy. By October 1945, 60,000 war brides were still waiting to be transported to the States. These 'wallflower wives' demonstrated outside the American Embassy in Grosvenor Square and paraded outside Mrs Roosevelt's hotel when she visited London, carrying placards bearing such slogans as 'Forgotten British Wives' and 'We Demand Ships', while their children clutched boards demanding 'We want our Dads'. But the answer was always the same – the shipment home of American troops took priority. While British women pined for their husbands, and some secretly worried that they might have been consigned to a far distant wartime memory, like Brussels sprouts, there were always kind friends to enquire solicitously – 'Oh dear! Hasn't he sent for you *yet?*'

When they finally got their embarkation orders, the brides – and their infants – were processed at Tidworth army camp, which was 'miserably cold' and regimented. There were endless physical checks for venereal disease and lice, lest, despite all the authorities' vigilance, someone who wasn't a 'nice girl' had slipped through the net. The women were waited on by German and Italian POWs, but for young girls already anxious about leaving their families and friends and apprehensive about life thousands of miles from home with a man they had only known for a short time, the bleak regime at Tidworth could be a devastating experience, and there were some desertions. Things didn't improve until the late spring of 1946 when the Red Cross was drafted in to provide some comfort and reassurance to the brides. The organization adopted a slogan which could well have served as a motto for the GI wives themselves: 'Be alert, adjustable and ready for change'.

The ships going back to America might not have been as crowded as they had been when the troops arrived, the food was certainly better, and the danger of U-boats had passed, yet the sea could be as rough, the seasickness as wearing and the anxiety about a foreign land no less acute. As a shipload of soldiers returning to Britain passed the *Argentina* in the Atlantic the men yelled, 'You'll be sorry!' 'No we won't,' chorused the brides, with more conviction than many probably felt. A booklet handed to each passenger as she walked up the gangplank in 'an attempt to answer 99,999½ of the

One for the album. Margaret Double (now Pilgrim) poses with a US airman on the wing of a Mustang fighter plane stationed at Raydon in Suffolk on 9 June 1945.

100,000 questions' about the life they could expect aimed to be comforting: 'remember, the Army will not send you to a destination unless it has been verified that "that man" is there waiting. In short, consider yourself parcel-post delivery. So relax and enjoy your cruise.'

A large map of the USA had been pinned up in the ship's library and the women marked their destinations on it: 'some girls had a fright when they saw how far they had to travel after they got to New York', and one woman 'found this a particularly lonely time . . . because when it came to my turn to look at the map, I was completely unable to find Amboy in Minnesota. I couldn't help but wonder what I was in for.' A group on the *Alexander* had prepared a show for the last night at sea; the finale was a rendering of 'There'll Always Be an England', which reduced the cast and audience to tears.

As the ships drew in to New York harbor – everyone was 'appalled' to realize that the Statue of Liberty was green – the quayside band struck up with 'Sentimental Journey' followed by 'America the Beautiful' and the passengers craned over the rail, hoping to recognize the husbands who had come to 'claim' them in their civilian clothes. A few women had received 'Not wanted, don't come' messages on the ship, and the odd one

*'It's been good knowing you.' A GI from Maine says goodbye
to his East Anglian 'mother'.*

Pack up your pin-ups in your old kitbag. Technical Sergeant M. H. Burakoff of Boston prepares to move out of Wilton camp near Salisbury.

couldn't face her husband after all when she saw him waiting on the shore and bolted herself in her cabin and refused to leave the ship; but the vast majority of brides clambered down the gangplank to start a new life in the States, living not only with a new husband but often with in-laws as well. Many of the GIs came from first-generation immigrant families who would greatly have preferred their boys either to marry within their own community or to secure their grip on American society by marrying an American girl – and sometimes showed it. For the women, this could mean that not only did they have to adapt to American ways, but also to embrace Italian or Polish or German culture as well. 'They thought *I* was the immigrant,' remembers Averil Logan of her husband's Italian family who had settled in New Jersey, 'and I thought that *they* were.'

The GI brides found that America was indeed a land of plenty and opportunity, at least for some; that there was a great deal of the USA in between New York and Hollywood; that a promised ranch could turn out to be a shack on the side of the hill; a 'chain of restaurants', a couple of hot dog stalls, and an icebox just that. But a surprising number did 'adapt and adjust', joining English Brides' Clubs to talk over the old country and re-create what they remembered as quintessentially English; they felt homesick a lot of the time, but stayed on to make successful marriages in a country they came to appreciate.

ON THEIR WAY 'OVER THERE'

ABOVE *GI wives and babies wave goodbye to England from SS* Argentina *on 26 January
1946 — exactly four years after the first US troops arrived in Britain.*
RIGHT *Together again. A GI from Florida is reunited with his English wife and baby
daughter on their arrival in New York in 1946.*

For those left behind, the rapid departure of so many GIs after D-Day and the exodus
from most of the huge air bases within months of VE-Day left a feeling of unfinished
business in those parts of Britain which the troops had dominated for as long as two and
a half years. After the GIs had left a camp in Wiltshire, a woman went down to clear up:

> The men had discarded an assortment of articles. I picked up three cartloads of
> wood, makeshift chairs and tables, shower partitions and stands, for instance.
> There was even food. I remember finding a 50lb bag of white flour and a partial
> crate of tomatoes. Hundreds of coat-hangers, some wooden with dry cleaners'
> names and addresses in the States on them. There are some of them at home
> today. There were Armed Forces pocket books, I collected perhaps fifty of them.

Inevitably, 'kids from a nearby school discovered this paradise later in the day. They also
discovered boxes of prophylactics . . . not knowing what they were they used them like
balloons and left them lying all over the place.'

" But, honey—where did you get the idea that all Americans live in skyscrapers ? "

One US infantry officer felt ashamed about the condition in which his men had left their campsite:

> it was a mess – a sloppy, wasteful, disgraceful mess. [They] had discarded everything which they considered not essential. They hadn't turned it in to the supply tent, but had just abandoned it where it lay or could be thrown. Lying in the mud of the tent and the company streets were articles of clothing of all descriptions: helmets, ammunition, grenade fuses, rifles, shelter tents, rations, mattress covers, some filled with straw and some empty – and a variety of personal items, including toilet articles, books, sweaters, and PX rations. The most disgraceful were an M-1 rifle sticking out of a stove with the stock partially broken off and a BAR which looked like it had been wrapped round a tree. I could hear the repercussions when a formal inspection was made of the area . . . I would like to have found out the British soldiers' reactions to that wasteful mess, but it was too embarrassing to even look them in the eye. For men who had been at war for years and under strict rationing, such waste must have given them the impression that Americans were, at best, very amateur soldiers.

But that impression was largely dispelled on the Normandy beaches. Those GIs who passed through Britain after D-Day or who returned from France found that any hostility their countrymen may have incurred earlier from British troops and civilians was mostly a thing of the past. They were comrades in arms now.

Harold Nicolson gave a lecture at an American mess a few weeks after D-Day and found that 'they all agree that British and American troops *always* get on badly when they first glower at each other in the streets and *always* get on well when they have a job of work to do. Their co-operation in Normandy has apparently been quite splendid. People are enormously cheered' – though the disasters of Arnhem and the heavy casualties in the Ardennes revived tensions between the Allied commanders and the reservations that some officers and men had about their allies' performance in battle.

Many of the British, slow to welcome the GIs when they first arrived, felt bereft when they left. A Suffolk woman remembers how when the 8th Air Force began to pull out of their East Anglian bases, 'everything became silent. The Yanks had come and now they were gone.' 'One moment,' recollects another East Anglian, 'it was all noise and then dead silence and everything deserted . . . It was as if everyone had fallen asleep. We shall never forget the boys who had come so far from their homes in America and now were gone.'

For Averil Logan, 'it was so drab when they had gone. The whole world had been opened up to me and then it was closed down again . . . We realized how confining England was, how dull the weather was . . . there always seemed to be clouds on top of my head . . . and the men, how small the gene pool was.'

A. P. Herbert penned a farewell in 1944:

> *Goodbye GI. Bud, now that you know the way*
> *Come back and see us on a brighter day.*
> *When England's free and 'Scotch' is cheap but strong*
> *And you can bring your pretty wives along.*
>
> *Goodbye GI. Don't leave us quite alone.*
> *Somewhere in England we must write in stone*
> *How Britain was invaded by the Yanks,*
> *And under that, a big and hearty 'Thanks'.*

Eric Westman remembers how it had been before the Yanks came:

> With no TV our outlook was narrow, parochial and jingoistic. Few families owned a motor vehicle; almost none had experienced an overseas holiday, and indeed any holidays were rare. There was mass unemployment, with desperately low wages . . . our material standing of living was low until the war began and full employment, mainly on armaments, came . . . At the same time, the British Empire, the greatest the world had ever known, owned one quarter of the earth's surface and held one quarter of the world's population in subjection. It was inconceivable to us that this situation could ever end. We regarded ourselves as the supreme race with all others inferior, and that was as it should be. [We had faith in] the universally believed tag, 'One Englishman is worth ten bloody foreigners.' We were very naive.

Or, as a twenty-five-year-old GI from New York State saw the British ways: 'What I thought funny . . . was the way in all these tea shops, specially in the country towns, they

Now this lousy war is over. GIs on their way home on
the Queen Mary *in August 1945.*

have plates stuck round the walls. You ask, "What are those plates there for?" And the girl says, "I don't know. They've always been there." And that goes for more than plates stuck around the walls.'

For it wasn't just the occasional broken heart, a considerable number of illegitimate babies, a far greater number of warm memories, and the detritus of wartime that the GIs left behind. It was a changed country. A lot of hostility to the US troops as coarse Johnny-come-latelies to the world stage as well as to the war came from people who had seen in their confident, classless, noisy consumerism the shape of the future of Britain – and hadn't liked what they had seen. Harold Macmillan, who would do as much as anyone in the post-war years as Prime Minister to forge the 'special relationship' between Britain and the US, found during the war 'the Americans much as the Greeks found the Romans, great big vulgar bustling people, more vigorous than we are and also more idle'. And for Harold Nicolson, distressed as he heard American accents echoing 'Auld Lang Syne' in Parliament Square on New Year's Eve in 1943; for Cecil King, the newspaper magnate, whose malice seemed particularly reserved for America, 'a country that plucks the fruit of victory by coming in late and leaving the casualties to others . . . the concern of senior officers is for "welfare" which seems to cover food, drink, games and whores, but fighting hardly enters their heads,' (despite the fact that 362,561 members of the US forces were killed in the Second World War); for all those who were spectators at the death of an old Europe that they had hoped for too long would survive, the new world order threatened a global economy dominated by the United States, and that in turn threatened the British Empire overseas and the existing social order at home. Already by 1944, there were clear signs that the peace would bring powerful demands from those who had fought the war. There were many now who were saying that it wasn't so much that the American troops were overpaid, it was that the British troops were underpaid.

As a Chippenham woman reflected: 'I cannot recall anyone who had the slightest idea of how tremendous an impact the Americans would have on our lives . . . the Americans changed England more than the English like to realize and admit. Americans challenged the British way of life, shook basic concepts.' For a Bristol schoolboy, 'life settled down a little bit . . . after the departure of the Yanks. It never has been, nor ever will be, quite like it was before. The Yanks introduced a whole new concept of life to the British Isles.'

And a Suffolk woman says wistfully, 'I still remember the Yanks almost more than I remember the war itself.'

SOURCES AND FURTHER READING

The letters and tapes sent to me and the interviews I conducted with Americans and Britons who experienced the GI years form the basis of this book. Some names are mentioned in the text: many are not, but a full list of all the people who have contributed their memories and impressions appears after this bibliography. In addition, I drew upon unpublished manuscripts, both in archival collections and private hands, which are acknowledged in the notes to each chapter.

Several books which have informed the entire work are listed below. There are also books and papers which have been invaluable for individual aspects of the US troops in Britain during the Second World War — these are listed under the relevant chapter headings.

Official and reference sources

The Chief Military History for the Department of the Army, *United States Army in World War II: The European Theater of Operations* series (Washington DC), in particular Roland G. Ruppenthal, *Logistical Support of the Armies* (2 vols, 1953); Forrest C. Pogue, *The Supreme Command* (1954); Special Studies series (Washington DC); Mattie E. Treadwell, *The Women's Army Corps* (1954); *The Army Air Forces in World War II*, ed. Wesley Frank Craven and James Lea Cate (Chicago), Vol. I, *Plans and Early Operations, January 1939 — August 1942* (1948); Vol. II, *Europe: Torch to Pointblank, August 1942 — December 1943* (1949); Vol. III, *Europe: Argument to V-E Day, January 1944 — May 1945* (1951); Randolph Leigh, *48 Million Tons to Eisenhower: The Role of the SOS in the Defeat of Germany* (Washington, 1945); A. Marjorie Taylor, *The Language of World War II* (New York, 1944); Harold Wentworth and Stuart Berg Flexner, *Dictionary of American Slang* (New York, 1975).

General Works

Charles B. Macdonald, *The Mighty Endeavour: American Armed Forces in the European Theater in World War II* (New York, 1969); Kenneth S. Davis, *Experience of War* (New York, 1965); John Morton Blum, *V was for Victory: Politics and American Culture during World War II* (New York, 1976).

Winston S. Churchill, *The Second World War* (London, 1959); Martin Gilbert, *Second World War* (revised edn, London, 1990); John Keegan, *The Second World War* (London, 1989).

Norman Longmate, *The GIs: The Americans in Britain, 1942—1945* (London, 1975); *The Yanks are Coming*, ed. Edwin R. W. Hale and John Frayn Turner (London, 1983); Edwin P. Hoyt, *The GI War: The Story of American Soldiers in World War II* (New York, 1988); Lee Kennett, *GI. The American Soldier in World War II* (New York, 1987).

Charles R. Cawthon, *Other Clay. A Remembrance of the World War II Infantry* (Colorado, 1991); John P. Downing, *At War with the British* (Florida, 1980); David Eisenhower, *Eisenhower at War 1943—1945* (London, 1986); Dwight D. Eisenhower, *Crusade in Europe* (London, 1948); Henry E. Giles, *The GI Journal of Sergeant Giles* (Boston, 1965); Ernie Pyle, *Brave Men* (New York, 1944) and *Here is your War* (New York, 1945).

John T. Appleby, *Suffolk Summer* (Ipswich, 1948); Robert Arbib, *Here We Are Together* (London, 1946); Angus Calder, *The People's War* (London, 1969).

Paul Fussell, *Wartime. Understanding and Behaviour in the Second World War* (Oxford, 1989); Studs Terkel, *The Good War. An Oral History of World War Two* (London, 1985).

The London edition of *Stars and Stripes* and *Yank*.

Novels

Len Deighton, *Goodbye Mickey Mouse* (London, 1983); Sarah Russell (Marghanita Laski), *To Bed with Grand Music* (London, 1946); Mary Lee Settle, *All the Brave Promises* (New York, 1966, London, 1984); Douglas Sheldon, *The Rainbow Men* (London, 1976); Nevil Shute, *Chequer Board* (London, 1947); Leslie Thomas, *The Magic Army* (London, 1981); Brian Thompson, *Buddy Boy* (London, 1977).

SOURCES AND FURTHER READING

Where books referred to in specific chapters have been mentioned in the general list above, the short title only is included. Books specific only to individual chapters are listed as much as possible in the order in which the information occurs in the chapter.

Chapter One War on a Far Front

Ross Gregory, *America 1941. A Nation at the Crossroads* (New York, 1989); Glen C. H. Perry, *'Dear Bart': Washington Views of World War II* (Westport, 1982); David Brinkley, *Washington Goes to War* (New York, 1988); Robert A. Divine, *Roosevelt and World War II* (Baltimore, 1969); Francis L. Lowenheim, Harold D. Langley and Manfred Jonas, *Roosevelt and Churchill: Their Secret Wartime Correspondence* (New York, 1975); Walter Lord, *Day of Infamy* (New York, 1957); John W. Blake, *Northern Ireland in the Second World War* (Belfast, 1956); Ian Henderson, 'The GIs in Northern Ireland' in *After the Battle*, no. 34 (London, 1981); John G. Winant, *Letter from Grosvenor Square* (London, 1947); *The London Observer: The Journal of General Raymond E. Lee. 1940–1941*, ed. James Leutze (London, 1972); Harold Nicolson, *The War Years, 1939–1945*, ed. Nigel Nicolson (London, 1967); Mollie Panter-Downes, *London War Notes, 1939–1945* (Harlow, 1972); Geoffrey Crowther, 'America in Total War' in *Current Affairs*, no. 12 (London, 1942); *Report to the Nation; The American Preparation for War* (Washington, 1942); Ted Hill, *'Tell Your Mother There's a War on.' The Wartime Memories of a Bedminster Boy* (Bristol, 1985); *The Times*; papers of Robert McCall, *Recollections of an Infantry Private in World War II* (Department of Documents, Imperial War Museum (IWM), nd).

Chapter Two Soldiers: Government Issue

Fred Huston, 'My Battle from Britain', Thomas Todd, 'From Leavenworth to Liverpool' and Robert Burns, 'Old Ironsides' in *The Yanks are Coming*, ed. Hale and Turner; Cawthon, *Other Clay;* Downing, *At War with the British;* Giles, *The GI Diary of Sergeant Giles;* Ralph Martin, *The GI War, 1941–1945* (Boston, 1967); Ralph Hammond, *My GI Aching Back* (New York, 1946); Robert Henrey (otherwise Madeleine Henrey), *The Siege of London* (London, 1946); Arbib, *Here We Are Together;* Orval Eugene Farbus, *In This Faraway Land* (Arkansas, 1971); E. J. Kahn, 'The Army Life: My Day' in *The New York Book of War Pieces* (New York, 1947); Lloyd O. Olson, *Front and Center: Lest We Forget* (unpublished, nd); *Stars and Stripes; Yank;* private, unpublished information.

Chapter Three The Goddamn Yankee Army's Come

Panter-Downes, *London War Notes;* Arbib, *Here We Are Together;* Ernie McDonald Leo, 'Anglophile Extraordinaire' and Bill Ong, 'Infantryman' in *The Yanks are Coming*, ed. Hale and Turner; Downing, *At War with the British;* Ruppenthal, *Logistical Support of the Armies: Vol. I;* Kennett, *GI: The American Soldier in World War II;* Hoyt, *The GI War;* Martin, *The GI War;* Cawthon, *Other Clay;* Nicolson, *The War Years;* Ian Hay, *America Comes Across* (London, 1942); Maurice Colbourne, *America and Britain: A Mutual Introduction* (London, 1943); John Langdon-Davies, *America Close Up: Portrait of an Ally* (London, 1943); Phyllis Bentley, *Here is America* (London, 1942); *A Short Guide to Great Britain* (Washington, nd); *Meet the Army* (London, 1943); Margaret Mead, *The American Troops and the British Community* (London, 1944); Jean Lancaster Rennie, *And Over Here* (Norfolk, 1976); Cecily Mackworth, 'Public Opinion and the Americans' in *The Outpost* (1943); Edward R. Murrow, 'A Reporter Remembers', *The Listener* (18 January 1979); papers from the collection of N. A. Forde (Department of Documents, IWM); Mass Observation Archive; private unpublished information.

Chapter Four 'Where the Hell Am I?'

Ruppenthal, *Logistical Support of the Armies: Vol. I;* Downing, *At War with the British;* William B. French 'Yanks in the Hayloft' in Hale and Turner, *The Yanks are Coming;* Arbib, *Here We Are Together;* Cawthon, *Other Clay;* Leigh, *48 Million Tons to Eisenhower;* Hammond, *My GI Aching Back;* William Weaver, *Yankee Doodle Dandy* (Ann Arbor, 1958); Philip Kaplan and Rex Alan Smith, *One Last Look: A Sentimental Journey to the Eighth Air Force Heavy Bomber Bases of World War II in England* (New York, 1983); R. Douglas Brown, *East Anglia: 1942* (Lavenham, 1988); *A Book of War Letters*, ed. Harry E. Maule (New York, 1943); private, unpublished information.

Chapter Five Getting to Know the Invaders

Arbib, *Here We Are Together*; Henrey, *The Siege of London (1946); Nicolson, The War Years, 1939—1945*; Longmate, *The GIs*; Kennett, *GI*; Kaplan and Smith, *One Last Look*; Mead, *The American Troops and the British Community;* Ted Hill, *'Tell Your Mother There's a War On'*; James Landon Hodson, *Home Front* (London, 1944); Maurice Gorham, *Sound and Fury: Twenty-One Years in the BBC* (London, 1948); *The Collected Essays, Journalism and Letters of George Orwell: As I Please, 1943—1945*, ed. Sonia Orwell and Ian Angus (London, 1968); Anthony Cotterell, *An Apple for the Sergeant* (London, nd); John Costelloe, *Love, Sex and War: Changing Values, 1939—45* (London, 1985); William Bostick, *England Under GIs' Reign* (Detroit, 1946); Charles Graves, *Women in Green. The Story of the WVS* (London, 1948); Robert S. Raymond, *A Yank in Bomber Command*, ed. Michael Moynihan (Newton Abbot, 1977); John Reed, 'London's Wartime Headquarters' in *After the Battle* no. 37 (London, 1979); papers of Mrs E. O. Scovell (Olivia C. Aykin) (Department of Documents, IWM); Mass Observation Archive; Public Record Office (PRO) FO 371/34123; private, unpublished information.

Chapter Six The Battle of the Mud

Arbib, *Here We Are Together*; Ruppenthal, *Logistical Support of the Armies*; Brown, *East Anglia, 1942*; Longmate, *The GIs*; Cawthon, *Other Clay*; Downing, *At War with the British*; Ong in *The Yanks are Coming*, ed. Frayn and Turner; Kaplan and Smith, *One Last Look*; Leigh, *48 Million Tons to Eisenhower*; *The Army Air Forces in World War II, Vol. 1*, ed. Craven and Cate; Roger A. Freeman, *The Mighty Eighth: Units, Men and Machines (A History of the US 8th Army Air Force)* (London, 1970); Michael J. F. Bowyer, *Action Stations: 1. Military Airfields of East Anglia* (Wellingborough, 1979 and 1990); J. Frank Dobie, *A Texan in England* (Boston, 1945); private, unpublished information.

Chapter Seven Warm Beer and Brussels Sprouts

Arbib, *Here We Are Together*; Cawthon, *Other Clay*; Kaplan and Smith, *One Last Look*; Longmate, *The GIs*; Downing, *At War with the British*; Cotterell, *An Apple for the Sergeant*; Bostick, *England Under GIs' Reign*; *A Book of War Letters*, ed. Maule; Murphy, *Dorset at War*; Rennie, *And Over Here*; Hill, *'Tell Your Mother There's a War On'*; *With Love, Jane. Letters from American Women on the War Fronts*, ed. Alma Lutz (New York, 1945); *Stars and Stripes*; *Yank*; papers of Mrs E. O. Scovell (IWM); PRO FO 371/34123; Mass Observation Archive; private, unpublished information.

Chapter Eight Furloughs and Passes

Downing, *At War with the British*; Winant, *Letter from Grosvenor Square*; Clarence Roesler, 'A Yank Abroad in London' in *The Yanks Are Coming*, ed. Frayn and Turner; Martin, *The GI War;* Arbib, *Here We Are Together*; Nicolson, *The War Years, 1939—1945*; Hammond, *My GI Aching Back*; Lutz, *With Love, Jane; The Home Front. An Anthology, 1939—1945*, ed. Norman Longmate (London, 1981); Longmate, *The GIs*; Pyle, *Brave Men*; Robert Henrey (otherwise Madeleine Henrey), *A Village in Piccadilly* (London, 1942); Geoffrey Williamson, *Star Spangled Square: The Saga of Little America in London* (London, 1956); A.S.F. Gow, *Letters from Cambridge, 1939—45* (London, 1945); *Stars and Stripes*; private, unpublished information.

Chapter Nine Islands of Little America

Downing, *At War with the British*; Hammond, *My GI Aching Back*; Graves, *Women in Green*; Virginia Graham, *The Story of the WVS* (London, 1959); Katharine Bentley Beauman, *Greensleeves: The Story of WVS/WRVS* (London, 1977); Robert H. Bremner, Minna Adams Hutcheson, Lucille Stein Greenburg, *The History of the American Red Cross: Vol. XXIII: American Red Cross Services in the War. Against the European Axis. Pearl Harbor to 1947* (Washington, 1950); George Korson, *At His Side: The American Red Cross Overseas in World War II* (New York, 1945); Vernon F. Gay, *Rainbow Corner* (Washington, 1944); Oscar Whitelaw Rexford, *Battlestars and Doughnuts: World War II Experiences of Mary Metcalfe Rexford* (St Louis, Missouri, 1989); Majorie Lee Morgan, *The Clubmobile: The Arc in the Storm* (Florida, 1982); *Stars and Stripes: Picture Post* (27 January 1945); WVS Archive: reports; American Red Cross Archive reports; private, unpublished information.

Chapter Ten 'Boy, Are We Going to Have Fun!'

Rennie, *And Over Here*; Longmate, *The GIs and The Home Front*; Costelloe, *Love, Sex and War*; Maule, *War Letters; A Short Guide to Britain*; James Belsey and Helen Reid, *West at War* (Bristol, 1990); *Stars and Stripes*; papers of Grace Eva Chawe (Mrs Alva H. Reinecke) (Department of Documents, IWM); private, unpublished information.

Chapter Eleven Piccadilly Commandoes

Kaplan and Smith, *One Last Look*; Belsey and Reid, *West at War*; Clarence Roesler in *The Yanks are Coming*, ed. Frayn and Turner; Arbib, *Here We Are Together*; Maule, *War Letters*; Henrey, *The Siege of London*; Costelloe, *Love, Sex and War*; Sadie Ward, *War in the Countryside: 1939—1945* (London, 1988); *Stars and Stripes*; PRO FO 371/34125; private, unpublished information.

Chapter Twelve Nice Girls and their Little Brothers

Roesler in *The Yanks are Coming*, ed. Hale and Turner; Mead, *The American Troops and the British Community*; Longmate, *The GIs*; Arbib, *Here We Are Together*; Rennie, *And Over Here*; Hill, *'Tell Your Mother There's a War On'*; Bostick, *England Under GIs' Reign*; Elfrieda Berthiaume Shukert and Barbara Smith Scibetta, *War Brides of World War II* (New York, 1988); *Stars and Stripes*; PRO FO 371/34125; papers of Avice Wilson (W 257/US), (Department of Documents, IWM); Mass Observation Archive; private, unpublished information.

Chapter Thirteen 'Come Home and Meet Father'

Longmate, *The GIs*; Shukert and Scibetta, *War Brides of World War II*; Pamela Winfield (in collaboration with Brenda Wilson Hasty) *Sentimental Journey: The Story of GI Brides* (London, 1984); Ron Glade, *Our Ron, that Chlöe* (Bristol, 1987); *Stars and Stripes; New York Times* 17 September 1946; papers of E. M. McMurdo, (Department of Documents, IWM); private, unpublished information.

Chapter Fourteen Fighting a War on Two Fronts

I am heavily dependent on information in Graham Smith's *When Jim Crow Met John Bull: Black American Troops in World War II in Britain* (London, 1987) and David Reynolds's 'The Churchill Government and the Black American Troops in Britain during World War II' in *Transactions of the Royal Historical Society* 5th series, vol. 35 (1985) for this chapter. Blum, *V for Victory*; Longmate, *The GIs*; Weaver, *Yankee Doodle Dandy*; Brinkley, *Washington at War; The Home Front*, ed. Longmate; Ulysses Lee, *The United States Army in World War II. Special Studies series: The Employment of Negro Troops* (Washington DC, 1966); Ralph Ellison, 'In a Strange Country' in *I Have Seen War*, ed. Dorothy Sterling (New York, 1960); Walter White, *A Rising Wind* (New York, 1945); Phillip McGuire, *Taps for Jim Crow: Letters from Black Soldiers in World War II* (Santa Barbara, 1983); *An Autobiography: Benjamin O. Davis Jnr: American* (Washington, 1991); Eisenhower, *Crusade in Europe*; Ian McLaine, *Ministry of Morale: Home Front Morale and the Ministry of Education in World War II* (London, 1979); Calder, *The People's War*; Susan Briggs, *Keep Smiling Through* (London, 1975); James Lees-Milne, *Ancestral Voices* (London, 1975); Frances Partridge, *A Pacifist's War* (London, 1978); Paul D. Casdorph, *Let the Good Times Roll: Life at Home in America during World War II* (New York, 1989); P. Wright, *Village at War* (Bristol, 1990); Ken Werrell, 'Crime in World War II: Mutiny at Bamber Bridge' in *After the Battle* No. 22 (London, 1978); *Stars and Stripes; Yank; New Statesman and Nation* 26 September 1942; *Sunday Pictorial* 6 September 1942; PRO CAB 66/29, WP (42) (456); PRO FO 371/34123; Mass Observation Archive; private, unpublished information.

Chapter Fifteen The Mighty Eighth

The Army Air Forces in World War II (3 vols.), ed. Craven and Cate; Kaplan and Smith, *One Last Look*; Bowyer, *Action Stations*; Roger A. Freeman, *The Mighty Eighth* (London, 1970), *Mighty Eighth's War Diary* (London, 1981) and *The American Airman in Europe* (London, 1991); R. J. Overy, *The Air War, 1939—1945* (London, 1980); Anthony Verrier, *The Bomber Offensive* (London, 1968); Lee Kennett, *A History of Strategic Bombing* (New York, 1982); Michael S. Sherry, *The Rise of American Air Power: The Creation of Armageddon* (New

Haven and London, 1987); Lowell Thomas and Edward Jablonski, *Doolittle: A Biography* (New York, 1976); Elmer Bendiner, *The Fall of the Fortresses* (New York, 1980); Dale O. Smith, *Screaming Eagle: Memoirs of a B-17 Group Commander* (New York, 1990); *B-17s over Berlin*, ed. Ian L. Hawkins (New York, 1990); Paul W. Tibbets, *The Tibbets Story* (New York, 1978); John M. Redding and Harold I. Leyshon, *Skyways to Berlin* (Indianapolis, 1943); James Good Brown, *The Mighty Men of the 381st. Heroes All* (Salt Lake City, 1984);

Allan Healey, *The 467th Bombardment Group* (privately printed, 1947); *The Bloody Hundredth*, ed. Horace L. Varian (privately printed, nd); *Letters from England*, ed. J. M. Bennett (privately printed, nd); David Lande, *From Somewhere in England* (London, 1991); Michael L. Gibson, *Aviation in Northamptonshire* (Northampton, 1982); the papers of William E. Ruck, John N. McClane Jnr and Norman A. Erbe quoted by kind permission of the authors; private, unpublished information.

Chapter Sixteen Operation OVERLOAD

Gordon A. Harrison, *The European Theater of Operations: Cross-Channel Attack* in *United States Army in World War II* series (Washington, 1951); Max Hastings, *Overlord: D-Day and the Battle for Normandy* (London, 1984); John Keegan, *Six Armies in Normandy* (London, 1982); Cornelius Ryan, *The Longest Day* (New York, 1959); Dwight D. Eisenhower, *Crusade in Europe*; David Eisenhower, *Eisenhower at War, 1943–1945*; Winston S. Churchill, *Triumph and Tragedy* (London, 1954); Stephen E. Ambrose, *The Supreme Commander* (New York, 1970); *Eisenhower. Soldier and President*

(New York, 1990); Edwin P. Hoyt, *The Invasion before Normandy: The Secret Battle of Slapton Sands* (New York, 1985); Ken Small, *The Forgotten Dead* (London, 1989); Muriel and David Murch and Len Fairweather, *The American Forces at Salcombe and Slapton During World War Two* (privately published, 1984); Bob Sheehan, 'The D-Day Build-Up and After' in *The Yanks are Coming*, ed. Hale and Turner; Longmate, *Home Front*; papers of J. M. White (Department of Documents, IWM); private, unpublished information.

Chapter Seventeen The Far Shore

Harrison, *Cross-Channel Attack*; Hastings, *Overlord*; Keegan, *Six Armies in Normandy*; Ryan, *The Longest Day*; Charles Whiting, *'44. In Combat from Normandy to the Ardennes* (New York, 1984); Omar N. Bradley, *A Soldier's Story* (London, 1951); Donald Burgett, *Curahee! A Paratrooper's Account of the Normandy Landings* (London, 1967); Jim Kurz, 'D-Day — Arnhem' in *The Yanks are Coming*, ed. Hale and Turner.

Chapter Eighteen Over There

Eisenhower, *Crusade in Europe*; Winfield, *Sentimental Journey*; Shukert and Scibetta, *War Brides of World War II*; Nicolson, *War Diaries*; Cecil King, *With Malice Towards None. A War Diary*, ed. William Armstrong (London, 1970); Mass Observation Archive; papers of Avice R. Wilson (W 257/US) (Department of Documents, IWM); private, unpublished information.

Films

Why We Fight a series of films made by the US War Department and produced by Frank Capra: see no. 1. *Prelude to War* (1942); 2. *The Nazis Strike* (1942); 3. *Divide and Conquer* (1943); 4. *Battle of Britain* (1943); 5. *Battle of Russia* (1944); 6. *The War Comes to America* (1945). *Know your Ally: Britain* produced by Frank Capra (Army Pictorial Services, 1943); *USA: The Land and its People* (1944) dir. Paul Rotha for the Ministry of Information.
Mrs Miniver (1942) dir. William Wyler; *A Letter from Ulster* (1943, Ministry of Information); *Welcome to Britain* (1943, Ministry of Information); *A Canterbury Tale* (1944) dir. Michael Powell and Emeric Pressburger; *The Memphis Belle* (1944) dir. William Wyler; *Journey Together* (1945) dir. John Boulting; *The Way to the Stars* (1945) dir. Anthony Asquith; *The True Glory* (1945) dir. Garson Kanin and Carol Reed; *A Matter of Life and Death* (1946) dir. Michael Powell and Emeric Pressburger; *Twelve O'Clock High* (1949) dir. Henry King; *Yanks* (1979) dir. John Schlesinger; *Memphis Belle* (1990) dir. Michael Caton-Jones, producer David Puttnam.

ACKNOWLEDGEMENTS

AUTHOR'S ACKNOWLEDGEMENTS
Great Britain

Gilbert Adams; Mrs J. C. Allen; Margaret Anderson; Philip Arnold; George Arthur; F. Austin; Dennis Bailey; Margaret Ball; Ken Banbury; Beryl Bann-Ashley (née McDermott); Frances Barton; A. Bates; Mrs E. Beeby; Mary Biggs; F. H. R. Birch; Quentin Bland; Peter Bottomley; Del Bradshaw; Joan Bridge; R. Brinkworth; Allah H. Buksh; C. Bull; Grace Burnett; S. Burns; G. R. Burrows; Margaret Busi; Catherine Butterworth; Peter Camp; Dorothy Candy; Oliver Carter; Marjorie Castle (née Hale); Muriel Cave; H. J. Charles; E. A. Cheney; Mr Chilvers; J. Chubb; Angela Church; Ambrose M. Congdon; Bernice Conway; Mrs L. Coombs; Nancy Coote; Cecilia Cousins; Renée Cracknell; N. T. Crosbee (née Hancox); F. T. Crowton; Kathleen Cruse; M. E. Davies; Pat Davies; Carmen de la Torre; Denis Dew; Tony Downe; Barbara Dring; G. F. Eady; Sylvia and Ronald Ebdon; A. K. Edwards; Olive G. Edwards; Dennis E. Elliott; Norah Ellis; Mrs Essexly; Patricia Everson; Bill Fey; F. Flood; Iris W. Ford; Vera Foster; F. H. Foyle; Arthur Garbett; G. Gilbert; Mrs D. C. Grant; Mrs Greenhow; Vera Haines (née Harper); M. G. Hall; Mary Hannon; Mac Hawkins; Gwendoline Haynes; Arthur Heath; Joyce Hector-Jones; Mrs M. J. Hopkins; E. Joan Houston; Mrs V. Howard; Margaret Hugo (née Manahan); James S. Hurd; Sheila Hussey; Jo James; Edna M. Kelly; Mary Kelly; John Kerrington; Dorothy Kilshaw; John King; Geoff Knott; G. B. Lambert; Patricia Lambourn; Doreen Le Gallienne; Eddie Malyon; Edwin Marley; R. D. McCoy; Beatrice McDougall; Jane MacGowan; May Mack; Betty Mallard; Ron Miles; D. Morgan; I. W. Morris; P. J. Morris; Anona Moser; Jean H. Newell; T. Norris; Jean Norton; Mrs M. Ockwell; F. E. and D. M. Oliver; L. V. Oliver; Brian Orme; Elizabeth Oxley; Catherine L. Pearse; John Pendlebury; Joan Perry; Margaret Pilgrim (née Double); June Pohl; Mrs J. Pollard; Daphne Price; Peter Pullin; the Countess of Radnor; Audrey Randall; D. G. A. Randall; Mollie J. Rees; Connie (née Stanton) and Gordon Richards; June Riggs; Pearl Roe; Barbara Rogers; T. G. Rookes; Peggy Ross; Jonathan Rowe; Mary Ruau (née Kemp); James Rutter; T. J. Sampson; Nora Schneider (née Lambert); Eunice Shaw; Ron Shepherd; Muriel J. Sherlock; F. B. Simpkins; Laurence Skinner; Jessie Slattery; Mrs A. M. Smith; Freda M. Smith; Eileen Smithers; Sandra Soer; Mrs O. Sprason; K. G. Stainer; Alan Staines; W. F. Stanton; Edith Steed; Florence Stubbs; Joyce E. Surman; Ruth Sutton; Dorothy Sweeney; Mrs Y. Talbot; Anne Tanne; Mrs Taylor; W. A. Tennear; Kathleen Thomas; V. J. D. Thomas; Kathleen Turner; George R. Vanden Heuvel; Aidan Vaughan; E. Vaughan; Rosamund Vincent (née Sewell) and Lewis John Vincent; Evelyn Wagner (formerly Jacob); Mrs J. Wainwright; Beryl J. Waller; J. E. Walsh; Margaret Ware; E. Watkins; Mrs D. P. Watson; J. Wealthy; Christopher Webb; Angela Weeks (née Grimsdale); Eric Westman; Gladys Whitehouse; Dick Wickham; Betty Williams; Lillian Willis; Betty J. Wilson; Mrs S. E. Winskill; Dorothy Wood; William Woodward; Samuel T. Wyatt.

USA

Frank Aleksandrowicz; Helen Fox Angell; Kitch Aydelotte; Edward L. Barebo; Eileen and William E. Barry; James W. Bell; Homer L. Briggs; Evelyn Brinkley; Philip S. Callahan; Mrs M. Castle; Forrest S. Clark; Mary Clark; Robert C. Coakley; Russell H. and Kathryn C. Cunningham; Fred A. Dale; Mrs E. L. Dobbins; George S. De Heus Snr; Jean E. and John Doktor; Joseph A. Dolan; Ralph L. Dorff; Robert A. Edberg; Norman Erbe; Benjamin L. Everett; Florence Harold A. Shebeck; William G. Shove; Dewayne B. Smith; Donald F. Stuart; William Swartz; Charles W. Taylor; Fred L. Taylor; Joyce and Richard van Duyn; Fellows; Mabel A. Forde; George C. Frederick; Myra Meredith; June Harris; Warren Holbrook; Clark Houghton; Donald B. Hyde; Clarence Johnson; Paul M. Jones; Nancy Jordison; Janet M. Kovac; Boyd Lewis; Averil Logan; Kenneth L. Mann; Carl Mantell; Eugene S. Norton; Leslie Pedersen; Eugene L. Peel; William Prince; Robert F. Reins; Bob Reynolds; John T. Robertson; Al Sadowsky; Samuel A. Schenker; William Schwinn; George W. Shaffer; Lindley Shaw; Sandy Vasquez; Jenal Virdel; John R. Walsh; Marshall W. Williams; Barbara and Edward P. Yeater; Edmund Zieba; Albert C. Zultz.

Grateful acknowledgement is made to the following for permission to reprint copyright material:

To Faber & Faber Ltd publishers of Randall Jarrell, *The Complete Poems*, for lines from 'Losses'; to John Murray publishers of John Betjeman, *Collected Poems*, for a verse from 'In Westminster Abbey'; to Malago Publications for permission to quote from *Tell Your Mother There's a War On. The Wartime Memories of a Bedminster Boy* by Ted Hill; to the University Press of Colorado for permission to quote from *Other Clay: A Remembrance of World War II Infantry* by Charles Cawthon; to John Frayn Turner for permission to quote from *The Yanks Are Coming* by Edwin R. W. Hale and John Frayn Turner; to Campbell Connelly & Co., London, for 'Choc'late Soldier from the USA' by Elton Box, Sonny Cox & Lewis Ilda, published 1944 by Dash Music Co., London; to the Trustees of the Imperial War Museum for access to its collections and to the individual copyright holders, or their estate (detailed in the appropriate chapter bibliography), for permission to quote from their papers; Mass Observation extracts reproduced with the permission of the Trustees of the Mass Observation Archive, University of Sussex. Every attempt has been made to trace copyright holders of material quoted and the author apologizes for any omissions.

ILLUSTRATION ACKNOWLEDGEMENTS

Frontispiece US National Air & Space Museum; 12 Imperial War Museum (IWM); 13 Popperfoto; 21 IWM; 25 *Punch*; 29 IWM; 34 *Punch*; 37 Hulton Picture Company; 42 (top) US National Archive, (bottom) IWM; 43 (top) Popperfoto, (bottom) by courtesy of Patricia Everson; 45, 49 Bruce Bairnsfather cartoons; 57 Popperfoto; 60 (top & bottom) IWM; 66 Hulton Picture Company; 69 Giles cartoon, permission *Daily Express* newspapers; 71 US National Archive; 75 Hulton Picture Company; 78 IWM; 82 (top) IWM, (bottom) Hulton Picture Company; 86 *Punch*; 90 Popperfoto; 91, 93 US National Archive; 94 IWM; 98 (top & bottom) Hulton Picture Company; 99 (top & bottom), 105 American Red Cross; 106 by courtesy of Charles W. Taylor; 109 Hulton Picture Company; 111 IWM; 112, 115 Hulton Picture Company; 117 Bairnsfather cartoon; 120 Hulton Picture Company; 122 Bairnsfather cartoon; 124 by courtesy of Philip Kaplan; 128 by courtesy of Robert Reynolds; 129 (top & bottom), 133 Hulton Picture Company; 134 IWM; 137 by courtesy of Connie and Gordon Richards; 143 Giles cartoon, permission *Daily Express* newspapers; 145 Hulton Picture Company; 146 (top) IWM, (bottom) by courtesy of Barbara and Edward Yeater; 151 US National Archive; 153, 157 Hulton Picture Company; 161 US National Archive; 163, 164, 166 Popperfoto; 170 by courtesy of Patricia Everson; 171 Popperfoto; 173 US National Archive; 174 Popperfoto; 175 Hulton Picture Company; 176, 177 Popperfoto; 181 (top & bottom) Hulton Picture Company; 183 (top) IWM, (bottom) Popperfoto; 189 (top & bottom), 195 IWM; 197 American Red Cross; 203 Giles cartoon, permission *Daily Express* newspapers; 205 by courtesy of Margaret Pilgrim; 206 Hulton Picture Company; 207, 208, 209 Popperfoto; 210 Giles cartoon, permission *Daily Express* newspapers; 212 Hulton Picture Company.

INDEX

Figures in *italics* refer to illustrations